CE: MYTH AND EVIDENCE

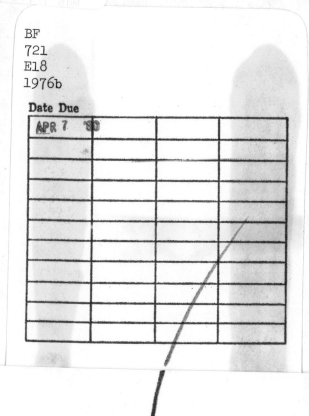

INDIAN VALLEY COLLEGES

EARLY EXPERIENCE: MYTH AND EVIDENCE

Ann M. Clarke and A.D.B. Clarke

The Free Press
A Division of Macmillan Publishing Co., Inc.
NEW YORK

The Free Press
A Division of Macmillan Publishing Co., Inc.
866 Third Avenue, New York, N.Y. 10022

Collier Macmillan Canada, Ltd.

Library of Congress Catalog Card Number: 76-21992

Printed in the United States of America

printing number

1 2 3 4 5 6 7 8 9 10

*To our sons, Robert and Peter, who
suffered maternal deprivation
and multiple foreign caretaking
during 'the critical period';
and to Patrick Taylor who insisted
that this book should be written*

Contents

Preface

During the last twenty-five years the impact of new biological and social knowledge has caused revision or reformulation of many theories about the development of behavioural processes. In particular the complexity of the interactions and transactions between nature and nurture are now more fully appreciated. There remains, however, one theory which is peculiarly resistant to change: that the environment in the early years exerts a disproportionate and irreversible effect on a rapidly developing organism, compared with the potential for later environmental influences.

The present editors have for some twenty years been highly sceptical about this view, and from time to time have said so. Until fairly recently, however, there has been a relative dearth of evidence. We feel that the time has now come to assemble the data and review the arguments. We believe that the theory has a marked environmental impact upon the early development of professional workers, altering the selectivity of their perceptual and cognitive processes. We are confident, however, that this early learning, which is so powerfully and cumulatively reinforced, is far from being irreversible, provided that different reinforcements (i.e. evidence as against myth) are offered. We hope, therefore, that this volume may form part of a rehabilitation programme.

The book is divided into five sections, each of which is linked to succeeding contributions. We have been fortunate in gaining the permission of our contributors, and their journal editors or publishers, to reprint a number of important papers, and in two cases over and above our own five original chapters, articles have been specially written for this book by Professor Jerome Kagan and Dr Jarmila Koluchová.

We are very grateful for typing and other assistance to Mrs M.L. Ewbank and Miss L.M. Plaxton. Mrs Moira Phillips has once again assisted us in preparing the book for publication, offering useful comments and undertaking the chore of preparing author and subject indexes. We are very grateful. Mr F. W. Garforth was most helpful in tracing the early history of the myth. The data provided in table 2.1 and the accompanying details of the subsequent development of earlier isolated twins were kindly supplied by Mr A. Sutton and Miss J. Francis. Messrs Harvey Goldstein and Ken Fogelman were good enough to offer us important unpublished data from the National Child Development Study. Finally we must express our thanks to Mr Patrick Taylor of Open Books, who overcame our initial reluctance and has throughout offered helpful advice and encouragement.

A.M.C.
A.D.B.C.
University of Hull
January 1976

Acknowledgements

The editors and publishers would like to thank the following for permission to reproduce material contained in this book: the author and the editor of the *American Journal of Sociology* for 'Final note on a case of extreme isolation'; the author and the editor of the *Journal of Child Psychology and Psychiatry* for 'Severe deprivation in twins: a case study'; the author and Prentice-Hall Inc. for 'Children of the Crèche: conclusions and implications'; the authors and the editor of *Child Development* for 'A comparison of the effects of adoption, restoration to the natural mother, and continued institutionalization on the cognitive development of four-year-old children'; the author and the editor of the *Journal of Child Psychology and Psychiatry* for 'Parent–child separation: psychological effects on the children'; the author and Columbia University Press for 'Adopting older children: summary and implications'; the authors and the editor of *Child Development* for 'The Early Training Project: a seventh-year report'; the author and D.H.E.W. Publications for 'Facts and principles of early intervention: a summary'; Dr J.W.B. Douglas and the editor of *Developmental Medicine and Child Neurology* for tables 6.1 and 6.2, and the data in table 6.3.

List of Contributors

Urie Bronfenbrenner Ph.D.	Professor of Human Development and Family Studies and of Psychology, Cornell University
Alan D.B. Clarke Ph.D.	Professor of Psychology, Department of Psychology, University of Hull
Ann M. Clarke Ph.D.	Reader in Educational Psychology, Department of Educational Studies, University of Hull
Kingsley Davis, Ph.D.	Ford Professor of Sociology and Comparative Studies; Chairman, International Population and Urban Research, Institute of International Studies, University of California, Berkeley
Wayne Dennis Ph.D.	Professor Emeritus, Department of Psychology, Brooklyn College
Judith Gould (*née* Rees) B.Sc., M.Phil.	Member, Scientific Staff, Medical Research Council Social Psychiatry Unit, Institute of Psychiatry, London
Susan W. Gray Ph.D.	Professor of Psychology, George Peabody College for Teachers
Alfred Kadushin Ph.D.	Professor of Social Work, School of Social Work, University of Wisconsin, Madison
Jerome Kagan Ph.D.	Professor of Human Development, Department of Psychology and Social Relations, Harvard University
Rupert A. Klaus Ph.D.	School Psychologist, Murfreesboro City Schools; Adjunct Associate Professor, George Peabody College for Teachers

Jarmila Koluchová
Ph.D., C.Sc.

Reader in Clinical Psychology, Department of Psychology, Palacky University, Czechoslovakia

Michael Rutter,
M.D., F.R.C.P.,
F.R.C.Psych., D.P.M.

Professor of Child Psychiatry, Department of Child and Adolescent Psychiatry, Institute of Psychiatry, London

Barbara Tizard
Ph.D.

Dr Barnado's Senior Research Fellow, Institute of Education, Thomas Coram Research Unit, London

Section I

Introduction

CHAPTER ONE

The Formative Years?

Ann M. Clarke and A.D.B. Clarke

THE BACKGROUND

It is well known that the ways in which we perceive reality are selective. Such selectivities may be shaped by current experience, past learning or the intergenerational transmission of 'received wisdom'. We thus build models of phenomena or events against which new experiences are compared, and with which they are then integrated. Such integration may require distortions of phenomena without which they cannot easily be accommodated. Our models may be narrowly specific, or fairly general (e.g. man's place in the universe). They may persist throughout the individual's life span, or they may be of brief duration. They vary in the ease with which they may be individually or popularly modified. Within any society the more general concepts become cultural assumptions which are rarely questioned, indeed they may be held tenaciously (sometimes contrary to all evidence), and form part of the fabric of its existence.

The notion that the planets revolve round the sun, for example, was advanced by Aristarchus, a contemporary of Euclid. So much did it clash with orthodox views that it produced a demand that he should be indicted for impiety. Copernicus (in 1543) merely revived or rediscovered the theory, which was greeted with violent hostility by Lutherans as well as Catholics. 'That in the end the great development of the scientific movement occurred mainly in protestant countries is due to the relative impotence of the national churches in the control over the opinion of its members' (Russell 1959). Galileo adopted the heliocentric theory and, as is well known, was twice called before the Inquisition (1616 and 1633) before he recanted.

This brief excursion into part of the history of cosmology offers in extreme form an example of the way in which a reinterpretation of well-known observations inspires resistance or hostility. All societies possess, in some sense, a model of man, including a conception of his development. Such models have profound implications, but it is only quite recently that it has become possible to cast light upon them and their validity, by means of empirical research. The most pervasive western model for human development, as the following quotations will indicate, is the view that the first few years of life necessarily have crucial effects upon later development and adult characteristics. Yarrow (1961) states this quite narrowly: 'The significance of early *infantile* experience for later development has been reiterated so frequently and so persistently that the general validity of this assertion is now almost unchallenged' (our italics). It is indeed the purpose of this book to indicate that such a view *must* be challenged in the light of growing evidence, and that the super-environmentalism with which the first few years of life have been regarded, and which is implicit in such statements, is no longer tenable.

Within our contributions to this volume we will use the terms early learning and early experience synonymously, for, as indicated later, experience which has anything more than merely ephemeral effects must involve the learning processes. In a useful book, Sluckin (1971) grapples with the problem of definition, rightly regarding the concept of learning as narrower than that of experience. Nevertheless he feels the distinction must not be over-stressed. Since the present volume is entirely concerned with extension in time of early experience effects, we trust that no confusion will result from our terminology.

The allegedly crucial importance of the pre-school years for future development is reflected throughout the whole history of western thinking, although the intelligent layman probably believes that this concept owes its existence only to Freud (1856–1939). A brief review of this area must start with Plato.

Plato (428–348 B.C.)

And the first step, as you know, is always what matters most, particularly when we are dealing with those who are young and tender. That is the time when they are taking shape and when any impression we choose to make leaves a permanent mark.

Quintilian (c. A.D. 35–100)

We are by nature most tenacious of what we have imbibed in our infant years, as the flavour, with which you scent vessels when new, remains in them . . .

Francesco Barbaro (1428)

According to Woodward (1905) the fifteenth-century humanists were keenly alive to the importance of the first years of infancy in the development of the child, quoting a chapter by Francesco Barbaro, *De Liberorum Educatione*, from his tract *De Re Uxoria*. The writings of Vergerius are also cited in this respect.

John Locke (1632–1704)

. . . Try it in a dog or a horse or any other creature, and see whether the ill and resty tricks they have learned when young are easily to be mended when they are knit; and yet none of these creatures are half so wilful and proud, or half so desirous to be masters of themselves and others, as man . . . Whatever [children] . . . do leaves some impression on that tender age, and from thence they receive a tendency to good or evil.

If . . . the difference to be found in the manners and abilities of men is owing more to their education than anything else, we have reason to conclude that great care is to be had of the forming of children's minds and giving them that seasoning early which shall influence their lives always after . . .

. . . I think I may say that of all the men we meet with nine parts of ten are what they are, good or evil, useful or not, by their education. 'Tis that which makes the great difference in mankind. The little or almost insensible impressions on our tender infancies have very important and lasting consequences . . .

. . . errors in education . . . carry their afterwards incorrigible taint with them through all the parts and stations of life. (Locke 1964)

James Mill (1816)

It seems to be a law of human nature that the first sensations experienced produced the greatest effects; more especially, that the earliest repetitions of one sensation after another produce the deepest habit . . . Common language confirms this law, when it speaks of the susceptibility of the tender mind . . . It is, then, a fact, that the early sequences to which we are accustomed form the primary habits; and that the primary habits are the fundamental character of man . . . as soon as the infant, or rather the embryo, begins to feel, the character begins to be formed; and that the habits, which are then contracted, are the most pervading and operative of all.

Sigmund Freud (1910)

On the other hand we must assume, or we may convince ourselves through psychological observations on others, that the very impressions which we have forgotten have nevertheless left the deepest traces in our psychic life, and acted as determinants for our whole future development.

J.B. Watson (1928)

But once a child's character has been spoiled by bad handling, which can be done in a few days, who can say that the damage is ever repaired? . . . some day the importance of the first two years of infancy will be fully realized . . .

Children's fears are home grown just like their loves and temper outbursts. The parents do the emotional planting and the cultivating. At three years of age the child's whole emotional life plan has been laid down, his emotional disposition set. At that age the parents have already determined for him whether he is to grow into a happy person, wholesome and good-natured, whether he is to be a whining, complaining neurotic, an anger driven, vindictive, over-bearing slave driver, or one whose every move in life is definitely controlled by fear.

Sigmund Freud (1949)

It seems that neuroses are only acquired during early childhood (up to the age of six), even though their symptoms may not make their appearance until much later . . . analytic experience has convinced us of the complete truth of the common assertion that the child is psychologically father of the man and that the events of his first years are of paramount importance for his whole subsequent life . . .

Bowlby (1951)

Among the most significant developments in psychiatry during the past quarter of a century has been the steady growth of evidence that the quality of the parental care which a child receives in his earliest years is of vital importance for his future mental health . . . it is this complex, rich, and rewarding relationship with the mother in the early years, varied in countless ways by relations with the father and with siblings, that child psychiatrists and many others now believe to underline the development of character and of mental health . . . the evidence is now such that it leaves no room for doubt regarding the general proposition – that the prolonged deprivation of the young child of maternal care may have grave and far-reaching effects in his character and so on the whole of his future life.

Bloom (1964)

It is the view of the writer that for these (personality) characteristics the early development is, at least quantitatively, in accord with the psychoanalytic literature . . . By an average age of about 2, it seems evident that at least one third of the variance at adolescence on intellectual interest, dependency, and aggression is predictable.

Rathbun and others (1965)

There is considerable clinical evidence that abrupt early separation of children from their mothers may inflict irreversible damage upon later personality development . . . a single separation experience, however, need not involve deprivation for a child if an adequate mother substitute, with whom there can be real interaction is then offered . . .

White (1971)

I will begin with the bold statement that the mother's direct and indirect actions with regard to her one- to three-year-old child are, in my opinion, the most powerful formative factors in the development of the pre-school child . . . Finally, I would expect that much of the basic quality of the entire life of an individual is determined by the mother's actions during these two years. Obviously I could be very wrong about these declarative statements. I make them as very strong hunches . . . as a kind of net result of all our inquiries in early development.

Storr (1975)

But, if we want our children to grow up happy, there is little doubt that the experience of the first few months and years of life is crucial. An infant who receives what he irrationally deserves during this period is likely to acquire an unshakeable sense of his own loveability and worth which will see him through most of the reverses of life without too much difficulty.

The issue of early experience and its later effects began to be revived in the immediate post-war years. Two main, separate and independent streams of work, each following entirely different methodologies and theoretical positions, could be seen as combining to strengthen the notion of the crucially formative role of early experience. The first sprang from a psychoanalytical approach, and was thus clinical and observational (Bowlby 1951). The second, based upon studies on the role of learning in development, was largely experimental (Hebb 1949).

Bowlby's (1951) monograph, published by the World Health Organization, concerning the relation between early mother–child relationships and subsequent mental health, had (and still has) a very considerable impact, both in research and in practice. But within a few years researchers began to voice criticisms of the confused concept of maternal deprivation (e.g. O'Connor 1956; Clarke and Clarke 1959, 1960; Yarrow 1961) and Bowlby himself reduced his claims (Bowlby and others 1956). In his summary he concluded that 'some of the workers who first drew attention to the dangers of maternal deprivation resulting from separation have tended on occasion to overstate their case . . .' (see also Ainsworth and others 1962).

Because of its continuing impact, some attention must nevertheless be devoted to the Bowlby thesis, which was based not merely on his own work, but particularly on researches reported by Spitz and by Goldfarb. The concept of maternal deprivation, as Bowlby indicated, covers 'a number of different situations'. This was an understatement, for it included short and long separations, privation in institutions, changes in the mother figure and even rearing in kibbutzim ('It is by no means certain that children do not suffer from this regime' [Bowlby 1951, p. 43]). All had in common a disrupted maternal bonding, or in the latter case some reduction in the continuous relationship which was seen to be essential for future normal development. But the quoted institutional researches involved not only lack of maternal care but very often extreme lack of care. Thus, as many writers have subsequently indicated, a very heterogeneous collection of studies, with differences in outcome, were subsumed within Bowlby's framework. This might be seen as a strength were it not for the poor quality of most of them.

Dramatic support for the maternal deprivation theory was claimed from the work of Spitz, reported in several interlocking papers (1945, 1946a and 1946b). The first was concerned with the effects of continuous institutional care of infants below the age of one year for reasons other than sickness. The second describes the development of the children in one of the two institutions over a two-year period; the third describes the depression observed in many of the infants in the other institutions. Spitz believed that there is a qualitative change after three months of deprivation, after which recovery is rarely, if ever, complete.

A truly horrifying picture emerges of developmental deceleration, high mortality from a measles epidemic and progressive dehumanization. In one study, the unexplained reappearance of mothers after absence produced rapidly accelerating development, which, however, it was believed, might not last. There is a great lack of essential detail, although it seems that the institutions, in two different and unnamed countries in the western hemisphere, were of very poor standard. As many writers have indicated, the most obvious error in the Spitz studies was his failure to distinguish separation from other possible (and more probable) causes of retardation. A detailed and comprehensive critique by Pinneau (1955a and 1955b; see also Spitz 1955) suggests that this whole series of reports is so riddled with omissions and doubts that they cannot be taken very seriously as throwing light on the general hypothesis. Moreover such workers as Klackenberg (1956) have failed to replicate the findings, possibly because they worked in much better institutions.

A number of studies by Goldfarb are quoted in detail by Bowlby. Of these Goldfarb (1943) is most favoured, since in it were reported details of fifteen pairs of children followed up to the ages of ten to fourteen. One group (fifteen) was reared in an institution from six months to three and a half years of age and then fostered, while the other fifteen had gone straight to foster homes. Goldfarb shows a marked inferiority of the former group, at the time of follow-up, in intelligence, attainment, social maturity, ability to form relationships and speech. This is attributed to the three years of institutional rearing. Goldfarb was satisfied that both heredity and the foster homes for the two groups were similar. It is, however, significant that one group was considered fit for fostering in the first few months of life, while this did not take place for the other until three years later. There is thus the possibility of the results reflecting unknown selective factors. Although the educational and occupational histories of the mothers had been ascertained, and those of the institutional group shown to be superior to those fostered at once, little or no information about the fathers was available. In any event length of follow-up may be relevant, for few studies are quoted with follow-up beyond early adolescence; and since some of the assessments were not carried out 'blind', the possibility of an experimenter effect cannot be ruled out. It is also interesting that Trasler's (1960) follow-up of children in foster care has been taken by some as confirming Goldfarb's work. There was a clear association between early rearing in institutions and subsequent breakdown in foster care. But Trasler's data indicate that a high proportion of those who broke down had been placed in foster homes which were themselves unsatisfactory, so that a more balanced interpretation would suggest that children affected by poor early rearing were further affected by adverse foster homes.

Our own data (Clarke and Clarke 1954) on deprived adolescents and young adults with initial deficits similar to those of Goldfarb's institutionally reared subjects nevertheless showed delayed recovery from extreme deprivation, and forced us even in those early days to regard this phenomenon as requiring some modification to Bowlby's theory. Within a few years (Clarke, Clarke and Reiman 1958) our experimental studies indicated that our subjects, in adult life, were 'very much less impaired than would have been expected from Bowlby's original theory . . . [it is possible] that when more deprived children are followed up through adolescence and adult life, it will be found that, in many, the initial psychological damage, as with our own deprived population, . . . [will tend] steadily to be repaired to varying extents . . .' (See pages 71–4.)

It became obvious that the concept of deprivation was much more complex than the blanket notion of mother–child separation, and that an analysis of different forms, extents and durations of experience, as well as of the situation before and after deprivation, was necessary (Clarke and Clarke 1960). Furthermore at that time no voice was raised against the almost unquestioning acceptance of the *post hoc ergo propter hoc* reasoning that appeared to dominate the thinking of social policy makers and many adoption agencies.

Moreover, there was a failure to delineate the various consequences of adversity such as (1) cognitive deficit; (2) social maladjustment; (3) emotional problems, including psychopathy; and (4) scholastic underfunctioning, and to establish the natural history of these. There was also an over-emphasis on *physical* separation of the mother from child ('any home is better than no home') and an under-emphasis on the possibility that many mothers in 'intact' families were damaging their children through cruelty and neglect. This has probably played a considerable part in the implicit policy that where possible, and where this is desired, illegitimate children should remain with their mothers. On average this procedure does not appear to be in the child's best interests, and in some cases is highly detrimental. As Seglow, Kellmer Pringle and Wedge (1972) indicate, as a result of a large-scale study of seven-year-olds, 'in contrast to the adopted in working class homes, who did better than could be expected, the illegitimate who remained with their own mothers did relatively badly, even when they grew up in a middle class home . . . it looks as if the generally favourable environment of adoptive homes was of overriding importance in compensating the children for their poor early start . . .' (p. 141). Other studies (e.g. Skodak and Skeels 1949; Kadushin 1970) certainly support this view of the generally more favourable outcome of adoption in comparison with expectancies based upon knowledge of parental history and adverse early circumstances.

Additionally there appeared to be a sequential problem inherent in many of (but not all) the data offered in evidence for the maternal deprivation theory, namely that children subjected to severe deprivation in infancy were more often than not reared in similar conditions throughout their whole period of physical and intellectual development. Similarly, those enjoying excellent circumstances early in life usually continued in such conditions.

These and other studies, then, were beginning to challenge both the concepts of maternal deprivation and the notion of irreversibility of effects induced by early experience. To say the least, therefore, by the 1960s Bowlby's conclusions were open to doubt and to alternative formulations.

Hebb's (1949) important book, as noted, initiated a different approach to the problem of early learning, and, like Bowlby's contribution, stimulated much important research, well summarised by such writers as Scott (1968) and Denenberg (1972). Hebb's thesis of the dependence of later learning upon earlier rested quite largely upon experimental work in the animal field (e.g. by Riesen) and upon a somewhat heterogeneous collection of reports, mainly clinical, summarised almost twenty years earlier by von Senden. As is well known, new findings in the animal field (degeneration of optic pathways in the absence of light) have given a different twist to Hebb's thesis, and the human work has also been criticised. But there remain some important facts which are very relevant to this discussion. As he succinctly states it: (1) more complex relationships can be learned by higher species at maturity; (2) simple relationships are learned about as promptly by lower as by higher species; (3) *the first learning is slower in higher than in lower species* (our italics). Hebb's view that adult learning may well be heavily loaded with transfer effects from earlier experience is a plausible hypothesis, relevant to the general theme.

We have given less emphasis to Hebb's book and the stream of research which it stimulated, for its effects on policy and on the traditional view of the role of early human development were far less marked than Bowlby's. It can be said, however, that new data and new thinking had, by the early 1960s at the least, greatly modified the interpretations of their work. To the best of our knowledge, however, no comprehensive, critical assessment of the alleged importance of early experience (as opposed to maternal deprivation)* had been made until one of us was invited to give the 42nd Maudsley Lecture in 1967. On that occasion it was argued, among other things, that (1) the notion of a critical period of development exercising a powerful influence on later characteristics did not accord with some evidence on the development of deprived children, and particularly of those who had experienced significant environmental change; (2) that normally, and for most children, environmental change does not occur, so in later life one may be looking at the outcome, not merely of early experience, but of continuing experience; (3) that experimental studies of extreme deprivation in animals, while important, must for a number of reasons be regarded with caution before extrapolation of the findings to humans; and (4) that important experiments on reversing the effects of early experience in animals remained to be carried out (Clarke 1968).

* For an excellent reassessment of the concept of maternal deprivation see Rutter (1972).

The situation as we now see it is as follows: our general hypothesis is that psychological experience which has anything more than merely transitory effects must involve learning, that is, a modification of behaviour possessing some extension in time. The crude facts about learning enable us to examine the question of whether early experience is likely to possess a potent effect on, or act as a crucial determinant of, adult behaviour. Such facts as the effects of repetition of learning sequences, of over-learning, of reinforcement and of extinction are clearly relevant. Early learning by definition has immediate effects. The size and duration of these, will, of course, depend upon the length and potency of the experience and the age of the learner, but more particularly on the amount, intensity and duration of subsequent reinforcement or repetition. Conversely, it was hypothesised that early learning will have effects which, if unrepeated, will fade with time. It will not *per se* have any long-term influence upon adult behaviour other than as an essential link in the developmental chain. Obviously here one is not referring to gross 'biological' experiences (e.g. malnutrition, brain damage), although even here the social context may be influential in amplifying or minimising particular effects (Sameroff and Chandler 1976).

The effects of social learning through modelling, identification with selected adults and peers and feedback from the environment operate on the maturing organism in ways as yet little understood. The child, of course, is not a passive receptor of stimulation, but rather is an increasingly dynamic being, who to some extent *causes* his own learning experiences (Rutter and others 1964). There is thus the possibility that early experience may produce particular effects which, acting upon later environments, result in reinforcing feedback, thus prolonging early learning effects. The disturbed institutional child, placed in foster care, may elicit from the foster mother antagonistic responses which strengthen the child's instability. The resulting correlation between early and later behaviour is, as implied, likely to reflect indirect rather than direct causality, and here the child may become the unwitting agent of his own later difficulties. The unsophisticated observer may attribute these to early adversity; in a sense he would be both right and wrong in so doing. All this underlines the prime importance of considering what follows particular early experience which may prolong what would otherwise be transitory effects, good or bad.

As Sameroff and Chandler (1975) indicate in a highly important chapter, some models of human development clearly fail to accommodate the data. Thus the 'Main Effect Model' implies that constitution and environment exert independent influences. Defective constitution is seen as leading to a particular effect, regardless of environment, or a pathological environment is regarded as solely responsible for the damaged individual regardless of constitution. Apart from extremes, there is clear evidence against this model. The Interactional Model much more easily accounts for research findings, but may be insufficient to reveal causal mechanisms leading to developmental problems. In particular it assumes the constancy of both constitution and environment, and this may sometimes be unwarranted. The Transactional Model, however, a variant of the latter, stresses 'the plastic character of the environment and the organism as an active participant in its own growth'.

A further possible qualification to the general hypothesis is that, if there are critical periods of learning or of development, with brief and intense responsivity to the environment, one might expect early experience to exercise disproportionate effects on later development But the notion of critical periods has not been argued very convincingly as applying to man, and anyway in its interpretation has undergone considerable modification. Thus Lenneberg (1967) regards the critical period for primary speech acquisition as lasting until puberty, a very long span of criticality. (For a recent review see Connolly 1972; while this deals mainly with animal experiments, some attention is devoted to man.)

A third qualification is that early learning may be first learning. By pre-empting neural mechanisms, it might exercise particularly crucial and long-lasting effects (e.g. Fuller and Waller 1962).

In spite of these caveats it will become apparent that, in studies of humans (as opposed to animals), the data fit the general hypothesis remarkably well, and certainly far better than the more commonly accepted alternative. Hence we offer a brief overview under five headings:

1 Animal studies are very commonly quoted as showing, firstly the importance of early learning and, secondly, their relevance to man. Four factors, however, combine to suggest that such extrapolations may be unwarranted:

(a) Commonly the duration and severity of early experience in animal research are such as could hardly permit survival of the human infant, as in Harlow's experiments with socially isolated monkeys (Harlow and Suomi 1970). Under similar conditions infants would fail to feed themselves. Where less intense experiences (e.g. handling of rat pups) are concerned, it is unclear whether the mechanisms which mediate the effects result solely from the brief experience, or are extended by important changes in maternal behaviour.

(b) Very few attempts appear to have been made systematically to establish whether the effects may be reversible. Where such attempts have been tried, reversion towards normality is usual (e.g. Woods 1959; Suomi and Harlow 1972; Wachs 1973; Novak and Harlow 1975). As the latter authors indicate, monkeys reared in total social isolation for the first year of life 'have been characterized as social vegetables ... Such debilitating effects have traditionally been considered to be not only pervasive, but also permanent. The findings of the present study, however, clearly demonstrate that monkeys raised without any social experience during the first year of life can learn to be social under appropriate conditions.' The authors add that their findings offer a compelling argument against the critical-period interpretation of the effects of social isolation.

(c) Rather few attempts have been made to establish whether these changes can be induced later in life by similar means i.e. whether they are age specific.

(d) Lastly, and most importantly, it seems obvious that the role of early experience in animals is entirely different from in man. With 'nature, red in tooth and claw', if learning is to play a part in development, it must do so very quickly. The newly hatched waterfowl, which is not imprinted rapidly, will either get lost or fall victim to predators.

Studies of animal behaviour will therefore not be included in this book. This is not to say that they may not offer useful hypotheses, particularly if they are concerned with the lower primates, which may be applied to human data.

2 The effects of short changes in early environment are most easily studied in relation to the better investigations of hospitalisation. Here there are often immediate effects which relate to age, to pre-hospital adjustment and to the ways in which the ward is organised. These effects fade with time, however (e.g. Prugh

and others 1953; Schaffer 1958). It is possible that they may be revived under stressful circumstances later, but there is little firm evidence. It is also possible that severely traumatic events have effects which are of a different order from the ordinary variations of experience, and may resist extinction *at any age* (e.g. Campbell, Sanderson and Laverty 1964, in their study of *adults*). Douglas (1975) indicates that children hospitalised in the pre-school years are not typical: they are, for example, more likely to come from large families, with manual-work occupations and with parents who take little interest in their schooling. The majority of the children studied (68 per cent) did not, according to their mothers, show changes of behaviour on leaving hospital. Ten per cent improved, while the remainder exhibited some deterioration in behaviour. The author shows associations between early hospital admissions (and particularly repeated admissions both before and after the age of five) and adolescent disturbance, which he regards as highly suggestive of a causal link. This interpretation seems to us to be improbable, and it is, in our view, more likely that these associations result from long-term influences. Early admission to hospital is thus considered to be an actuarial symptom of present and future disadvantages, rather than a cause of adolescent problems. (For more detailed discussion of Douglas's important evidence, see pages 81–7.) More frequent hospital admissions may, however, be causally linked with later disturbances.

3 Prolonged early experience, according to the hypothesis, may have more powerful and more permanent effects, but they, too, can be shown to fade with time. Many of the contributions in this book will endorse this argument, so no particular references will be offered here.

4 Miscellaneous studies, the results of which support the hypothesis, range from an investigation of visual imagery in persons blinded at different ages (Schlaegel 1953) to later memory for non-meaningful material read to a young child daily between the age of fifteen months and three years. (Burtt 1932) In such cases the non-repetition of experience was associated with a gradual fading of effects.

5 Lastly the stability of psychological characteristics over lengthy periods in longitudinal studies must be considered. If, in early life, the basic characteristics of the individual are laid down as a result of genetic /environmental interactions, then later assessment

should yield a reasonably high correlation with the earlier measures. Such was the view of Kagan and Moss (1962) and of Bloom (1964). Our (1972) evidence disputed this, and it is of great interest that Kagan himself has now independently reached a similar conclusion. (See below, and also section III.) Bloom's (1964) contribution is generally regarded as offering the firmest documentation of the belief in stability of characteristics. In it were reviewed, most usefully, the results of a number of longitudinal studies of normal children reared in their own homes. The book was, however, marred by a certain naivety both in Bloom's concept of 'half development' (perhaps unwisely using an analogy from the half life of radioactive substances) and by an undemanding criterion (one of three) that a correlation of 0·5 or above between developmental measures over a substantial period of time indicated the existence of a stable characteristic.* The half development of a characteristic is that chronological age at which 0·7 correlations with adult status emerge; such correlations are indeed often found towards the end of the pre-school years. 'This fact', writes Jensen (1969), 'has led to the amazing and widespread, but unwarranted and fallacious, conclusion that persons develop 50 per cent of their mature intelligence by age four!' The fact that a 0·7 correlation accounts for half the variance of one measure from the variance of the other thus cannot identify the age by which half development of a characteristic has occurred. Indeed the notion of half development is meaningless with scales not possessing an absolute zero, or with non-equal interval units. Bloom argues that a fully developed characteristic is by definition one that is no longer subject to environmental influence. The problem, however, is to define full development;

---

* For those unfamiliar with the use of correlations it should be stated that these are coefficients of association between two (or more) variables, ranging from + 1·0 (perfect positive co-variation) through zero (no association) to − 1·0 (perfect inverse co-variation). It should also be noted that correlations do not themselves imply any causal link between variables; indeed if causality is present, its direction may be ambiguous. Correlations may reflect the operation of a third agency; for example, there is said, perhaps apocryphally, to be a correlation between the annual increase in banana consumption and the annual increase in the issue of television licences. Finally, high correlations (e.g. + 0·9) do not indicate a total stability of ordinal position on each variable compared with the other; a minority may exhibit considerable changes. Elementary textbooks of statistics should be consulted by those wishing for an elaboration of these points.

at one time cognitive measures were supposed to reach their limits in late adolescence. For some groups such a view is no longer tenable, and non-pathological changes at quite late ages have been recorded. But with his alleged half developments occurring in the pre-school years, the implication is strong that later environmental shifts have smaller and smaller chances of effects. Elsewhere we have termed this a 'wedge' theory, representing at the thick 'young' end, maximal responsiveness to the environment and at the extreme thin 'older' end, no responsiveness at all. It is our argument that the thin end lies well up the chronological age range, and that the possibilities for alteration in response to a changing environment remain open far longer than has been commonly accepted (Clarke and Clarke 1976).

As noted, we have discussed the relative consistency and variability during development of height, intelligence, scholastic attainment and personality measures. It was concluded that the strong arguments for individual consistency in development were based upon both the preconception that individual development *should* be fairly stable, and upon a misinterpretation of the meaning of correlational coefficients quoted in longitudinal studies. Obviously, however, if the measures of change are crude, then consistency will predominate. If they are sensitive, then variability will be more striking. In either event the earlier the first measure, and the longer the period over which measurement takes place, the greater the likelihood of individual variability. Yet there are wide and unexplained individual differences in developmental variability, even within an apparently constant environment. Where environmental change occurs, such variability is commonly much greater (Clarke and Clarke 1972).

Our main general conclusion is that, in man, early learning is mainly important for its foundational character. By itself, and when unrepeated over time, it serves as no more than a link in the developmental chain, shaping proximate behaviour less and less powerfully as age increases. Other conclusions will be outlined in the final chapter, but it can be stated here that our major research need in this important area is to determine more precisely the factors that initiate, accentuate and maintain alteration in human characteristics, as well as to determine the ultimate limits of these effects and the causes of individual differences in responsiveness to change.

No doubt several factors conspire to make our theme unfamiliar to many readers. The apparent consistency with which authorities from several disciplines hold similar views about the role of early experience is naturally impressive. There is resistance to abandoning such widely held attitudes; some researchers seem more concerned with modifications rather than with rethinking the problem. Moreover most studies in developmental psychology relate to children living in the relatively unchanging circumstances of their own homes. That development is correlated with home background is well established. Particularly where adult deviant behaviour is involved, clinicians and others will tend, through their pervasive frame of reference, to seek information about the early years. Commonly such data show abnormalities in early rearing and a causal link is thought to be established. As already implied, however, this is a *non sequitur*, for it ignores the probability that later experiences were also deviant (see Rutter's contribution to this book, pages 153–86.) One could argue, then, that the cumulative effects of deviant rearing are responsible; or that later rearing is prepotent. Without environmental change as an independent variable it is indeed very difficult to determine the nature of this type of relation between early and later development.

EARLY CRITICAL PERIODS: SOME IMPLICATIONS

There are three clear implications stemming from the belief that the first few years of life are experientially critical for the development of characteristics much later in life.

Experiences in early childhood

If the view is to be accepted that early experiences exercise a disproportionate influence upon later development, the conclusion is inescapable that learning at this stage is particularly efficient and persistent. There is no evidence that this is the case, and a considerable amount of data which negates it.

Continuities in development

It is not disputed that statistically significant predictions of adult status can be made for some important characteristics in the pre-school years. Indeed, in most cases they can be assessed from an estimate of genetic and environmental variables before the child is born. What is in dispute, however, is the extent and, under appropriate circumstances of environmental change, the relative ease of reversibility of early environmentally induced characteristics. Most is known about the later development of children who had experienced early adversity. It must, of course, be assumed that children whose early experiences were superior, but whose later nurture became unsatisfactory, have shown later underfunctioning or deviant behaviour. Clinical experience suggests that there are many such children whose cases have not, however, been well documented. The only systematic evidence on this point is to be found in an as yet unpublished report arising from the large British National Child Development Study. To present these data, on the association between downward mobility and attainment, the authors have kindly sketched the wider context. They write:

The British National Child Development Study has investigated changes in reading and mathematics attainments between seven and eleven years of age. In addition to the pre-existing social class differences at the age of seven, further differences between the social classes have emerged by the age of eleven. Thus the average difference in reading attainment between non-manual children and children from the registrar general's social classes III manual and IV (skilled and semi-skilled manual) is about 0·9 years of reading attainment at age seven, with an additional 1·1 years by the age of eleven. Of considerable further interest is the finding that children from upwardly socially mobile backgrounds also had a gain in score. Thus those who moved from social classes III manual and IV at age seven into the non-manual group at age eleven had gained on average an additional 0·5 years of reading attainment, compared to those who remained in classes III manual and IV. Likewise those who were downwardly mobile between these groups had lost an additional 0·7 years of reading attainment compared to those who had remained in the non-manual group. Similar results hold for mathematics attainment. It would appear, therefore, that social class is associated with increasing differences in the educational attainments during the primary school years. The increase in the differences after the age of seven are at least as great as the differences associated with social class up to that age. (Personal communication from Ken Fogelman and Harvey Goldstein; report in press, 1976.)

These findings endorse the view that environmental shift (between the ages of seven and eleven) in either direction is actuarially associated with corresponding personal changes.

The notion of continuity underpins all developmental theories. Each stage is held to depend upon, and be influenced by, the integrity of previous stages. As noted, however, longitudinal studies involving repeated measurements do not suggest the existence of *powerful* continuities. Indeed, as Kagan, who formerly espoused the view that developmental consistencies were common, stated in a speech which formed the basis for a paper by Kagan and Klein (1973) that in his earlier work he had:

. . . uncovered fragile lines that seem to travel both backward and forward in time, the breadth and magnitude of those continuities are not over-whelming, and each seems to be easily lost or shattered . . . I rationalised the modest empirical support for continuity by arguing that although behaviors similar in manifest form might not be stable over long term periods, the underlying structures might be firmer. (See also pages 97–121.)

It seems obvious that genetically programmed growth shows accelerating and decelerating phases, which are themselves responsible for changes in developmental status. And in so far as learning (in its broadest sense) interacts powerfully with constitutional factors in development, it seems that part of its role is *unlearning* formerly appropriate responses which have become inappropriate. Such responses do not require modification, they need extinction and replacement. Hence one would expect (and one finds) discontinuities in normal development even in a situation where there is some degree of long-term environmental constancy. Thus prediction of later from earlier characteristics is on the whole poor, not primarily because of imperfect measurement, but because it is confounded both by discontinuities as well as by individual continuities which show variability over time (Clarke and Clarke 1976).

Any general statement about continuities and discontinuities must, however, be qualified by reference to the characteristics of a particular population. Thus, over lengthy periods, personality measures in normal children exhibit a strong tendency towards variability, compounded both by poor short-term reliability of measurement, as well as by systematic trends. On the other hand, the bizarre features of early childhood autism show very strong continuities for the vast majority, with only a minority shifting in their degree of deviance. Or again, in Lee Robins's (1966) study of the long-term outcome for those originally referred to a child guidance clinic, about age twelve, the continuities into adult life of those originally diagnosed as sociopathic were far stronger than for other conditions which at the time of referral also gave rise to concern for the child. Even the sociopaths, however, for whom the outcome was generally rather poor, contained some for whom the severity of disorder shifted towards or into normality. A number of studies, such as that by Mellsop (1972) confirm that childhood neurosis tends not to develop into adult neurosis. Summarising some of his own work Rutter (1976) indicates that more than half the children who had shown an emotional disorder at age ten were without disorder in adolescence, but in contrast this was so for less than a quarter of those who had shown a conduct disorder.

An approach to discontinuities in normal development similar to our own has been provided by Kadushin (1970; see pages 187–210 of this book). He writes that

... we may need a reorientation in emphasis with a greater respect being accorded to the present and the more recent, proximate experiences. The past does, of course, intrude to shape perception, and in the case of the psychotic and seriously neurotic it may even be decisive. But for those less ill ... the present is a countervailing force which exerts a constant pressure, demanding that we live by it ...

The belief in a necessary and powerful continuity has influenced policies concerning the age at which children can safely be offered for adoption, although fortunately there are signs that this is changing.

Social policy and early experience

The third implication of the traditional model has been studied by Patricia Morgan (1975) who offers a broad critique of one aspect of the current theme, namely the maternal deprivation theory which she sees as underpinning current child-rearing ideology, and the role of women in society. She states correctly:

... for about twenty years, the public, including the most influential bodies responsible for social policy-making, has been persuaded that the connection between maternal deprivation and personality damage has been scientifically established, and that it enjoys the same kind of authoritative standing as other medical discoveries ... But the true position is not remotely like this. By experimental standards as strict and coherent as those applied in the case of rubella, for example, the Maternal Deprivation Theory has no significant scientific support, and there is sufficient counter-evidence to make it decidedly improbable. (Morgan 1975, pp. 17–18)

She goes on interestingly to argue that a rejection 'of the erroneous view of childhood must involve us in very wide reappraisals of our assumptions about society'.

There is little difficulty in justifying these arguments whether from earlier official documents or from the 'experience' of intelligent people who perceive problems in the light of this model. Thus a World Health Organization Expert Committee (1951) regarded the use of day nurseries and crèches as leading to 'permanent damage to the emotional health of a future generation'. Baers (1954) claimed the children's normal development is dependent on the mother's full-time role in child rearing, and that 'anything that hinders women in the fulfilment of this mission must be regarded as contrary to human progress'. At a more popular level a mother refers to persistent school phobia in her daughter and to 'endlessly examining myself and her home to find the reason; I accept that it was the mother-separation anxiety she suffered in her most formative years' (*Guardian*, 27 August 1975).

The quasi-mystical bond between mother and child, seen as the great shaper of the future by psychoanalytic writers, has led in practice (and particularly among social workers) to the adoption of the slogan that a bad home is better than a good institution. There is also much talk about the sanctity of the family, and the need to keep deviant families 'propped up' with support, rather than remove the children to alternative forms of care. And yet, inconsistently, such workers are ready to point to the perpetuation of disadvantage through poor parent–child interactions; privately many admit that a regular weekly visit is hardly likely to produce significant change, and it is, of course, a common finding that those most in need of help are least likely to seek it, use it or profit by it.

In recent years there has been much talk about labelling and its effect in closing options for the individual. The wholesale acceptance that poor experiences in the first few years inevitably lead to doom has also tended to set in motion administrative decisions which confirm the implication. The disturbed young child, taken away from parents, on a 'fit person' order, is sent to an institution rather than a foster home because the prognosis is bad. Only later, if miraculously the child improves, will he be considered for non-institutional care. But by then the next slogan ⸮waits his case. 'Children adopted, or fostered late, do badly', so this option is seldom in fact open. (See Kadushin's contribution in section III.)

Indeed, the whole field of child care is so bedevilled by case law and by outmoded theories that it is small wonder that increasing criticisms from the voice of common sense are being levelled against its practitioners. In a sense this is unfair to them, for their past training, which in most cases had little effect in encouraging critical attitudes, and instead offered superficial generalisations, is ultimately responsible. In every part of this book the inadequacy of such received wisdom is made manifest, not by exchanging one set of clichés for another, but by examining facts dispassionately, outlining areas of ignorance and uncertainty and drawing appropriate, if modest, conclusions. To anticipate a little, such a survey makes it clear that a child's future is far from wholly shaped in the 'formative years' of early childhood. Rather, human development is a slow process of genetic and environmental interactions, with sensitivities (rather than critical periods) for different processes at different times. The implications of such a view are far from being merely academic; they challenge what Morgan (1975) has termed our current ideology of childhood.

Section II

The Study of Formerly Isolated Children

CHAPTER TWO

Formerly Isolated Children

A.D.B. Clarke and Ann M. Clarke

INTRODUCTION

Children who have been isolated from normal human contact are fortunately very few in number. It has long been appreciated that their study, following such privation, would throw important light upon the mechanisms of human development. Thus Itard, writing in 1801, noted that a few cases of wild children had been reported in the seventeenth and eighteenth centuries. However, 'in those unenlightened times so retarded was the progress of science – given up as it was to the mania for explanation, the uncertainty of hypothesis, and to explanation undertaken exclusively in the armchair – that actual observation counted for nothing and these valuable facts concerning the natural history of man were lost.' Itard goes on to note that the accounts left of these children were reduced to insignificant details:

... from which the most striking and most general conclusion to be drawn is that these individuals were susceptible to no very marked improvement. This was doubtless because the ordinary method of social instruction was applied to their education, without consideration for the difference of their organs. If the application of this method was entirely successful with the wild girl found in France towards the beginning of the last century, it is because, having lived in the woods with a companion, she already owed to that simple association a certain development of her intellectual faculties. (Itard 1932)

Itard's own study of a 'wild boy', who may well have been autistic or aphasic, was a monument to scientific endeavour. Indeed it was the first experimental study of one human being by another, and its place in the history of psychology has been underestimated. Similarly the case of Kasper Hauser, discovered in 1828, has been widely quoted as showing how isolation could produce severe retardation, but in this case largely made good over a five-year period until his death from a stab wound under mysterious circumstances (Tregold and Soddy 1956).

There have also from time to time been reports of children allegedly reared by animals (e.g. Romulus and Remus). Studies of such feral children cannot, however, be taken very seriously. One of the best known investigations (Gesell 1940) has been strongly criticised on several grounds, most notably and devastatingly by Ogburn and Bose (1959) who sifted fact from fancy in reinvestigating the famous 'wolf children'. Ogburn (1959) has also written an amusing paper about the 'wolf boy of Agra'.

Bettelheim (1959), among others, has suggested that feral children may be recently abandoned psychotic, autistic or severely retarded children. They are by definition always discovered in remote countryside and myths to account for their strange behaviour easily arise.

MODERN STUDIES

There are just a few cases of children whose early histories, to varying degrees, were known, who subsequently were isolated by deranged parents or grandparents, and who were ultimately discovered. The first modern account of such children was given by Kingsley Davis (1940, 1947) and his second paper is reprinted as the next contribution to this book. These children, Anna and Isabelle, were both discovered separately and at about the same time, both being aged about six. Anna received no specialist treatment and her general level of functioning, though showing improvement, remained severely retarded up to the time when she died at the age of ten and a half years from haemorrhagic jaundice.

The changes induced in Isabelle were, however, rapid and remarkable. It is important that this case was independently reported upon by Mason (1942) who was in charge of the girl's speech remediation. It is a great pity that the authors were unable to discover very much about the parentage of these girls; little was known about paternity. Nor is there any exact indication of the emotional state of Isabelle when followed up finally at age fourteen. Educationally she was then apparently a little below average but in general was considered normal. We do not know whether she herself had memories of her early years, or of her responsiveness to a radical change of environment (as had, for example, Helen Keller). But the case is sufficiently well documented to make it clear that one child showed substantial recovery to normality from a level of severe retardation. Moreover deprivation of language experience during the normal period of development of this function did not prove to be critical. It is of interest that Lenneberg (1967), basing his views on a wealth of experimental evidence, is quite cautious in qualifying his conclusion that ' . . . we may speak of a critical period for language acquisition' (1967, p. 174). But his concept is very wide: 'Between the ages of three and the early teens the possibility for primary language acquisition continues to be good . . . After puberty, the ability for self-organisation and adjustment to the physiological demands of verbal behaviour quickly declines' (1967, p. 158). Thus the data presented by Davis, and later in this section by Koluchová can certainly be accommodated within Lenneberg's (as opposed to narrower and less sophisticated) concepts of critical periods for language. What is surprising, however, in the light of the traditional model of the role of early development, is that barren early experience (though in the company of a deaf-mute mother, of unknown intelligence) had not set for Isabelle an irreversible path.

Stone (1954) has written an important critique of the earlier studies of infant isolation. He begins by indicating that until recent times a narrow view of potential environmental influences led to the study of specific training for skills. It was possible 'to show, for example, that just as the growth of grass pushed boulders apart, the developmental impetus in the individual produces walking when the child is ready to walk, even though he has been held down or even wrapped up in the preceding months' as in some cultures. This led to an acceptance of the view that

. . . it really mattered very little what one did in the course of the first year, since development, by and large, would take care of itself. Of course it was necessary for parents to see that babies received adequate nutrition, and beyond that it was their obligation to train the infant in such a way that the responses, as they unfolded, were made to appear on appropriate rather that inappropriate signal. It was a period of simultaneous excesses both in Watsonian empiricism and Gesellian nativism somehow wrapped together.

Stone argued that 'within this structure, so firm and tight that it was virtually sound-proof, it was difficult even to hear the clamorings of the psychoanalysts and such, who seemed to feel that what was done to the child in the first year . . . made all kinds of a difference.' In effect at that time there were two child psychologies, although these did not produce active conflict because they were virtually insulated from one another. Although more than twenty years old, this paper remains an important review and reinterpretation of knowledge up to that time and still repays study.

The two reports by Koluchová (1972, and a second, hitherto unpublished) are the most satisfactory in the literature, and are reprinted in full in this section. The monozygotic twin boys who suffered severe and prolonged deprivation have case histories which bear some resemblance to that of Isabelle, but the detailed analysis and descriptions, as well as the prolonged and intimate knowledge by the investigator, put these studies into a special class.

As Clarke (1972) indicated, it is possible to make a direct comparison of the development of Isabelle and the twins. All three were rachitic on discovery at ages six and seven, respectively, but Isabelle showed a greater intellectual deficit and even rudimentary speech was not present since she had been imprisoned from birth with her deaf-mute mother. While Isabelle's initially very low I.Q. trebled in eighteen months, the mental ages of the twins increased from three to eight years in a two-year period, and I.Q.s from about 40 to 95 and 93 in four years, a slower rate of advance but still an immense acceleration in development. Now at age fifteen they have I.Q.s of about 100, and, as the author suggests, the delayed maturation may not yet be complete.

It may be of importance that the twins spent the first eighteen months of life in nutritionally adequate environments, for this is the post-natal period where the developing brain is most vulnerable to damage from undernutrition (Dobbing and Smart 1974). The bases for perceptual and linguistic development were probably also laid during this period.

The failure of the twins to speak and to understand the meaning of pictures, and their relation to reality, is independent testimony to the length and severity of their deprivation. Yet malnutrition from eighteen months to seven years, cruelty, neglect and isolation (yet not from one another) had not predestined them to a permanent condition of quite severe mental handicap which they exhibited on discovery.

Koluchová's second report, written specially for this book, amplifies the picture considerably. She attributes the boys' continued progress to a number of factors, but in particular to an immensely dedicated adoptive family which could provide therapeutic help not normally available in institutions or in children's homes. She also draws attention to diagnostic problems, and in effect implies that there may be a number of other children like the twins who are not recognised as such, and whose inadequate treatment reinforces the handicap produced by abnormal rearing. Her brief account of another severely deprived child's progress is a useful addition to the report.

It is also of interest that the experts whose early prognostications about the twins were so gloomy, continue to maintain that 'severe deprivational damage at an early age is irremediable' and that the twins are no more than an exception to this rule. On the contrary, Isabelle (though not the untreated Anna) and the three cases reported by Koluchová all show, in extreme and rare form, the recovery processes which are much more commonly apparent in smaller amount in those children rescued from less adverse conditions. What is, however, astonishing is the existence of such potential resilience after such prolonged privation.

Mr A. Sutton (University of Birmingham) and Miss J. Francis (The Hospital for Sick Children, Great Ormond Street, London) have reported (personal communication) a study of twin girls who experienced severe deprivation.

The twins' father was an itinerant musician, who was accompanied on his travels by his wife, aged nineteen on marriage. Because of his erratic moods she left him when six months pregnant with the twins. They were born in February 1969, were cared for by some friends for three months, and then moved to some distant relatives with the hope that they might be adopted. This couple's marriage broke up, however, and the children were taken into care for a few weeks. Thereafter they lived with a maternal uncle and aunt until aged one year. During this time the mother joined up with her husband again, became pregnant and left him. In mid-1970 she settled in a slum in a large city and took over the children, and has had care of them and their younger brother ever since. She moved house in November 1971 and remarried in 1973.

The mother became depressed in her poor accommodation and

her remarriage did little to alleviate this, both because her second husband worked long hours, and because of some conflict between them.

The headmistress of a nursery school became at this time very concerned about the by-now four-year-old twins' development. Speech was rudimentary and unintelligible, play was under-developed and it was feared that by virtue of their mental sub-normality they would not benefit from normal school at age five. The headmistress referred them to a specialised pre-school agency, and the family appeared to benefit from help and advice.

Subsequent events took place in the light of some remarkably fortunate coincidences. The agency's psychologist was very familiar with the work on perhaps similar twins reported by Luria and Yudovich (1971). It was arranged that the family should be rehoused in an outer-suburban estate, and the infants school to which the twins were sent was fully aware of the nature and purpose of the subsequent experiment. The headmistress already had experience of taking a previously isolated child into her own home and habili-tating her. The experiment was also unique in that the twins were not removed from their home, and that their successful treat-ment depended primarily upon the school. After a term together in the reception class they were separated into different classes and base-line measures were taken by means of the W.P.P.S.I. and Reynell scales. During the next term a psychologist visited weekly and daily language training was given by the regular staff of the school. Test—retest measures before and after separation of the twins and their subsequent language training showed very large increases in the second half of the first year. At the end of the period the girls were regarded as normal children. The results are shown in figure 2.1 opposite.

It should also be noted that over the course of the year (from age 5—4 to 6—4) the language development of the twins accelerated sharply. The Reynell Developmental Language Scales showed that on Comprehension Twin A advanced from 3—4 to above 6; Twin B from 3—8 to 5—1. For Expression Twin A changed from 3—0 to 6—0, and Twin B from 3—6 to 5—3.

These cases, then, seem to have arisen because of early consider-able disruption in caretaking, and a subsequent degree of isolation arising in circumstances of very poor housing, and maternal depres-sion. The remarkable outcome may be attributable to a number

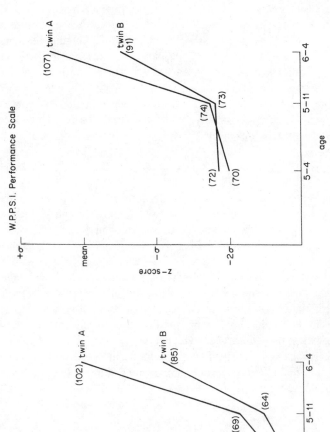

Figure 2.1   W.P.S.I. Verbal Scale, W.P.S.I. Performance Scale

The twins' intellectual growth measured psychometrically with the Wechsler Pre-school and Primary Scale of Intelligence (W.P.P.S.I.) before separation, after separation with no training, and after separation with language training. I.Q.s (in brackets) are in fact a form of linear standard score (15z + 100). The test permits separate presentation of tasks that are primarily verbal in nature and those which involve visuo-motor performance.

of circumstances, among which the prime ones probably included unusual awareness of the problem by the headmistress, and hence her staff, the special role of the psychologist, the separation of the twins after the first term, the introduction of a language-teaching programme, and the ability of the parents to respond to help and advice. There seems little doubt that if these interventions had not occurred, transfer to an E.S.N. school would have been inevitable, and a self-perpetuating chain of events would have ensued. Once again there was clearly no critical period after which normalisation became impossible.

CONCLUSIONS

These studies are important as extreme cases of early environmental deprivation of long duration, and have therefore been treated in this book outside the context of more common forms. They are, furthermore, the only cases where something approaching adequate evidence on the rearing conditions is available, unlike Itard's 'wild boy' and 'feral children' in which the antecedent conditions were assumed. It is, of course, impossible to be sure what the outcome for these children might have been, granted favourable early experience. However the consistent picture of substantial recovery, coupled with the absence of evidence suggesting potential genetic superiority, calls seriously into question the possibility of an early period in which the organism is irreversibly vulnerable to environmental influence.

CHAPTER THREE

Final Note on a Case of Extreme Isolation

Kingsley Davis

Early in 1940 there appeared in this *Journal* an account of a
girl called Anna. She had been deprived of normal contact and
had received a minimum of human care for almost the whole
of her first six years of life. At that time observations were not
complete and the report had a tentative character. Now, however,
the girl is dead, and, with more information available, it is possible
to give a fuller and more definitive description of the case from
a sociological point of view.

Anna's death, caused by hemorrhagic jaundice, occurred on 6
August 1942. Having been born on 1 or 6* March 1932, she
was approximately ten and a half years of age when she died.
The previous report covered her development up to the age of
almost eight years; the present one recapitulates the earlier period
on the basis of new evidence and then covers the last two and
a half years of her life.

EARLY HISTORY

The first few days and weeks of Anna's life were complicated
by frequent changes of domicile. It will be recalled that she was
an illegitimate child, the second such child born to her mother,
and that her grandfather, a widowed farmer in whose house her
mother lived, strongly disapproved of this new evidence of the
mother's indiscretion. This fact led to the baby's being shifted about.

Two weeks after being born in a nurse's private home, Anna
was brought to the family farm, but the grandfather's antagonism
was so great that she was shortly taken to the house of one of

Reprinted from *American Journal of Sociology* 45 (1947), 554 – 65

* The records are not clear as to which day.

her mother's friends. At this time a local minister became interested in her and took her to his house with an idea of possible adoption. He decided against adoption, however, when he discovered that she had vaginitis. The infant was then taken to a children's home in the nearest large city. This agency found that at the age of only three weeks she was already in a miserable condition, being 'terribly galled and otherwise in very bad shape'. It did not regard her as a likely subject for adoption but took her in for a while anyway, hoping to benefit her. After Anna had spent nearly eight weeks in this place, the agency notified her mother to come to get her. The mother responded by sending a man and his wife to the children's home with a view to their adopting Anna, but they made such a poor impression on the agency that permission was refused. Later the mother came herself and took the child out of the home and then gave her to this couple. It was in the home of this pair that a social worker found the girl a short time thereafter. The social worker went to the mother's home and pleaded with Anna's grandfather to allow the mother to bring the child home. In spite of threats, he refused. The child, by then more than four months old, was next taken to another children's home in a nearby town. A medical examination at this time revealed that she had impetigo, vaginitis, umbilical hernia, and a skin rash.

Anna remained in this second children's home for nearly three weeks, at the end of which time she was transferred to a private foster home. Since, however, the grandfather would not, and the mother could not, pay for the child's care, she was finally taken back as a last resort to the grandfather's house (at the age of five and a half months). There she remained, kept on the second floor in an attic-like room because her mother hesitated to incur the grandfather's wrath by bringing her downstairs.

The mother, a sturdy woman weighing about 180 pounds (81 kilograms), did a man's work on the farm. She engaged in heavy work such as milking cows and tending hogs and had little time for her children. Sometimes she went out at night, in which case Anna was left entirely without attention. Ordinarily, it seems, Anna received only enough care to keep her barely alive. She appears to have been seldom moved from one position to another. Her clothing and bedding were filthy. She apparently had no instruction, no friendly attention.

It is little wonder that, when finally found and removed from the room in the grandfather's house at the age of nearly six years, the child could not talk, walk, or do anything that showed intelligence. She was in an extremely emaciated and undernourished condition, with skeleton-like legs and a bloated abdomen. She had been fed on virtually nothing except cow's milk during the years under her mother's care.

Anna's condition when found, and her subsequent improvement, have been described in the previous report (1940). It now remains to say what happened to her after that.

LATER HISTORY

In 1939, nearly two years after being discovered, Anna had progressed, as previously reported, to the point where she could walk, understand simple commands, feed herself, achieve some neatness, remember people, etc. But she still did not speak, and, though she was much more like a normal infant of something over one year of age in mentality, she was far from normal for her age.

On 30 August 1939 she was taken to a private home for retarded children, leaving the county home where she had been for more than a year and a half. In her new setting she made some further progress, but not a great deal. In a report of an examination made 6 November of the same year, the head of the institution pictured the child as follows:

Anna walks about aimlessly, makes periodic rhythmic motions of her hands, and, at intervals, makes guttural and sucking noises. She regards her hands as if she had seen them for the first time. It was impossible to hold her attention for more than a few seconds at a time – not because of distraction due to external stimuli but because of her inability to concentrate. She ignored the task in hand to gaze vacantly about the room. Speech is entirely lacking. Numerous unsuccessful attempts have been made with her in the hope of developing initial sounds. I do not believe that this failure is due to negativism or deafness but that she is not sufficiently developed to accept speech at this time . . . The prognosis is not favorable . . .

More than five months later, on 25 April 1940, a clinical psychologist, the late Professor Francis N. Maxfield, examined Anna and reported the following: large for her age; hearing 'entirely normal'; vision apparently normal; able to climb stairs; speech in the 'babbling stage' and 'promise for developing intelligible speech later seems to be good.' He said further that 'on the Merrill-Palmer Scale she made a mental score of 19 months. On the Vineland Social Maturity Scale she made a score of 23 months.'*

Professor Maxfield very sensibly pointed out that prognosis is difficult in such cases of isolation. 'It is very difficult to take scores on tests standardized under average conditions of environment and experience', he wrote, 'and interpret them in a case where environment and experience have been so unusual.' With this warning he gave it as his opinion at that time that Anna would eventually 'attain an adult mental level of six or seven years'. †

The school for retarded children, on 1 July 1941, reported that Anna had reached 46 inches (1 2 metres) in height and weighed 60 pounds (27 kilogrammes). She could bounce and catch a ball and was said to conform to group socialization, though as a follower rather than a leader. Toilet habits were firmly established. Food habits were normal, except that she still used a spoon as her sole implement. She could dress herself except for fastening her clothes. Most remarkable of all, she had finally begun to develop speech. She was characterized as being at about the two-year level in this regard. She could call attendants by name and bring in one when she was asked to. She had a few complete sentences to express her wants. The report concluded that there was nothing peculiar about her, except that she was feeble-minded – 'probably congenital in type'. ‡

A final report from the school, made on 22 June 1942, and evidently the last report before the girl's death, pictured only a slight advance over that given above. It said that Anna could follow directions, string beads, identify a few colors, build with blocks, and differentiate between attractive and unattractive pictures. She had a good sense of rhythm and loved a doll. She talked mainly in phrases but would repeat words and try to carry on a conversation. She was clean about clothing. She habitually washed her hands and brushed her teeth. She would try to help

* Letter to one of the state officials in charge of the case
† Letter to state official
‡ Progress report of the school

other children. She walked well and could run fairly well, though clumsily. Although easily excited, she had a pleasant disposition.

INTERPRETATION

Such was Anna's condition just before her death. It may seem as if she had not made much progress, but one must remember the condition in which she had been found. One must recall that she had no glimmering of speech, absolutely no ability to walk, no sense of gesture, not the least capacity to feed herself even when the food was put in front of her, and no comprehension of cleanliness. She was so apathetic that it was hard to tell whether or not she could hear. And all this at the age of nearly six years. Compared with this condition, her capacities at the time of her death seem striking indeed, though they do not amount to much more than a two-and-a-half-year mental level. One conclusion therefore seems safe, namely, that her isolation prevented a considerable amount of mental development that was undoubtedly part of her capacity. Just what her original capacity was, of course, is hard to say; but her development after her period of confinement (including the ability to walk and run, to play, dress, fit into a social situation, and, above all, to speak) shows that she had at least this much capacity — capacity that never could have been realized in her original condition of isolation.

A further question is this: What would she have been like if she had received a normal upbringing from the moment of birth? A definitive answer would have been impossible in any case, but even an approximate answer is made difficult by her early death. If one assumes, as was tentatively surmised in the previous report, that it is 'almost impossible for any child to learn to speak, think, and act like a normal person after a long period of early isolation', it seems likely that Anna might have had a normal or near-normal capacity, genetically speaking. On the other hand it was pointed out that Anna represented 'a marginal case, [because] she was discovered before she had reached six years of age', an age 'young enough to allow some plasticity' (Davis 1940, p. 564). While admitting, then, that Anna's isolation *may* have been the major cause (and was certainly a minor cause) of her lack of rapid mental progress during the four and a half years following her rescue from neglect, it is necessary to entertain the hypothesis that she was congenitally deficient.

In connection with this hypothesis, one suggestive though by no means conclusive circumstance needs consideration, namely, the mentality of Anna's forebears. Information on this subject is easier to obtain, as one might guess, on the mother's than on the father's side. Anna's maternal grandmother, for example, is said to have been college educated and wished to have her children receive a good education, but her husband, Anna's stern grandfather, apparently a shrewd, hard-driving, calculating farmowner, was so penurious that her ambitions in this direction were thwarted. Under the circumstances her daughter (Anna's mother) managed, despite having to do hard work on the farm, to complete the eighth grade in a country school. Even so, however, the daughter was evidently not very smart. 'A schoolmate of [Anna's mother] stated that she was retarded in school work; was very gullible at this age; and that her morals even at this time were discussed by other students.' Two tests administered to her on 4 March 1938, when she was thirty-two years of age, showed that she was mentally deficient. On the Stanford Revision of the Binet-Simon Scale her performance was equivalent to that of a child of eight years, giving her an I.Q. of fifty and indicating mental deficiency of 'middle-grade moron type'.*

As to the identity of Anna's father, the most persistent theory holds that he was an old man about seventy-four years of age at the time of the girl's birth. If he was the one, there is no indication of mental or other biological deficiency, whatever one may think of his morals. However, someone else may actually have been the father.

To sum up: Anna's heredity is the kind that *might* have given rise to innate mental deficiency, though not necessarily.

COMPARISON WITH ANOTHER CASE

Perhaps more to the point than speculations about Anna's ancestry would be a case for comparison. If a child could be discovered who had been isolated about the same length of time as Anna

* The facts set forth here as to Anna's ancestry are taken chiefly from a report of mental tests administered to Anna's mother by psychologists at a state hospital where she was taken for this purpose after the discovery of Anna's seclusion. This excellent report was not available to the writer when the previous paper on Anna was published.

but had achieved a much quicker recovery and a greater mental development, it would be a stronger indication that Anna was deficient to start with.

Such a case does exist. It is the case of a girl found at about the same time as Anna and under strikingly similar circumstances. A full description of the details of this case has not been published, but, in addition to newspaper reports, an excellent preliminary account by a speech specialist, Dr Marie K. Mason, who played an important role in the handling of the child, has appeared (1942). Also the late Dr Francis N. Maxfield, clinical psychologist at Ohio State University, as was Dr Mason, has written an as yet unpublished but penetrating analysis of the case. Some of his observations have been included in Professor Zingg's book on feral man (Singh and Zingg 1941, pp. 248–51). The following discussion is drawn mainly from these enlightening materials. The writer, through the kindness of Professors Mason and Maxfield, did have a chance to observe the girl in April 1940, and to discuss the features of her case with them.

Born apparently one month later than Anna, the girl in question, who has been given the pseudonym Isabelle, was discovered in November 1938, nine months after the discovery of Anna. At the time she was found she was approximately six and a half years of age. Like Anna she was an illegitimate child and had been kept in seclusion for that reason. Her mother was a deaf-mute, having become so at the age of two, and it appears that she and Isabelle had spent most of their time together in a dark room shut off from the rest of the mother's family. As a result Isabelle had no chance to develop speech; when she communicated with her mother, it was by means of gestures. Lack of sunshine and inadequacy of diet had caused Isabelle to become rachitic. Her legs in particular were affected; they 'were so bowed that as she stood erect the soles of her shoes came nearly flat together, and she got about with a skittering gait'.* Her behavior toward strangers, especially men, was almost that of a wild animal, manifesting much fear and hostility. In lieu of speech she made only a strange croaking sound. In many ways she acted like an infant. 'She was apparently utterly unaware of relationships of any kind. When presented with a ball for the first time, she held it in the

* Maxfield, unpublished manuscript

palm of her hand, then reached out and stroked my face with it. Such behavior is comparable to that of a child of six months' (Mason 1942, p. 299). At first it was even hard to tell whether or not she could hear, so unused were her senses. Many of her actions resembled those of deaf children.

It is small wonder that, once it was established that she could hear, specialists working with her believed her to be feeble-minded. Even on non-verbal tests her performance was so low as to promise little for the future. Her first score on the Stanford-Binet was nineteen months, practically at the zero point of the scale. On the Vineland Social Maturity Scale her first score was thirty-nine, representing an age level of two and a half years.* 'The general impression was that she was wholly uneducable and that any attempt to teach her to speak, after so long a period of silence, would meet with failure' (Mason 1942, p. 299).

In spite of this interpretation, the individuals in charge of Isabelle launched a systematic and skilful program of training. It seemed hopeless at first. The approach had to be through pantomime and dramatization, suitable to an infant. It required one week of intensive effort before she even made her first attempt at vocalization. Gradually she began to respond, however, and, after the first hurdles had at last been overcome, a curious thing happened. She went through the usual stages of learning characteristic of the years from one to six not only in proper succession but far more rapidly than normal. In a little over two months after her first vocalization she was putting sentences together. Nine months after that she could identify words and sentences on the printed page, could write well, could add to ten, and could retell a story after hearing it. Seven months beyond this point she had a vocabulary of 1,500–2,000 words and was asking complicated questions. Starting from an educational level of between one and three years (depending on what aspect one considers), she had reached a normal level by the time she was eight and a half years old. In short she covered in two years the stages of learning that ordinarily require six' (Mason 1942, pp. 300–4). Or, to put it another way, her I.Q. trebled in a year and a half.† The speed with which she reached the normal level of mental

* Maxfield, unpublished manuscript
† Maxfield, unpublished manuscript

development seems analogous to the recovery of body weight in a growing child after an illness, the recovery being achieved by an extra fast rate of growth for a period after the illness until normal weight for the given age is again attained.

When the writer saw Isabelle a year and a half after her discovery, she gave him the impression of being a very bright, cheerful, energetic little girl. She spoke well, walked and ran without trouble, and sang with gusto and accuracy. Today she is over fourteen years old and has passed the sixth grade in a public school. Her teachers say that she participates in all school activities as normally as other children. Though older than her classmates, she has fortunately not physically matured too far beyond their level.*

Clearly the history of Isabelle's development is different from that of Anna's. In both cases there was an exceedingly low, or rather blank, intellectual level to begin with. In both cases it seemed that the girl might be congenitally feeble-minded. In both a considerably higher level was reached later on. But the Ohio girl achieved a normal mentality within two years, whereas Anna was still marked inadequate at the end of four and a half years. This difference in achievement may suggest that Anna had less initial capacity. But an alternative hypothesis is possible.

One should remember that Anna never received the prolonged and expert attention that Isabelle received. The result of such attention, in the case of the Ohio girl, was to give her speech at an early stage, and her subsequent rapid development seems to have been a consequence of that. 'Until Isabelle's speech and language development, she had all the characteristics of a feeble-minded child.' Had Anna, who, from the standpoint of psychometric tests and early history, closely resembled this girl at the start, been given a mastery of speech at an earlier point by intensive training, her subsequent development might have been much more rapid.†

The hypothesis that Anna began with a sharply inferior mental capacity is therefore not established. Even if she were deficient to start with, we have no way of knowing how much so. Under ordinary conditions she might have been a dull normal or, like

* Based on a personal letter from Dr Mason to the writer, 13 May 1946
† This point is suggested in a personal letter from Dr Mason to the writer, 22 October 1946.

her mother, a moron. Even after the blight of her isolation, if she had lived to maturity, she might have finally reached virtually the full level of her capacity, whatever it may have been. That her isolation did have a profound effect upon her mentality, there can be no doubt. This is proved by the substantial degree of change during the four and a half years following her rescue.

Consideration of Isabelle's case serves to show, as Anna's case does not clearly show, that isolation up to the age of six, with failure to acquire any form of speech and hence failure to grasp nearly the whole world of cultural meaning, does not preclude the subsequent acquisition of these. Indeed, there seems to be a process of accelerated recovery in which the child goes through the mental stages at a more rapid rate than would be the case in normal development. Just what would be the maximum age at which a person could remain isolated and still retain the capacity for full cultural acquisition is hard to say. Almost certainly it would not be as high as age fifteen; it might possibly be as low as age ten. Undoubtedly various individuals would differ considerably as to the exact age.

Anna's is not an ideal case for showing the effects of extreme isolation, partly because she was possibly deficient to begin with, partly because she did not receive the best training available, and partly because she did not live long enough. Nevertheless her case is instructive when placed in the record with numerous other cases of extreme isolation. This and the previous article about her are meant to place her in the record. It is to be hoped that other cases will be described in the scientific literature as they are discovered (as unfortunately they will be), for only in these rare cases of extreme isolation is it possible 'to observe *concretely separated* two factors in the development of human personality which are always otherwise only analytically separated, the biogenic and the sociogenic factors' (Singh and Zingg 1941, pp. xxi-xxii).

Sincere appreciation is due to the officials in the Department of Welfare, Commonwealth of Pennsylvania, for their kind cooperation in making available the records concerning Anna and discussing the case frankly with the writer. Helen C. Hubbell, Florentine Hackbusch and Eleanor Mecklenburg were particularly helpful, as was Fanny L. Matchette. Without their aid neither of the reports on Anna could have been written.

CHAPTER FOUR

Severe Deprivation in Twins: A Case Study

Jarmila Koluchová

CASE HISTORY

The background of deprivation

This is a case record of monozygotic twins, two boys P.M. and J.M., born on 4 September 1960. Their mother died shortly after giving birth to them and for eleven months they lived in a children's home. According to the records their physical and mental development was normal at that stage. Their father then applied to take them into the care of his sister, but soon afterwards he remarried and the boys were again placed in a children's home until the new household could be established. This new family included two natural elder sisters of the twins, and two children (a boy and a girl) of the stepmother – six children altogether, the oldest being nine years old. The married couple M. bought a house in the suburbs of a small town where nobody knew them. All the subsequent events concerning the twins could only be reconstructed after their discovery in the autumn of 1967.

For five and a half years the twins lived in this family under most abnormal conditions. Some of the neighbours had no idea of their existence, others guessed there were some little children in the family although they had never seen them. It is surprising that this could happen in a quiet street of family houses where the environment and social relations are very like those in a village. During the trial, however, the people next door testified that they had often heard queer, inhuman shrieks which resembled howling, and which came from a cellar leading to the back court. The father was once seen beating the children with a rubber hose until they lay flat on the ground unable to move. The neighbours,

Reprinted from *Journal of Child Psychology and Psychiatry* 13 (1972), 107 – 14 however, did not interfere in any way because they did not want to risk conflict with the children's stepmother, who was known to be a selfish, aggressive woman, unwilling to admit anyone into her house.

In spite of very good and extensive child welfare services in Czechoslovakia, the true situation of these children was somehow undetected by the authorities concerned. The children had never been medically examined either routinely or because of illness. They were not registered for school attendance at the appropriate age. The relatives of the natural mother of the twins complained that the children were very poorly cared for, but their complaints were never properly investigated by a personal visit to the family from a social welfare officer. It was a quite exceptional case which, because of its severity, was scrutinized very closely by the jury when the matter came to light.

The central figure in the family, and in the tragedy involving the twins, was the stepmother. All the investigations, and especially the trial at the district and regional court, showed that she was a person of average intelligence, but egocentric, remarkably lacking in feeling, possessing psychopathic character traits and a distorted system of values. The father was a person of below average intellect, passive and inarticulate; the stepmother dominated the family. Her own two children (the first of them illegitimate and the second the product of a disturbed marriage which ended in divorce) were reared in early childhood by their maternal grandmother. The stepmother therefore had little experience with small children and showed no interest in them. When the twins joined the family she fed them, but the other aspects of their care were left to their father. This disinterest developed into active hostility towards the twins, and she induced a similar attitude towards them in other members of the family. The other children were forbidden to talk to the twins or to play with them. The father, who worked on the railways, was often away from home and took little interest in the boys. He probably realized that they were not receiving proper care but he was incapable of changing the situation. The twins therefore grew up lacking emotional relationships and stimulation, and were totally excluded from the family. Relationships between the other members of the family were also unnaturally cool due to the mother's abnormal personality. The elder children were well dressed, their homework was supervised and so on, but these measures seemed to have been motivated by the mother's ambitions. She accepted the two stepdaughters into the family though she preferred her own children, but with none of the children did she have a genuine maternal relationship.

The boys grew up in almost total isolation, separated from the outside world; they were never allowed out of the house or into the main living rooms in the flat, which were tidy and well furnished. They lived in a small, unheated closet, and were often locked up for long periods in the cellar. They slept on the floor on a polythene sheet and were cruelly chastised. They used to sit at a small table in an otherwise empty room, with a few building bricks which were their only toys. When one of their natural sisters was later examined for another reason, she depicted this scene in a drawing entitled 'At Home'.

The twins also suffered physically from lack of adequate food, fresh air, sunshine and exercise. At the end of August 1967 the father brought one of the boys to a paediatrician, asking for a certificate that his son was unfit to enter primary school. Because the boy looked as if he were three years old rather than six, hardly walked, and was at first sight severely mentally retarded, the doctor agreed to postpone school entry, but insisted that the twins should be placed in a kindergarten, and that the family situation should be investigated by a social worker and a district nurse. The stepmother objected to these visits, criticized everybody concerned, and stressed that she was overworked at home. Probably anticipating further intervention by the welfare authorities, she tried to remove traces of the way in which the twins had been living.

Gradually it became clear that this was a case of criminal neglect. In December 1967 the twins were removed from the family and placed in a home for pre-school children, while legal proceedings were taken against the parents. Several days after their admission to the home it was found that the twins suffered from acute rickets, a disease which has been practically eliminated in modern Czechoslovakia. The children were admitted to an orthopaedic clinic and at the same time examined by a multi-disciplinary team.

PSYCHOLOGICAL FINDINGS

On admission to hospital attempts were made to assess the mental status of the twins. It was clear that the improvement in their living conditions during the three months prior to hospital admission had allowed some progress to take place. For example on admission to the kindergarten the twins did not join in any activities but were timid and mistrustful. They had to be brought to the kindergarten in a wheelchair, because they could barely walk, and when given shoes could not walk at all. During their last three months with the family they were not locked in the cellar and their little room was better equipped, but at the same time the stepmother's negative attitude towards them became even more acute, because she saw in them the cause of the unwelcome interference from outside.

While in hospital, the children were psychologically examined. They were encouraged to become familiar with the testing room and adapted to it very well. At first it was impossible to use a diagnostic tool which required their direct cooperation, and the preliminary step in assessment was the observation of their spontaneous behaviour, and in particular of their free and controlled play. Later it was possible to establish direct contact and to move on to more formal testing in which the author used Gesell's scale and the Terman–Merrill test.

The boys' restricted social experience and very poor general information was most strikingly shown in their reactions of surprise and horror to objects and activities normally very familiar to children of their age – e.g. moving mechanical toys, a TV set, children doing gymnastic exercises, traffic in the street, etc.

However their inquisitiveness gradually prevailed, the reactions of terror disappeared, and they began to explore their environment, although often they were easily distracted. Their shyness with people was reduced during their stay in the children's home, and in the hospital ward they were the centre of interest. They related to adults positively and indiscriminately, in a way that is typical of deprived children. Their relations with other children were at an immature and uncontrolled level for their age.

The spontaneous speech of the boys was extremely poor. In order to communicate with each other they used gestures more characteristic of younger children. They tried to imitate adult speech, but could repeat only two or three words at a time with poor articulation. They could not answer questions, even if it was evident from their reactions that they had understood them. It was obvious that they were not used to speech as a means of communication.

Their spontaneous play was very primitive, and predominantly at first it was only the manipulation of objects, but imitative play soon developed. As they became familiar with the toys and with their surroundings in the clinic their play gradually reached more mature levels, but they continued to need adult intervention to initiate and develop a play activity and were unable to join in the play of other children.

A remarkable finding was that the boys could not understand the meaning or function of the pictures. It was impossible therefore to measure the extent of their vocabulary by means of pictures, because they had never learned to perceive and understand them. We started therefore with pictures which were of the same size and colour as the real objects which they represented. After repeated comparisons of picture and object, understanding of the relationship emerged and extended to a constantly widening range of phenomena.

The author felt that to express the boys' intellectual level in terms of an I.Q. would be quite inadequate. Their I.Q.s at that stage would have been within the range of imbecility, but qualitative analysis of their responses, their total behaviour, and their considerably accelerated development since they had been taken away from their family, all unambiguously suggested that this was a case not of a primary defect in the sense of oligophrenia, but of severe deprivation. It seemed more appropriate therefore to consider their mental ages, which in December 1967 varied for both boys round the three-year level, with a range of ±1 year for separate component items. At this time their chronological age was seven years and three months.

After the period of hospitalization the children returned to the children's home where they made good progress. They began to participate with the children there; this was made easier for them by the fact that the other children in the home were some two to three years younger. Relationships with adults and children improved and they acquired much of the knowledge and many of the skills appropriate to pre-school children. As their health improved so their motor abilities developed; they learned to walk, to run, to jump, to ride a scooter. Similar progress was also noted in their fine motor coordination.

After six months' stay in the children's home the boys were

readmitted to the clinic for a short time to enable paediatric, audiological and psychological examinations to be made. Their mental age was by this time approximately four years, with a narrower range of passes on the component items than on the previous examination. There was evidence of considerable progress in habit formation, experience and the development of knowledge.

THE FORENSIC PROBLEM

During the first period of hospitalization the investigating authorities requested a report from a forensic paediatrician, who in turn asked for a consultant psychologist's report. However, the problem of assessment seemed too complex to be handled on the basis of one or more consulting examinations. We therefore asked the investigating authorities to assign an expert psychologist to the case, who would have both the support of the court and the right of a forensic expert as well. The panel of forensic specialists followed the progress of the boys for a period of six months while they were in the children's home, and undertook careful control examinations during the second period of hospitalization. The problem for the panel was to assess the total developmental picture presented by the children, and to decide whether their disabilities were likely to have been congenital or acquired. The psychologist, moreover, had also to try to answer the question as to whether the twins were likely to grow up to become mentally and emotionally normal people.

The psychologist's report was of considerable importance in this case. It was necessary to disprove the statement of the defendant that the children had been defective from birth, and to prove that their disabilities were caused by severe neglect and lack of stimulation. For this reason a lengthy period of six months' observation was necessary, although it was apparent much earlier that the children were developing more quickly in the environment of the children's home than they ever had in their family home. During the trial, too, we had to refute the statement of the defendant and her husband that the children had had experience of picture material and play opportunities at home.

It was more difficult to answer the question about the future development of the twins. There was no evidence from the literature on deprivation, and because the case was so exceptional we had no personal experience to guide us. We could therefore only outline a probable prognosis and assume that in a good environment the children would develop in every respect, that their developmental deficits would show a tendency to be reduced, but that it was necessary to take into account the possible consequences of such severe deprivation on the development of personality. We pointed out to the judges some of the handicapping effects of this deprivation: entry to school delayed by three years, the probable necessity for the boys to attend a school for mentally retarded children, the effects on employment prospects, and the possibility of other difficulties in their social and intellectual development. We recommended that the children be placed as soon as possible in a compensating foster home, on the grounds that even the best children's home could not be the. optimal solution in the long term.

The main trial at the district court lasted for three days, all the forensic specialists being present. The defendant did not admit to having damaged the twins in any way. She denied that anything unusual had happened and maintained that they had been handicapped since infancy and that she had done her best for them by cooking and cleaning. She poured out her own troubles and expressed again her sense of being overworked. The court sentenced her to four years' deprivation of liberty and both father and stepmother also lost their parental rights.

In his final speech the public prosecutor and the chairman of the senate of judges, in confirming the verdict, emphasised the importance of the experts' reports in their evaluation of the defendant's guilt.

THE FURTHER DEVELOPMENT OF THE CHILDREN

In the school year 1968/9 the boys remained in the pre-school children's home. Their mental development was better than the original prognosis had suggested. Whereas some experts were doubtful about their educability, a psychologist's assessments showed that the retardation was diminishing and that the boys had reached a level of readiness for school. Because of their retarded speech, and relatively poor fine motor coordination and powers of concentration, we thought that a school for mentally retarded children was indicated as an initial step, since there were greater possibilities of individual teaching and a slower pace of learning.

Simultaneously with their starting school we tried to solve the problem of their foster home placement. A number of families were willing to take the children, but we had to assess the motivation of the applicants very carefully, considering the personalities of the potential substitute parents, and existing family structures. Finally in July 1969, the boys were placed with a family who have been able to accept them as natural and loved children. After two years' observation we still consider this to be the optimal placement, although in the conventional sense the family is not a complete family at all. It consists of two unmarried middle-aged sisters, both intelligent, with wide interests, living in a pleasant flat, and capable of forming very good relationships with the children. One of these sisters had already adopted a baby girl some years before, and this child is now an intelligent well-educated thirteen-year-old. The second sister became the foster mother of the twins. Our observation and information from many sources, show that deep emotional bonds have been formed between the children and their foster family, and many of the consequences of deprivation – e.g. a narrow outlook, a small range of emotional expression, etc. – which had remained during their stay in the children's home, are gradually diminishing. The boys have re-collections of their original home, and though the foster family tries to avoid reviving the past, the boys themselves will sometimes begin to talk about it; we also have touched on this during our psychological examinations. Until recently the boys did not have sufficient language ability to describe even in outline their life in their original family. If we compare their story now with the facts established during and before the trial, it is evident that their account is reliable. They have a completely negative attitude to their stepmother, and refer to her as 'that lady' or 'that unkind lady'. They remember the names of their brother and sisters, and they recollect how they used to be hungry and thirsty, how they were beaten about the head (their scalps are badly scarred), and how they used to sit at the small table. The stepmother often carried them into the cellar, thrashed them with a wooden kitchen spoon until it broke, and put a feather-bed over their heads so that no one would hear their screaming.

For a long time they had a dread of darkness. They appreciated the physical warmth of their new home, the good food they received, and the fact that they were no longer beaten. During our first visit to them in the foster home we had to reassure them that we would not take them away from their foster mother.

In September 1969 they were admitted to the first class in a school for mentally retarded children. On the basis of our observations of the children in class, the teacher's records, and our further examinations, we found the boys soon adapted themselves to the school environment and began to outstrip their classmates. Their writing, drawing and ability to concentrate improved remarkably in the second term, and it became clear that this type of school

Twin P. I.Q.		Twin J. I.Q.	
8 years 4 months			
verbal	80	verbal	69
performance	83	performance	80
full scale	80	full scale	72
9 years			
verbal	84	verbal	75
performance	83	performance	76
full scale	82	full scale	73
10 years			
verbal	97	verbal	94
performance	85	performance	86
full scale	91	full scale	89
11 years			
verbal	97	verbal	96
performance	93	performance	90
full scale	95	full scale	93

Table 4.1   Wechsler Intelligence Test Scores (W.I.S.C.)

would not extend them sufficiently. Accepting that there was a risk involved, we recommended a transfer to the second class of a normal school from the beginning of the next school year. In spite of the difference in curriculum and teaching methods, they proved to be capable of mastering the subject matter of the normal school, and did well enough to suggest that they have the ability to complete successfully the basic nine-year school course which, however, they would finish at the age of eighteen instead of the normal age of fifteen. Their schoolmates are three years younger, and it remains to be seen how relations between them and the twins develop, particularly as they enter puberty; the effects on the self-confidence and personality of the twins may be considerable but only extended observation will give us the answer to this.

A summary of the psychological test findings shows that in the fifteen months from June 1968 to September 1969 the mental age of the twins increased by three years; this was an immense acceleration of development, indicating how the change of living conditions provided a rapidly effective compensation for the consequences of earlier deprivation.

At first the children were assessed using Gesell's Developmental Scale and later the Terman-Merrill Scale in which their verbal level was markedly below non-verbal test items. Since the age of eight years and four months the boys have been examined by means of the Wechsler Intelligence Scale (W.I.S.C.). The test scores are presented in table 4.1 and indicate the low-level verbal response initially, especially in the Twin J., and the subsequent improvement over three years. Both children now seem to be functioning almost at an average level for their age.

CONCLUSIONS

This is a very exceptional case of deprivation, firstly because of the lengthy period of isolation, and secondly because of the unusual family situation which by outward appearances was a relatively normal and orderly one.

The children suffered from a lack of stimulation and opportunity for psycho-motor development. The most severe deprivation, however, was probably their poverty of emotional relationships and their social isolation. The stepmother did not even partially satisfy their need for maternal nurturance. She was on the contrary, as the dominating person in the family, the instigator of hostile attitudes towards the children and an active agent in their physical and mental torment. The influence of the father was confined to occasional repressive actions. The stimulating influence of brothers and sisters was also lacking. Thus we may speak of a combination of outer and inner causes of deprivation, the inner or psychological ones being primary.

We have not found in the literature a similar case of such severe and protracted deprivation in a family. Following Langmeier and Matějček (1968), we can define the situation of the twins as one of extreme social isolation, where the children are still fed by people, but are almost completely isolated from human society. Cases in the literature differ from ours both in recording a shorter period of social isolation, and in showing more severe consequences of deprivation than we have so far found. We assume, therefore, that the twins were able to bear the onerous situation better than any single child would have done.

Almost four years of observation of the twins have shown that in comparison with analogous cases in the literature their mental and social development has been very good. It is, however, difficult to foresee how their intelligence will develop, what the course of their development will be, how their personalities will be formed, and what residual effects of the deprivation will remain. The comparison between these monozygotic twins, living in essentially the same environment, will also be of interest.

In the presentation of this paper, the assistance of Professor A.D.B. Clarke, University of Hull, and Geoffrey A. Dell, Principal Psychologist at the Child Guidance Clinic, Glasgow, is gratefully acknowledged.

CHAPTER FIVE

A Report on the Further Development of Twins after Severe and Prolonged Deprivation

Jarmila Koluchová

This paper follows up a previous study of severe and prolonged deprivation of twin boys born in 1960 (Koluchová 1972). Although their development had been surprisingly good even at the time of the first report, and it was possible to exclude gross damage of their intellect and personality, there remained a number of problems, which could only be solved in a long-term study. The importance of observing the case over a long period was also emphasised in Professor A.D.B. Clarke's (1972) commentary. The author would like to express her gratitude to him here for his interest in her work, which she hopes to continue. Having observed the twins until now she wants to record their further development after an interval of three years, to mention similar cases and to arrive at some more general conclusions concerning the diagnosis and remediation of severe deprivation.

In the school year 1971-2 the twins, now aged between eleven and twelve, attended the third class. Their speech was entirely adequate to their age both in form and content. As the prediction of phoniatricians and paediatricians concerning the development of speech had been rather pessimistic, an attempt will be made to explain the fact that the twins' speech is at a good level and allows full social integration.

Until the eleventh month of their life the children had lived in an infants' home, then – for a shorter period of time – in a family of their relatives and later, in a home for toddlers. According to the available records of the infants' home, the children had been developing adequately for their age. It is possible to presume that at that time, which is usually regarded as a preparatory period of speech, and during which a mainly passive knowledge of a language is developed, the children had mastered actively several words and had comprehended the communicative function of speech. They had probably retained those abilities during the whole period of deprivation, mostly in a latent form only, because the small amount of speech they had been used to hearing between eighteen months and seven years had not had a communicative character for them. The basic prerequisite for the development of speech had also been missing, i.e. the individual contact of an adult with a child and the resulting positive stimulating relationship. But, although the period until their third year, which is usually considered the terminal limit for generating the ability to speak, had been missed, the twins' speech started to develop in spite of the fact that they had scarcely spoken at all until the age of seven. The development was quickest after their ninth year when they came to their foster family, which provided them with all the prerequisites both for the development of speech and the whole personality. At school and in a collective of children, the boys were agile, cheerful and popular; there were no signs of eccentricity or troubles in the social sphere. Until the fourth class of their school attendance their results were very good – they used to have a grade two only in the Czech language (mother tongue). They were the best pupils of the class in arithmetic (grade one), which arose, first, by a quick compensation of the retardation in the sphere of intellectual functions, and second, by their being two to three years older than their fellow pupils.

Gradually they began to feel older in comparison with their schoolmates and began to be aware of their late start at school, both these being due to the acceleration of their growth and a rather delayed commencement of pre-puberty. Both the teachers and the foster mother supported their natural ambition to master, during the fourth class, also the subject matter of the fifth class. They succeeded in their effort and after the holidays passed the examinations of the fifth class; then they were moved up from the fourth, direct to the sixth class. Thus they found themselves among children of more approximate age and their self-confidence was reinforced. Their results fell to the average, but the situation has been gradually improving hitherto. Both of them like attending school and, naturally, some subjects are favourite and others less attractive for them. They love reading, ride bicycles, can swim and ski, they play the piano well and they have both creative and technical talent. It is interesting that musical ability started to develop only at about the age of ten, but it is now at a good level. In the present school year (1974/75) the boys attend the seventh class; their schoolmates are on the average one and a half years younger. As their adolescence began about a year late in comparison with the average of our population, the whole status of their development and interests now corresponds approximately with the standard of their present schoolmates. After finishing basic education (nine classes) they would like to study at a secondary vocational school, for which they show sufficient aptitudes.

The development of the twins' intellectual level has been observed continually by means of several methods; to compare previous scores with more recent findings the author presents here the boys' I.Q.s obtained by means of the W.I.S.C.:

Age	Twin P. I.Q.	Twin J. I.Q.
8	80	72
9	82	73
10	91	89
11	95	93
12	95	104
13	98	100
14	100	101

It will be recalled that shortly after their discovery, I.Q.s were probably in the 40s but later, on the W.I.S.C. Test, it was evident that their development was quickest between the ninth and tenth years, namely the first year of their stay in the foster family and the first year of their school attendance. According to the past trend it is possible to anticipate that their intelligence scores may be raised a little. In the non-verbal scale of the W.I.S.C. and in Raven's Matrices Test the achieved scores are a little higher than in the verbal, which may be explained by the fact that the verbal score is to a certain extent dependent on education, which is still retarded according to their age. In spite of initial differences in the intellectual level of the boys, and distinctive differences in their development, their general standard has now come to be equal; however some features of their character have continued to differ. J. is a little slower in comparison with his brother, but he is in general of calmer disposition. P. perceives more quickly, he reacts more promptly, but his attention is rather labile, he is a little preoccupied and shows symptoms of autonomic lability.

In the development and forming of the personalities of the boys no psychopathological symptoms or eccentricities appear at present. It is possible to say that there are no consequences of the deprivation remaining which would cause retardation or damage to their development. It does not mean, however, that five years of hardship and ill-treatment by their cruel stepmother have not left any traces at all. The dread of darkness, which outlasted for a long time, has already faded, but under oppressive or unusual conditions the boys sometimes show the feeling of fear and their reaction is neurotic. For example, once they happened to come to a cellar similar to the one in which they had often been imprisoned. This frightened and upset them, and again revived the recollections of past suffering. In the cheerful environment of their new family, and with the help of their foster mother, who is always ready to understand, the boys will calm down quite easily and revert to their normal mood.

The twins hate recalling the conditions of their deprivation, and are even unlikely to speak about it with one another. However, by occasional remarks and the reactions mentioned above, it is evident that some recollections have remained and will probably be retained for ever. The boys' foster mother mentions that they will tell her something about their cheerless childhood now and then, but always each of them separately in an intimate talk. Comparing their previous and present recollections, it is apparent that there is no tendency to distort or exaggerate their experiences; their evidence conforms with the data stated in the judicial trial of their stepmother. The boys' recollections of the past are no longer associated with fear of possible recurrence of such living conditions and of losing their new family.

The awareness of the relations with the family is really profound and makes the boys feel safe and assured. Natural emotional bonds with all members of the family have arisen; apparently the relation with their foster mother, who is in a dominant position in the family, is emotionally deepest. Her sister is an aunt for them. As mentioned in the 1972 paper, the latter had adopted a girl – now sixteen years old – and besides her there is another ten-year-old girl (staying with the family during the last four years), whose brief history will follow. Thus, there are two foster mothers and their four children, who have very nice brother and sister relations with one another, although they of course know they are not consanguineous relatives. There is a happy atmosphere in the whole family, full of mutual understanding. Undoubtedly, it is possible to object to such a family without a father, whom the boys would need just at present in the period of their puberty. The boys' foster mother is aware of this and is trying to compensate for the lack of a man in the process of bringing up the boys by their frequent meeting with her brother and other relatives and friends, who have close relations with the boys.

The fact that has intensified their awareness of firm relationships in this family and has helped to establish the feeling of safety and assurance, was the agreed change of surname to that of their foster mother. Even before the change was completed, the boys had been using this surname; they have never uttered their original surname as it has evidently raised negative emotions in them.

As the most important factor in the conditions of deprivation of the twins from eighteen months until seven years of age was almost total social isolation and hostile relations of the members of that family, especially with their stepmother, a question arises – how has it been reflected in their social relations and behaviour?

In the 1972 report, the relations of the twins to one another, to other children and also to adults were described. The situation has been developing as follows: immediately after they had been removed from the family and placed in the children's home, a strong emotional bond with one another was evident. Apparently it had developed because it had been the only positive emotion that could have been built up and, moreover, it had helped them to bear the difficult living conditions. The outer demonstration of their relations, however, corresponded with a much lower age: they used to make themselves understood like toddlers, using mostly mimicry and gestures. Their original shyness with people and re-actions of terror had disappeared rather quickly and the children related both to adults and children positively in a way that is more characteristic of younger children. Mainly they showed a lesser differentiation of emotional relations and a prevailing interest in adults.

The children's gradual socialisation was facilitated by the fact that they had lived for a longer period of time among children approximately three years younger, which corresponded with their developmental deficit. Starting to attend a school for mentally retarded children at the age of nine, they were for the first time with a larger well-organised group of children, which they joined in successfully; undoubtedly the individual attention of their teacher, who had been informed of their history, helped a lot. There were no striking features in their social contacts, they did not show any symptoms of timidity, shyness or some other kind of abnormality and they never behaved aggressively either at the school for mentally retarded children or at the normal school later on. The boys have always had close relations with one another – an emotional bond much firmer than is usual with brothers of their age. But common teasing or petty conflicts are present of course, as is usual with children in normal families.

Making the boys acquainted with their suffering during the early and pre-school age appears to be a relatively difficult educational and psychotherapeutic problem. They can remember that period of time only in fragments without being able to comprehend the essentials of the whole event, its circumstances and causes. We consider it advisable to make them acquainted with the main facts concerning their parentage, family, the trial, and further events until their coming to this family, from the point of view of realisation of the continuity of their personalities, self-evaluation and also as a precaution against possible trauma caused by an incidental information or experience in later life. It is necessary to respect the long-standing aversion to reverting to the past, but at the same time their pubescent inquisitiveness and their efforts to know and to evaluate themselves should be employed. The foster mother is aware of the gravity of this task and she is thought to manage it well. The author wants to focus her attention on those problems too, in her talks with the twins within the framework of their psychological observation, naturally in close cooperation with their foster mother.

Appreciating the children's general development as highly successful – in contradiction with the original prediction of doctors – it is also necessary to evaluate the therapeutic factors that have contributed to this. As already stated in the 1972 report the children had been treated at an orthopaedic and paediatric clinic after their withdrawal from the family and after their rickets had been overcome. At the same time they had been examined at some other clinics – psychiatric, optic and in a phoniatric ward. Their somatic condition having improved, they were then placed in a children's home. Also, there, exceptional individual care was bestowed upon them and their future was discussed and planned carefully. The most important factor for solving that problem was a good prediction consequent to psychological examinations. The present foster family was selected from several families interested. Having been placed in this family the children started to attend speech training and they were also practising their pronunciation intensively at home. Consequently they managed to inhibit their nasal speech and in general to modify their poor articulation. The children have also been carefully looked after by a district paediatrician, who knows everything about the family and about the children themselves. Another important curative factor is the attitude of their teachers, which is individual and full of sympathy, although they expect the boys to meet reasonable scholastic claims without any preference or special tolerance.

Continuing care, carried out during the whole period by the same psychologist (the author), has proved to be fortunate. Besides the experimental direction, she also acts as an adviser and passes psychological reports to school and other institutions. In the author's opinion the main advantage of such a procedure lies in her detailed knowledge of the whole history, including court reports. Moreover the twins trust her, which has enabled her to observe the dynamism of their development over seven years.

Even if all the above mentioned curative factors are by no means significant, it is necessary to emphasise that the most effective and integrative curative factor is their foster mother and the whole environment of their family. Although the lady is employed, she devotes all her leisure time to the children with a lot of self-sacrifice; her solicitude for them is the content and purpose of her life, without spoiling the children or adopting uncritical attitudes.

The specialists, who had not believed in any possibility of remedying the severe deprivation damage in the twins, later referred to their quick development as an exception to the rule which states that severe deprivational damage at an early age is irremediable. According to the author's experience, however, there is a number of similar cases, but they are not usually correctly diagnosed, professionally observed and described.

As an example of the importance of a correct diagnosis and the difficulty of remedying severe deprivation, we want to mention a brief history of a girl, L.H., born in 1965, living now in the same family as the twins. This girl was withrawn legally from her own family at the age of four as a consequence of almost total social isolation and cruel treatment by her psychopathic mother. The child had been hated by her mother, tormented by hunger, she had been constantly kept alone in an unfurnished room, had slept on a straw mattress and had not acquired the basic habits of body hygiene. All of her mother's seven elder children had earlier been withdrawn from her legally. This girl was placed in a children's home, where she behaved anxiously, agitatedly, even aggressively; her language ability was almost totally undeveloped and she was still incontinent. The schoolmasters in the home considered her ineducable and it was decided that she should be placed in a mental home. For diagnostic and therapeutic reasons the child was admitted to a psychiatric hospital and dismissed after a month with the diagnosis of severe mental handicap.

The family in which the twins live happened to hear about this girl. Encouraged by the good development of the twin boys, they decided to adopt the girl into the family as a foster daughter in spite of the fact that the prediction of her development was rather pessimistic, being based on a supposition that she had been primarily an intellectually defective child. Even though the child was difficult to care for in the family during the first weeks, due to her agitation and anxiety, soon both the ladies understood that she had been damaged by cruelty and isolation and that she had a good intellectual capacity. During our first examination of the child soon after her arrival in the family we were able to eliminate mental subnormality even if her retardation was considerable and deprivation symptoms conspicuous. The child started learning to speak rather quickly, she was bright and she began to attend a kindergarten.

On the whole, however, this child has always been an incomparably greater educational problem than the twins. She attends a school for normal children, she can read and write well and she has an outstanding talent for music, but her attention is very labile, she is not able to take adequate pains while learning and she shows some shortcomings in the functions of her memory, which might be due to her having suffered meningitis, caused probably by frequent, uncured otitis, from which she still suffers. She has continued to have some problems in the social sphere, though, thanks to kind-hearted and consistent upbringing, there has been some improvement and rectification even here, which could not have been achieved in a children's home. The girl joins in with other children or the collective of pupils in her class with great difficulties; sometimes she is aggressive and intolerant with her contemporaries, while she is gentle and kind with younger children.

It is interesting to compare the girl with the twins. The deprivational history of the three children is rather similar; they live in the same family now and are given the same attention. Their different development in the social sphere can be explained by distinct congenital dispositions but mainly by the fact that the twins had mutually reduced their isolation and terrible living conditions. The girl's mother is a severely psychopathic person with disorders in character and the social sphere. There are no valid data about her father. On the other hand the twins' mother was quite normal in intelligence and personality structure. The father of the twins was already characterised in the 1972 report as passive and of below-average intellect. According to preserved photographs and to reliable reports the twins seem to possess their mother's features, both in the somatic and psychological sphere. But their better development in the social sphere should be explained in the first place by the fact that they could build up emotional relations with one another, and that they could stimulate one another to some extent and thus they did not experience the tormenting feeling of loneliness as intensely and destructively as would a child totally isolated.

We have recorded more cases similar to the twins and the above-mentioned girl, but their detailed history has not yet been obtained and they have been observed only for a shorter period. The author could often confirm, in her work as a clinical psychologist, that children who suffered severe and prolonged deprivation, coming either from inadequate families, often chastised and socially isolated, or living for a long time in a children's home environment, are misdiagnosed as mentally subnormal both by paediatricians, paedopsychiatrists and psychologists. The clinical picture of severe deprivation and mental subnormality is similar in certain symptoms, which can lead to a confusion of the two diagnoses when the subjects are only routinely examined, when the test methods are mechanically used or are misinterpreted and when the history is not known in detail. Both the cases are typical of general retardation of development and speech, social immaturity and a lowered ability to learn. Especially the development of children up to the third year of age may be so profoundly affected as a consequence of all the external and internal conditions of a children's home environment lacking stimulation, that it is rather difficult to differentiate such cases from mental subnormality.

As these children are usually socially forlorn – i.e. their parents cannot or do not want to look after them – it is necessary to solve the problems of their future and therefore a correct diagnosis is of immense value. The author thinks that, in understanding the difficult task of differential diagnosis, particular attention should be paid to psychological findings. Only psychological examination can reveal subtle differences between severely deprived and mentally subnormal children. However, cursory, non-residential examination will not do; it is absolutely necessary to carry out a detailed repeated examination by means of both test and non-test methods, aimed at the structure and dynamics of their development deficit. Such an examination enables a skilled psychologist to differentiate deprivation from subnormality and to determine the prognosis for its development. Here the psychological diagnosis is not only a theoretical problem, but above all a basis for educational, juridical and therapeutic actions.

In cases of severe deprivation, originating at an early age, the therapeutic prognosis has usually been considered poor. But the above-mentioned cases of deprived children, together with others that are still being observed, prove that even gross damage, previously considered to be irreversible, can be remedied. Our experience with the development of speech, too, contradicts the traditional view concerning the critical period for the development of speech. In the twins, as well as other cases, a successful development of speech was observed three to six years after their passing to a stimulating environment, sometimes even later. Thus, the prediction for the retarded development of speech in deprived children seems to be more optimistic if the defect is not organically or genetically conditioned, and when the child is given sufficient professional care and, above all, placed in a kind-hearted family environment.

The view that the effects of severe deprivation were irreparable arose from the fact that severely deprived children usually could not be found a new family. According to our experience the environment of a family, stimulating and full of understanding, giving them a feeling of safety and a firm relationship, is the only effective therapy, very exacting and time-consuming. This conclusion, together with the fact that the family is considered to be the most important educational factor, led to several arrangements for the care of children living outside their own families in our country, which are designed to prevent deprivation or remedy existing deprivation. There has been a general effort to assimilate a children's-home environment to a family environment e.g. to integrate a number of children of different ages into so-called 'family groups' with unchanging tutors.

Besides the standard children's homes there have arisen new forms of substitute family care – so-called 'children's villages' in which foster mothers with eight to ten children live in separate houses; then, there are so-called 'big families', where a married couple looks after a similar number of children. These 'big families' are not concentrated in 'villages', but they live in normal houses, both in towns and in the country. 'The father' is employed somewhere like the father of a normal family and 'the mother' looks after the children and is paid by the state on the same basis as 'mothers' in 'children's villages'. There are also cases of paid foster parentage in natural families. Both such families and the people interested in the work either in 'children's villages' or in 'big families' are carefully selected, including by psychological examination; all the forms of substitute family care are paid and methodically guided by the State authorities and advisory boards, in which psychologists also work. A special advisory service has also been established with psychologists and paediatricians, and, if necessary, other experts can be summoned, for example, paedopsychiatrists.

Several years' experience with these forms of care indicate the great therapeutic prospects offered by a stimulating family environment. To observe and evaluate them is a task for long-term studies which might be a valuable contribution to the diagnosis and remediation of deprivation.

Section III

Changing the Course of Human Development I

CHAPTER SIX

Studies in Natural Settings

A.D.B. Clarke and Ann M. Clarke

INTRODUCTION

The previous section on *Studies of Formerly Isolated Children*, with its four contributions, could have been subsumed under the above heading, but as noted earlier, it seemed appropriate to treat the extreme cases separately. What emerged clearly was that severe and prolonged social isolation (Davis 1947) accompanied by cruelty (Koluchová 1972 and second report) until age six and seven, respectively, did not predestine the children to permanent mental handicap or emotional maladjustment. The careful descriptions in these papers indicated a dramatic initial rise in ability, a rapid initiation of speech in the year or so following rescue, and slow but continuing improvements thereafter. The second Koluchová report represents the most weighty argument against the notion of early critical periods of development for speech, intelligence, personality and even some aspects of perception. It may be relevant that Isabelle was not alone during her early childhood, having been incarcerated with her deaf-mute mother; and the Koluchová twins were with one another, as were the twins described by Sutton and Francis, thus differing from the apparently more damaged girl whom Koluchová described in her second report.

Similarly Freud and Dann (1951), reporting an observational study on the first six children rescued from the concentration camp at Tereszin and brought to Britain in 1945, ascribe much importance to peer relations. All had been orphaned at twelve months or earlier and reared by a succession of concentration camp inmates until aged about three. In a one-year follow-up it was clear that they were hypersensitive, restless, aggressive and difficult to handle, 'but they were neither deficient, delinquent nor psychotic. They . . . had mastered some of their anxieties, and developed social attitudes.

That they were able to acquire a new language in the midst of their upheavals, bears witness to a basically unharmed contact with their environment.' This is attributed to the relations these children had formed with one another in the camp. Their feelings towards one another 'show a warmth and spontaneity which is unheard of in ordinary relations between young contemporaries'. The same point has been made by Koluchová.

In the present section attention is turned to studies of groups of children who have experienced environmental changes of varying kinds, mostly not documented in detail. Here one is considering the average outcome, described in global terms, of groups whose early environments were probably heterogeneous but on average were unsatisfactory, who later were placed in a range of more favourable circumstances. It is assumed, therefore, that personal changes, if any, can only be considered as reflecting a general direction.

It is a useful convention to review previous work chronologically. The researches of the Iowa school in the 1930s attracted much attention and abuse (McNemar 1940), but although there were certainly weaknesses in methodology, the findings of such investigators as Skeels and Skodak have largely been substantiated by their own and others' subsequent research. It is of interest that, as a service agency, the Iowa Child Welfare Research Group was always primarily concerned with the effect of desirable changes in environment, reflected in improved functioning in children, or a better outcome than predicted from parental or personal history. Skeels himself, was, however, scarcely immune to the notion that early experience is crucial, for his 1966 monograph was entitled 'Adult status of children with contrasting *early* life experiences' (our italics). On the contrary, the very early life experiences of the children in the orphanage were similar; it was in their subsequent *life* experiences that they differed. The most important Iowa studies will be reviewed in section IV.

A little later, unlike the Iowa Group, such workers as Spitz and Goldfarb concentrated upon the damaging effects of early environment, and their reports had a marked impact upon public policy via Bowlby's (1951) monograph. (See section I for a review.)

Thus two streams of contemporaneous work, well insulated from one another, held in common, and helped to perpetuate, the view that early experiences were highly formative, the one concentrating upon improvement and the other upon deterioration or long-term damage.

In the present section, with one or two exceptions (e.g. the work of the present authors) we shall concentrate upon studies concerning children removed from adversity and placed in better than average homes. Environmental changes were thus quite large in amount.

In analysing much material on natural experiments arising from environmental change, we have experienced some problems in deciding which reports should be reprinted in full and which should be briefly reviewed. Indeed each investigation to be outlined could have justified reprinting. Recency of publication has been a guiding principle in selecting papers or extracts from books for full quotation.

The studies to be reviewed are very heterogeneous in character. Some concern intelligence, others adjustment and attainment, yet others, personality factors, and some involve all of these. This adjacency within one chapter may yield a confused picture, perhaps to be reduced by the use of rather broad subheadings relating to type of study. Equally, however, those who have urged the long-term potency of early experience have suggested that effects may indeed be found in cognitive, scholastic personality and conduct areas. To varying extents, and with varying success, the studies that follow have a bearing upon these possibilities.

It should also be stressed that neither the environment nor environmental change operate upon the individual in a rigid and mechanical way. They interact and transact (see section I) with both strong constitutional factors and previous life experiences. One certainly expects to find strong actuarial trends following particular experiences, but there are commonly a range of individual differences arrayed round such trends.

SOME NATURAL EXPERIMENTS

Early adversity, withdrawal from parents and alternative care

In 1953 Clarke and Clarke reviewed the general problem of I.Q. inconstancy and reported preliminary results on a group of adolescent and young adult mildly retarded persons resident in an institution for the mentally retarded, and with records of either early adversity or exceptional adversity. These had unexpectedly shown sometimes large increments in I.Q. after quite short periods of a year or two. In view of the precautionary control conditions, it was argued that such changes could not be explained as artefacts, were relatively large in relation to test–retest time interval, were mainly in the direction of improvement, and occurred at ages when, in those unenlightened times, intellectual growth was assumed to have ceased. Further investigations (Clarke and Clarke 1954, 1959; Clarke, Clarke and Reiman 1958) amplified this picture, suggesting that I.Q. increments in this population were common and that many of these institutionalised young people reverted towards, and sometimes achieved, intellectual normality.

Several hypotheses were advanced to account for these surprising results. The only one which was repeatedly confirmed related to early adversity; the worse the early social history, the better the prognosis for change. After the pilot experiment, social histories were independently and objectively scored for severe adversity by researchers who knew neither these young people nor their previous or present test scores. Retesting was undertaken by someone who knew neither the previous test scores nor the social-history rating. It was then possible to compare the I.Q. increments from those originally drawn from exceptionally bad homes with a residual group where either early experiences were rather less adverse, or where the history was fragmentary. It should be stressed that the various studies originated in a sample of fifty-nine young persons, the *total* which entered the institution in 1949. Another sample of sixty represented the *total* 1953 intake. Clear evidence indicated that sample shrinkage, as time interval increased, was due to the discharge from care of the more successful members of the various groups, whose social histories on average were exceptionally adverse. Hence all estimates in the longer-term studies were conservative.

It will be noted from figure 6.1 that, firstly, a larger proportion of those drawn from exceptionally adverse conditions made the large changes, and secondly, an increasing proportion of different but comparable groups made such changes with increasing test–retest time interval. It was also apparent that those drawn from the worst conditions also had a better social prognosis. It was also clear that those from exceptionally adverse homes made rather rapid and larger initial increases in I.Q., followed by slower and smaller increments, reminiscent of the findings from studies of formerly isolated children. Others from less adverse backgrounds showed smaller but steadily increasing increments over time.

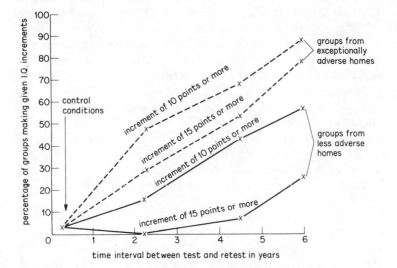

Figure 6.1   I.Q. changes in relation to social background

This shows the increasing proportion of different but comparable groups of mildly retarded young persons exhibiting increments in I.Q. of ten and fifteen points with increase in time interval between test and retest. Increments of twenty points or more are not shown, but for the six-year interval 33 per cent of the group from exceptionally adverse homes, and 5 per cent of those from less adverse homes, made gains of this order.

Since neither the material nor psychosocial conditions prevalent in the institution at that time could be described as good, it was suggested that the increments were a delayed effect of withdrawal from very bad conditions rather than entry into better ones. Attempts were then made to see whether such changes could themselves be accelerated by specially stimulating conditions. While experimental subjects showed a better social competence than controls, the two did not differ significantly on I.Q. increments. Overall the results were thought to represent the effects of recovery from early adversity.

The authors drew attention to individual differences, to the fact that the environment does not operate in a rigid and uniform way, and to the obvious resilience of many of these young people. They indicated that this delayed maturation was probably one factor in the markedly reducing prevalence rates for mild retardation from adolescence onwards, and pointed to some parallels with recovery from malnutrition. Finally, they showed that the quite large increments in I.Q. probably represented minimal estimates for total change in the life of the individual. A number of studies, reviewed by Clarke and Clarke (1975) have confirmed these findings, and when others have failed to do so there have been obvious differences in the degree of early adversity or the amount of environmental change.

Hilda Lewis (1954) reported on the progress of five hundred children taken from their families, or referred by caring agencies, and place initially in a special reception centre. They were regarded as 'the most difficult cases the county could produce'. Two hundred in the study had been removed from home on a 'fit person' order, and orders on a further seventy-five were later made on the centre's recommendation.

The precipitating cause of admission, often masking several other interlocking causes, included pilfering (50); uncontrollable at home or school (90); neglected (111) and loss of parental care (78). Age range was as follows: under five, 12·4 per cent (62); five to seven, 23·2 per cent (116); eight to eleven, 46 per cent (230); twelve to fifteen, 17·4 per cent (97); a further 1 per cent were over fifteen years. Thus the vast majority were above five years. The 500 children came from 363 families; 218 from 81 families came accompanied by at least one brother or sister. Thirty-two per cent came from a family of five or more children. The general background was poor, and sixty-six of the families were regarded as multiply deprived 'problem families'. The children had experienced many changes of school as well as of home.

A quarter of all the children admitted were regarded as normal in behaviour, but normal behaviour in some cases masked poor general mental well-being. Thirty-two per cent were delinquent, 18 per cent severely neurotic, 3 per cent psychopathic, and 21 per cent normal but with slight neurotic symptoms. This was clearly a heterogeneous group of deprived children for whom some special measures were deemed advisable.

Lewis was able to demonstrate, in line with previous work, quite significant associations between type of background and differing types of behaviour in the children. It is in the follow-up data, however, that special interest lies. She took a hundred consecutive admissions (a 20 per cent sample) between April and December 1948, omitting only eighteen who were too far away to be visited. These were replaced by the next child in the list, which must overall have been reasonably representative. Two years later, detailed interviews of foster parents, or staff in children's homes or residential schools, took place, with systematic recording of home and school data, including the child's behaviour. It was surprising that, in spite of severe deprivation, some 40 per cent of these children had been assessed on admission to the centre as being in 'good' (15 per cent) or 'fair' (25 per cent) psychological conditions. Using similar criteria this increased to 75 per cent after two years, with 39 per cent in 'good' and 36 per cent in 'fair' conditions. A postal inquiry, relating to a hundred and forty other children yielded substantially the same picture. As with the Clarke and Clarke data, but at an earlier age on follow-up, there is a fading of the effects of non-repeated early experience, even though the majority of these children had suffered considerable adversity. It is also noteworthy that individual differences were quite marked in response to such adversity.

No one type of placement had a monopoly of success, and none had a generally adverse effect. This is an important finding because no doubt selective factors dictated type of placement.

There are many other findings of interest in Lewis's book. As she says: 'If the contentions of Bender, Lowrey, Goldfarb, Bowlby and Spitz were correct, many of the Mersham children who had been separated from their mothers at an early age should not only exhibit an affectionless, psychopathic character, but should be relatively fixed in this mould . . .' While children separated from their mothers at some age were rather less satisfactory than the rest, two years after reception, the difference is not substantial. Nor did those separated for long periods or permanently before the age of two years exhibit a conspicuously worse condition. In any event Lewis was clear that 'separation' was a symptom of a much wider range of disadvantages, including lifelong institutionalisation.

In summary Lewis's report shows, among other things, that not all children are equally affected by adverse experiences, and that, where damage does occur, a substantial fading of its effects, granted an appropriate change of environment, tends to occur over as short a period as two years.

The findings of Trasler (1960) have sometimes been taken as confirmatory of Goldfarb's researches. (See section I.) This worker investigated the causes of failure in foster-home placements which in Britain appear to amount to between a third and two-fifths of all long-term placements. The technique employed was an intensive and detailed study of a limited number of cases and the collection of statistical information; the author regarded his study as exploratory and believed that his findings must be interpreted with caution. More than three-quarters of those children admitted into public care before the age of five years, who subsequently failed in foster homes, spent at least half of the first three years of life in institutions whereas only 40 per cent of the successful placements had this background. No straightforward interpretation is, however, possible for the following reasons: (1) as Trasler implies, it is not known what selective factors delayed the different proportions of institutional children from being adopted; (2) there is little evidence concerning hereditary factors, and (3) above all, an examination of the data presented by Trasler shows that forty-four out of fifty-seven unsuccessful first placements were known to have been with foster parents who were regarded as unsuitable in a variety of ways. Hence disturbance induced by early institutionalisation may have been cumulatively reinforced in those foster homes. Moreover comparable data regarding the foster homes of the controls, the successful placements, were not presented. If, indeed, these were better parents it is small wonder that their foster children were better adjusted. The institutional background in the early years may thus have been of small relevance by itself.

Early adversity, cultural transplantation and adoption

Rathbun, Di Virgilio and Waldfogel (1958) briefly reviewed the work of Bowlby and Spitz, and believed that their evidence of the adverse effects of early deprivation was impressive. Nevertheless, since the studies were for the most part retrospective, the investigators were in no position to evaluate what attempts were made at rehabilitating these children. They believed:

... knowing the severe traumata to which the children had been exposed, one would expect that special ameliorative measures would be needed to counteract their destructive effects. There is no evidence that such measures were undertaken in any of the studies reported. Until one explores this possibility, it is premature to conclude that these effects of severe, early deprivation are irreversible. (1958, p. 40)

The authors were fortunate in having a remarkable opportunity to observe the beginnings of the restitutive process in a group of young children brought to the United States under the Inter-Country Adoption Program set up by the Refugee Relief Act of 1953. These thirty-eight young children were placed directly in their permanent adoptive homes, and there could be no gradual transition period as normally favoured by adoption agencies. They were allocated in advance to their prospective homes, and the necessary legal steps were taken. The child travelled by plane and met his new parents at the airport, where social and children's workers were present to give as much support as possible. During the initial period the social worker kept in touch by telephone and by personal visits.

Thirty-three families took the thirty-eight children; one family took three siblings and three took two children each. Only fourteen of the families had no children of their own. At the time of arrival the refugees ranged in age from five months to ten years; there were an equal number of boys and girls. Many were illegitimate and others were foundlings whose age, background and early history were unknown. Greece and Korea were the countries sending most children, and others were of Japanese, Italian, Armenian, Austrian or mixed parentage. Little or no information was available regarding early mothering experiences and nearly all had been in institutions for varying lengths of time. In Korea, particularly, the plight of illegitimate children was so desperate that the main problem was keeping them alive rather than of meeting other less pressing needs.

A record was kept of the child's behaviour from the time he arrived at the airport. Particularly during the early period, a detailed note was made of the intensity and duration of these responses to cultural transplantation. It must be remembered, for example, that none of the children knew any English, although a few of the adoptive parents were able to talk to the children in their own language. At the airport, some cried and struggled, while others seemed passive. In the new homes the most common problems were over-eating and sleep disturbance. Bedtime in particular seemed to reactivate the fears of separation which ran through all age groups, and many needed the presence of the adoptive mother until they went to sleep. Nightmares occurred often, especially among the older children.

Among the children who were toilet trained on arrival, there were no cases of serious regression. Several Korean children showed fear of the bathroom because of lack of familiarity with its use. Most of the children reacted to their changed life by making excessive demands on their new parents. They would often cling, solicit demonstrations of love, and express resentment to the presence of their new siblings. While many appeared sad on arrival, there were only four cases out of the thirty-eight where this continued long enough to justify a diagnosis of reactive depression. This is indeed remarkable in view of the radical changes which they had undergone, and as the authors write, 'the outstanding feature of this group of children is their almost incredible resiliency' (1958, p. 412).

An attempt was made to employ a three-point rating for initial reactions of the children; these were termed mild where there was little evidence of disturbance or where there might be an initial acute reaction which disappeared within a week or two; where intensity was great, duration long and the effects pervading the whole personality, the reactions were regarded as severe; and moderate reactions were those occurring between these two extremes. Only eight out of thirty-eight (about 20 per cent) were regarded as severe, with about 40 per cent moderate and another 40 per cent mild. The authors consider that a major factor limiting these initial reactions was the understanding and help given by the adoptive parents. For example, there were only two severe reactions in the twenty-four children below the age of four years; yet this is the age range which other investigators have believed to be the most vulnerable. In fact, however, persistent difficulties were more common in the older children and seemed usually to have preceded their adoptive placement.

The authors recognised that the fact that most had quickly re-established their mental equilibrium did not necessarily imply that they had worked through the disturbing emotions connected with the disruptions they had experienced, but there was evidence that their adjustment was not merely a surface one. Almost without exception they acquired English with remarkable speed, and they made excellent school progress, with not a single case of serious learning disability. Most impressive was the fact that with only a few exceptions the children did not seem to be suffering from either the emotional 'freezing' or the indiscriminate friendliness described by Bowlby. The authors indicated that later developmental crises might possibly reactivate difficulties, but also pointed out that the degree of recovery then observed could never have been predicted from the classic writers on deprivation. They did not reiterate, however, that in many cases these children had little to be *separated from*, and this surely is relevant. But, as they wrote, their data indicated that 'for the child suffering extreme loss, the chances of recovery are far better than had previously been expected.' They added that selective factors clearly operated in the adoptive parents, in their readiness to accept a foreign child with little or no history, and that the children, too, for a variety of reasons may have been better endowed or may have experienced close relationships in the chaos of their early existence. Finally the authors challenge Bowlby's statement (1951) that 'good mothering is almost useless if delayed until after the age of $2\frac{1}{2}$ years', and believe that their results are of special significance in an era where rupture of family ties is so common.

A follow-up of this group has been provided by Rathbun and others (1965), six years after arrival in the United States. With the exception of five children whose adoptive families had moved, the complete sample was restudied. The findings were primarily based upon semi-structured interviews with the adoptive families, conducted by an experienced case worker not previously acquainted with them. With parental consent additional information was obtained from schools in twenty-six cases. A two-part rating scale was developed, referring to twelve factors comprising personal competence, home, school and community relationships. Independently the four authors rated each case, and after discussion these were reconciled as a pooled evaluation. Ages at the time of interview ranged from six to sixteen years. Findings indicated that these children were placed in better-than-average American homes and were possessed of better-than-average personal assets. On average they were physically very healthy, of above average I.Q. and socially competent. Adjustment for the majority was judged adequate and in some cases notably superior. Specifically, five children were classified as possessing superior adjustment; sixteen were considered adequate; ten were viewed as having a problematic adjustment. The two remaining children were rated as clinically disturbed and in need of professional help. The authors indicate, however, that current problems could be attributed as readily to the emotional climate of the adoptive home as to the trauma of their early experiences. Of course many of the children, in their pre-adoptive lives, had shown an ability to tolerate stress, and the adoptive homes, too, were selected as older and 'more established' than the typical couples who adopt American children. Nevertheless, as the authors write, the description earlier given of 'almost incredible resiliency' which characterised their adjustment in the first year in adoptive homes is still applicable to twenty-one of the thirty-three children. 'The evidence', they write, 'points in the direction of a considerable degree of reversibility of the effects of early psychic damage.'

Early hospitalisation and its later effects

There is no doubt that entry to hospital is an upsetting experience for young children, and that to varying extents they show disturbances of behaviour. The question is, however, whether and to what extent such disturbances persist. The studies to be reviewed differ in length of hospitalisation, length of follow-up and methods of assessment. But one would expect to find at least some consistencies in the data. In section I attention was drawn to Bowlby's (1951) monograph, and to the way in which it reinforced the view that early experience, and especially separation from the mother, might possess long-term effects. It is thus of interest that a too little known yet well-controlled study by Bowlby and others (1956) modified some of Bowlby's earlier conclusions. Sixty children reared in a good but orthodox tuberculosis sanatorium for an average of eighteen months below the age of four years were followed up between the ages of seven to thirteen years. As a group their intelligence was average, as was their capacity for friendship. They were, it is true, more maladjusted than their controls, but, according to these authors, maladjustment in ordinary children is common (42 per cent), and their excess maladjustment (63 per cent) might equally be an effect of the sort of homes from which the tubercular child has come – often overcrowded and with a background of death or disablement in close relatives. Contrary to expectation these children had not become affectionless, warped characters of dull intelligence.

In section I we noted that much work on the effects of hospitalisation had been prompted by Bowlby's claims. The better studies, such as those by Prugh and others (1953) and Schaffer (1958) were concerned with short periods of hospitalisation and fairly short follow-up. In the former study a large proportion, some 68 per cent of those from a 'humanised' ward, showed significant disturbance, dropping to 44 per cent after three months, and none after six months. (Controls under orthodox conditions showed greater disturbance, reducing to 15 per cent after six months.) Schaffer (1958) found that eighty days marked the upper limit of disturbance for older children, and that some disturbance was typical of 72 per cent of the children. Thus both investigations concentrated upon fairly immediate effects. In contrast a recent study by Douglas (1975), which we would have wished to reprint but for constraints upon space in a book already about to go to press, has reported very minimal immediate post-hospital effects. In addition his very long follow-up to adolescence yields results which he believes may reasonably be interpreted as arising from early hospitalisation. Since such an interpretation is contrary to other evidence in this book, we propose to offer his evidence in some detail. Dr Douglas has kindly given permission for the reproduction of some of his data.

The present study is part of the national survey of children born in the first week of March 1946, excluding twins and illegitimate children. Apart from these, all the children of non-manual workers and farm labourers, and one quarter of those born to the wives of other types of manual workers and self-employed persons, were included. Douglas's major reports are to be found in *Children Under Five* (Douglas and Blomfield 1958); *The Home and the School* (Douglas 1964) and *All Our Future* (Douglas, Ross and Simpson 1968). The data were collected from a variety of sources: health visitors, parents, teachers, school medical officers, school nurses and so forth throughout Britain.

Douglas challenges the now widespread acceptance of the view that hospital admission in the pre-school years is seldom followed by persistent disturbance. His report is based on a large national sample which is well documented for a number of important variables, including number and length of hospital admissions, mother's assessment of behaviour on returning home, standard of maternal care at age four and six, and ratings in adolescence for 'nervousness', 'troublesomeness', 'poor reading', 'delinquency' and 'unstable job pattern' between fifteen and eighteen years.

adverse ratings (in percentage)	no admissions age 0–5	number of admissions age 0–5			length of stay (single admissions)		
		one	two	three or more	7 days or less	1 week + to 1 month	over one month
nervous	15·7 (2625)*	13·1 (525)	16·5 (85)	8·8 (34)	13·0 (284)	12·4 (194)	17·0 (47)
troublesome	14·8 (2625)	17·3 (525)	21·2 (85)	41·2 (34)	15·5 (284)	19·1 (194)	21·3 (47)
poor readers	14·0 (3218)	15·4 (644)	17·9 (106)	23·8 (42)	11·6 (353)	17·4 (230)	29·5 (61)
delinquent	12·3 (1589)	16·8 (346)	10·0 (60)	19·2 (26)	13·1 (199)	20·8 (120)	25·9 (27)
unstable job	14·5 (1658)	16·3 (349)	31·6 (57)	25·9 (27)	15·6 (167)	15·0 (140)	23·8 (42)

* Figures in parentheses throughout are numbers on which percentages are based

Table 6.1   Adverse ratings in adolescence related to history of hospital admissions in pre-school years (from Douglas 1975)

According to mothers' reports, 68 per cent of pre-school children showed no *disturbance or change in behaviour* on return home (in marked contrast with 67–72 per cent who showed *disturbance* in the Prugh and Schaffer studies). There are several possible explanations for this large discrepancy. A further 10 per cent were said to have improved, and only 22 per cent to have deteriorated. Douglas points out that children admitted in the pre-school years are atypical, and compared with those who have not been in hospital during this period are more likely to return to hospital one or more times between age five and fifteen; to have some persisting physical disability; to be boys; to come from large families; to be the children of manual workers; and to have parents who take little interest in their schooling. These figures suggest that early entry to hospital is actuarially associated with present and future disadvantage. The main interest in the study, however, arises from the long-term effects which Douglas believes may be consequent upon early hospitalisation. Tables 6.1 and 6.2 summarise the

	estimated marginal proportions					
	no admission after five			one or more admission after five		
adverse ratings (in percentage)	admissions before five			admissions before five		
	none	short	long or repeated	none	short	long or repeated
troublesome	14·5	18·7	20·5 †	14·8	15·1	22·5 †
poor readers	14·3	13·5	19·5 †	13·0	10·3	19·7 †
delinquent	12·6	10·1	13·3	10·6	12·6	20·5 ‡
unstable job	13·2	11·0	13·5	15·5	26·0*	26·8 §

* $0.1 > p > 0.05$; † $0.05 > p > 0.02$; ‡ $0.02 > p > 0.01$; § $p < 0.01$.
(Logit analysis: estimated marginal proportions after adjusting for parents' interest, father's occupation and family size)

Table 6.2   Adverse ratings in adolescence related to history of hospital admissions before five and between five and fifteen years (from Douglas 1975)

relation between early admission and adolescent ratings. Here we may be on firmer ground than with mothers' or health visitors' reports. Poor reading or delinquency, for example, are much more objectively assessed.

'Nervousness' shows no association with hospital admissions. With regard to 'troublesomeness' in adolescence, there is a steady increase in relation both to number of admissions and to duration compared with the 'no admissions' group. A rather similar pattern is found for 'poor reading', 'delinquency' and 'unstable job history'.

Table 6.2 indicates the findings for admissions before and after five years.

'Troublesome behaviour' and 'poor reading' are increased among those who experienced long or repeated early admissions, whether or not they were readmitted after five. 'Delinquency' and 'unstable job history' are increased only if there are admissions after five as well as before, and 'even short admissions before five have a statistically significant association with later job instability' (Douglas 1975). One notes the consistently more powerful associations with the longer periods in which hospital admissions take place after five, exactly as one might expect from our own thesis concerning the cumulative effects of repeated experience.

Douglas argues that 'absence of disturbed behaviour upon returning home' (typical of 78 per cent) 'does not imply freedom from the longer-term effects of hospital admission'. The correlations between the four adverse ratings among those who had long or repeated admissions in the pre-school years were surprisingly low, and none higher than 0·26. It is concluded, therefore, 'that different children show different long-term effects of pre-school admissions, and that it is rare for a child to be affected in more than one way'.

Douglas suggests that the ages of admission carrying the highest risks for adolescent disturbance (for those hospitalised for more than one week) are: one to two years for 'troublesome behaviour'; seven months to one year for 'poor reading' and 'delinquency'; and one to two years for 'unstable job patterns'. This is somewhat reminiscent of a 'critical-period' hypothesis, not supported in other studies. For example, Gardner, Hawkes and Burchinal (1961) reported a well-controlled retrospective study of twenty-nine children who had experienced an average five months' care by twenty to thirty house mothers during the second half of their first year. During this period they lived in a university home-management house before local adoption. At follow-up, between eight and seventeen years, the children were assessed for school achievement, personal and social adjustment, anxiety level and response to frustration. In none of these variables, which were compared with similar measures derived from matched control subjects, could differences be attributed to differing early experiences in the first year of life.

As noted earlier two 'rough assessments of maternal care' had been made by health visitors when the children were aged four and six. Both these were related to adverse assessments and poor reading in adolescence (but the author fails to mention how strongly). Those whose mothers were seen as offering poorest care 'were the most likely to be troublesome, poor readers, delinquent or unstable in work. But within each maternal care-level the relationship persists of long and repeated early admissions to adverse assessments in adolescence.' Again, however, the author fails to mention the strength, or the decreasing strength, of such relationships. Dr Douglas (personal communication) has, however, kindly supplied data relating to the four-year assessment. (See table 6.3.) Here we note the difference between 'no admissions' and 'long or repeated admissions' for 'good' and 'poor' care in relation to sex, social class and 'no persisting disability' or 'persisting disability'. These powerful statistically significant differences amount to about 4 to 6 per cent as between various categories, which in absolute terms are thus not very large. In other words if the relation between care and outcome were to be a causal one, then its strength is limited. The repeated hospitalisation association is much stronger. (See table 6.2.)

Douglas is careful to point out that 'the evidence so far presented, though highly suggestive does not establish the existence of a causal relationship between early hospital admissions and later behaviour. For that an experimental situation would be required.' He then considers a number of studies with monkeys (see our comments on analogies from animal work, pages 14–15). He summarises the foregoing, together with the results of additional analyses not outlined here, by suggesting that his study:

. . . provides strong and unexpected evidence that one admission to hospital of more than a week's duration or repeated admissions before the age of five years (in particular between six months and four years) are associated with an increased risk of behaviour disturbance and poor reading in adolescence. The association . . . is explained neither by initial selection of children for hospital nor by the physical disabilities they sometimes carry in later life. The interpretation . . . is complicated by the fact that some pre-school children appear to benefit from hospital stay. The . . .

		boys				girls			
		non-manual		manual		non-manual		manual	
		good care*	poor care*	good care	poor care	good care	poor care	good care	poor care
no persisting disability	no admission 0–5	12·8%	16·9%	14·8%	19·3%	11·2%	14·8%	13·0%	17·1%
	long or repeated admissions	17·4%	22·5%	19·9%	25·5%	15·3%	20·0%	17·6%	22·7%
persisting disability	no admission 0–5	17·4%	22·5%	19·8%	25·4%	15·3%	19·9%	17·5%	22·7%
	long or repeated admissions	23·1%	29·3%	26·1%	32·8%	20·5%	26·2%	23·3%	29·5%

* care Maternal care levels assessed by health visitors when children were four years old (mother management of child and willingness to accept advice)

significance of effects
disability   ·01–·001
maternal care   ·01–·001
hospital admission (0–5)   ·01–·001
sex   ·2–·1
goodness of fit x² 22·95 d.f. 26 0·7 p 0·5 (i.e. no interaction effects)

Table 6.3 Estimated proportions of troublesome children (data supplied by J.W.B. Douglas)

most vulnerable . . . are those who are highly dependent on their mothers or who are under stress at home in the time of admission . . .

We have devoted considerable space to Douglas's paper because its findings, which are very carefully outlined and discussed, appear to be antagonistic to our general theme. Its interpretation, as the author clearly indicates, suffers the doubts that must apply to all correlational studies. While the relations are, with some inconsistencies, quite plain to see, the problem is equally obvious. Is hospitalisation in the early years and subsequently either a significant actuarial symptom of present and future disadvantages which surround the child during his development, or is it a cause of later difficulties? Douglas's inference from his own data favours the latter; our own, from the many other studies we quote, suggests the former. As he most fairly puts it, 'there is the possibility that children admitted to hospital were also selected on the basis of family or environmental factors which we did not record' (1975). Neither interpretation of the present data is in itself certain, and it thus illustrates the difficulties of this type of approach. What is probable, however, is that the study will be regarded as providing support for the view that quite limited early experiences exert long-term influences.

A more recent and more powerful criticism has been provided by Quinton and Rutter (personal communication). Moreover, new data were available from two recent epidemiological studies. Single hospital admissions lasting a week or less were again not associated with any form of later emotional or behavioural disturbance, while repeated admissions were significantly related to such problems. Multiple admissions were more likely to come from disadvantaged homes. Quinton and Rutter's conclusion from this is substantially similar to our own. The case is succinctly argued in the addendum to Rutter's paper. (See page 184.)

In a rather different field, a similar point has been made by Wolkind, Kruk and Chaves (1976), who have reported preliminary findings from a study of over 500 primiparous women. They have related early separation experiences, their type and timing, to the women's psychosocial status at the time of pregnancy. The data emerged from detailed interviews and questionnaires. A separation was recorded for any reported absence from either parent for one month before age 5, and for 3 months after that age, unless an admission into local authority care had occurred after 5, when again one month was counted as a separation. Almost 20 per cent reported separation, so defined, and these were less likely to be married, and more likely to be teenage, to have housing difficulties and a significantly higher score for pre-pregnancy malaise. The separations 'should, however, be seen not as a cause of later difficulties, but rather as a sensitive index of other experiences which might lead to these difficulties'. The authors offer evidence that it is only separation occurring within the context of a disrupted childhood which is of importance, and that it is not critical that this separation should occur at an early age. The women concerned seem to have experienced a continuity of social and family difficulties through childhood and into early adult life. It may, of course, be objected that memory for events, and particularly for their timing, is notoriously unreliable, and that to some extent it might be possible that the women's statements were inaccurate, or at least weighted by misperceptions. The authors intend to check the reliability of this evidence, both by repeated interviews, and by seeking corroboration from earlier records (Wolkind, personal communication). This is clearly important to do.

COMMENTS ON REPRINTED CONTRIBUTIONS

Kagan's article was specially written for this book. It represents a considerable reorientation in his theoretical position, which earlier (Kagan and Moss 1962) stressed the importance of continuities in behaviour. (See page 21.) Outlining three alternative meanings of this concept, he deals primarily with two, the 'rank order' (i.e. the child's retention of a particular position for a particular attribute over a time-span), and the 'ipsative' (the child's tendency to display the same hierarchical organisation of behavioural dispositions over time). His major theme is that an environmental retardation in the emergence of universal psychological competences during the child's first two years 'has no important implication for the eventual attainment of universal intellectual competences during pre-adolescence if the environment after infancy is beneficial to growth'. He describes in detail the Guatemalan study which caused him to re-evaluate his position. Kagan concludes that 'the first messages written upon the *tabula rasa* may not necessarily be the most difficult to erase', a view which the rest of this book confirms, although one may query the comment that the infant is a *tabula rasa*. We suspect that Kagan would agree, and that he has used this metaphor rather loosely. His article, like others in this book, draws attention to the friendliness of developmental psychology for most of this century 'toward the pole of the irreversibility–reversibility theme that posited irreversible effects of early experience'. He hopes his contribution will 'persuade the receptive reader to move just a little closer' to the view that accepts some resilience in the human organism.

The inclusion of Dennis's 'Conclusions and Implications' from his book (1973) *Children of the Crèche* requires comment. Since the 1930s this author has been active in his interest in environmental effects on intellectual growth and has had access to some unusual and important data in two middle-eastern countries. His findings on the intellectual competence of adopted foundlings are in line with those of other studies, although it may be important to note that the mean I.Q. is lower than reported for many. He also believes, and presents evidence in support of the theory, that there *is* a critical period for the ultimate development of *average* intellectual status. Thus, the excerpt from Dennis presents a formulation which is, in this sense, contradictory to the thesis of this book. We believe it to be of special interest, and will thus comment in some detail upon the findings.

Returning to the Lebanon where he had worked earlier, Dennis took advantage of a natural experiment when for the first time (1956) adoption was legalised. The investigation is of importance in that it followed the after-careers of children adopted from an exceedingly poor institution upon which earlier data existed. Rearing therein was associated with marked developmental retardation. However those adopted before age two soon reached a mean I.Q. of nearly 100. Those adopted at a later age developed at a normal rate without showing a greater acceleration. Hence they did not overcome their pre-adoption retardation. For example, those adopted at age four were then two years retarded; by age fourteen they were still two years retarded (but had shown large I.Q. increments). Hence Dennis believes that there is a critical period for the ultimate attainment of average status of about two years.

Dennis does not, in his book, devote much attention to his earlier study in Beirut (Dennis and Najarian 1957). Here the foundlings, from I.Q.s averaging 63 between three and twelve months of age, advanced within the institution to averages of 93 and 95 between four and a half and six years on Goodenough and Porteus Maze (Performance) Tests. The current research employed mainly the Stanford-Binet Test which at later chronological ages is largely verbal. Cattell or Stanford-Binet results on institutionalised children tested between one and seven years averaged, however, only 53; most of these were later adopted. So there seems to be a large discrepancy, perhaps understandable in view of the impoverished verbal stimulation of the children, between verbal and performance measures at different times within the same institution.

Dennis's findings parallel Goldfarb's, but are unique in showing differential acceleration of mental growth among children adopted from adverse circumstances, the critical factor assumed being age of removal (before two or after two). They cannot readily be reconciled with the evidence from various other studies, notably Koluchová, Davis, Skeels (pages 35–66, 214–21), nor even our own (pages 71–4); it thus becomes mandatory to seek other possible explanations. It is one of the major assets of the Dennis book that all basic data are published, so that further analyses could be carried out.

The extent of sample bias is not precisely known, but none of the children adopted by French citizens could be followed up, probably about one-third of the total adopted (personal communication by Dennis), and less than half the American sample could be located and assessed. Moreover some of the children returned from the orphanage to their own families.

In explaining the results there appear to be two additional possibilities:

1 *Selective policy, or adoptive preference, factors concerning age of adoption* There are clear indications of these; for example, for birth dates up to 1951, the average age at adoption is about five years (N = 9); for 1956, average age four years (N = 6); for 1961, between two and three (N = 8); and for 1962, about nine months (N = 11). Moreover there was a difference in the proportion of boys to girls adopted in the early years of the study. The later samples (early adopted) contained a higher proportion of boys.

Whatever the reasons for the difference in policy, the fact is that the differential changes in I.Q. with age of adoption were directly parallel with the policy changes, and year of birth correlates significantly with I.Q. Table 6.4 gives a summary of our analysis of the Dennis data. This relates only to those adoptees upon whom full data exist. Thus five have been excluded from the Lebanese sample. Further, it seemed worth excluding one 'deviant' case (LA4F) from the latter, since both her age at adoption (7·1 years) and first and second I.Q.s (53 and 54, respectively) are very different from the rest of the sample.

	American sample	Lebanese sample	Lebanese sample minus deviant
mean age at adoption	3·6 yrs (S.D. 4·2 yrs)	2·5 yrs (S.D. 2·0 yrs)	2·4 yrs (S.D. 1·9 yrs)
mean 1st I.Q.	85·2 (S.D. 14·9 points)	85·9 (S.D. 17·8 points)	86·8 (S.D. 17·2 points)
mean 2nd I.Q.	—	92·1 (S.D. 17·5 points)	93·1 (S.D. 16·6 points)
N	42	38	37
year of birth × I.Q.[1]	0·324*	0·385*	0·330*
year of birth × I.Q.[2]	—	0·525†	0.478†
age adopted × I.Q.[1]	−0·448†	−0·731†	−0·707†
age adopted × I.Q.[2]	—	−0·557†	−0·439†

* significant at the 0·05 level
† significant at the 0·01 level

Table 6.4   Basic data and intercorrelations

It will be noted that in the Lebanese sample the correlation between age adopted and I.Q. decreases over the two-year test−retest time interval, from −0·731 to −0·557. With the removal of the 'deviant' case the discrepancy (−0·707 to −0·439) becomes more marked. Clearly the I.Q. changes are diminishing the 'effect' of age at adoption, such that whereas on first test it accounts for half the I.Q. variance, two years later it accounts for only 19 per cent.

2 The second possible alternative is that *children adopted at different ages tended on average to go to different types of home*, with those adopted later living in less adequate homes than those adopted early. This seems unlikely, but there are insufficient data available to evaluate it.

Dennis also presents interesting evidence on the fate of children not adopted but who, from about age six onwards, were moved to two institutions, Zouk (for the girls) and Brumana (for the boys). At the time of transfer there was no difference in mean I.Q. according to sex, and these means were slightly above 50. The average Zouk girl remained at the same average level at and beyond age sixteen. The average boy, however, attained a mean I.Q. of 80. These differences were associated with marked differences in the institutional programmes and there seems little doubt that this relationship was a causal one.

All the data presented by Dennis indicate average I.Q. shifts in the direction of environmental change, with the sole exception of girl foundlings moved from the Crèche to another very unstimulating orphanage (i.e. no real environmental change). The American adoptees averaged 85 (S.D. 14·7), only five points higher than the adolescent foundlings left at Brumana. Lebanese adoptees averaged 85 on the first test and 92 (in both cases with S.D.s of about 17) two or three years later. The non-adopted Crèche boys, moved to a much better institution, averaged I.Q. 80 compared with the non-adopted girls' average of 53·7 and two or three years later, 59·3 (S.D.s about 9 and 10, respectively).

The crucial question, which available data do not unequivocally resolve, is whether these reflect a critical age (about two) below which adoptees not only improve but catch up to normality, and above which considerable improvement occurs but, within the age limits of the study, complete catch-up does not take place. In our opinion the more plausible of two alternatives is that selective policy factors, or selective preference of adopters, dictated early versus late adoption. As the author has indicated, with limited data on the foundlings, the nuns could hardly be expected to predict outcome, but the present writers believe it possible that changing policies or preferences about the age for adoption may have picked out different sorts of children. Again this cannot be resolved, but interpretation may legitimately be swayed by the findings of other studies. It is, however, important to note that if Dennis is completely correct in his interpretation, the 'critical period' is not one after which adoption produces no change, but rather a more limited (but none the less considerable) change in ability. In addition, it is, as he notes, quite possible that some individuals will continue to improve and that his study will not necessarily have spanned the total increments in individuals.

The paper by Tizard and Rees (1974) lays to rest any remaining belief that young children cannot develop normally in an institution. It has long been clear to many that the cognitive outcome for children reared in orphanages such as those described by Goldfarb (1943) or Skeels (1966) was unlikely to be simply the result of the lack of a permanent, affectionate caretaker. The question of social development and emotional stability is, however, another matter; these might well be seriously impaired by a variety of caretakers and lack of opportunity to form stable emotional bonds. Dr Tizard has been persuaded to add to the paper published in 1974 a preliminary account of a follow-up at age eight and a half of this cohort of children. The I.Q.s and reading ages are included, but as yet no evaluation of emotional adjustment has been made. However, it is known that the parents are happy with the children; although the group as a whole were rated by their teachers as presenting more difficulties than a comparison group. Since none of them was adopted or restored to his parents below the age of two, it is tempting to draw a comparison between this study and that of Wayne Dennis. This would probably be unwarranted; the samples are discrepant in too many respects, including the material conditions in the institutions, and the staff–child ratios.

Rutter's (1971) paper on parent–child separation represents an important epidemiological approach to childhood disorder and arose from an intensive study of two samples of children on the Isle of Wight and in London. The author agrees that separation of the child from his family is a potential cause of short-term distress and emotional disturbance. His data indicate that it is of little importance in the genesis of long-term disorder. In considering *permanent* separations, Rutter compared delinquency rates for boys, whose parents were divorced or separated, with those whose parental loss had been through death. In three studies these rates were nearly doubled for the former and insignificantly raised for the latter. Where separation experiences have some association with later anti-social behaviour this arises not from the separation itself, but from the discord which precedes and accompanies it. In any event, 'children differ in their response to family discord; these differences are associated with both sex and temperamental factors.' Rutter's article is an outstanding example of how vague concepts such as 'separation' can be analysed with some precision, and how hypotheses can be tested against epidemiological data in naturalistic settings.

Attention should also be drawn to the addendum to the paper. This argues convincingly against the view of Douglas on the probable causes of the association between early hospital admissions and later disorder. (See pages 81–7.)

The 'Summary and Implications' from Kadushin's (1970) important book are included here for the light this study casts upon the adoptive parents' evaluation of children with poor social histories taken into adoption much later than usual. Typically these came from large families living in substandard homes, often below the poverty level. Marital conflicts were common, as was promiscuity, mental retardation, psychosis, alcoholism and imprisonment. While 31 per cent of the children had experienced a 'normally warm and accepting relationship' and physical abuse was rare, these children were most often characterised as suffering physical neglect. They had been removed from their homes by court order at an average age of three and a half, placed for adoption at an average age of just over seven years, *after on average 2·3 changes of foster home*, and were followed up at an average of almost fourteen years. Their case files indicated average ability, but they had originally been selected as 'healthy' and this implied, among other things, an I.Q. of 80 + . Kadushin (personal communication) writes that the number of older children placed for adoption below I.Q. 80 was very small, perhaps 2–3 per cent; it is these who were excluded from the study. How many more below this level and of this age were excluded from adoption by virtue of poor intellectual capacity is unknown. As Kadushin (personal communication) indicates, placement of older children for adoption in the 1950s and 1960s was anyway undertaken with considerable hesitancy by the adoption agencies and 'adding an additional hard-to-place factor would have seriously reduced the feasibility of placement.' Hence Kadushin's sample concerns children not already handicapped by disabilities other than those thought to be imposed by age and very poor social background. This is understandable but a pity in view of the work of Skeels, and Clarke and Clarke who were dealing with initially more intellectually impaired subjects from very bad backgrounds. But research workers employing natural experiments are frequently faced with such constraints.

Adoptive parents were older than the natural parents and at a considerably higher socioeconomic level. These children were in general a source of satisfaction to their adoptive parents and 'showed a greater degree of psychic health and stability than might have been anticipated given the nature of their backgrounds and developmental experiences.' The closest parallel here is the work of Rathbun and others (1958, 1965) already referred to, but the principle, that outcome is related to improved circumstances, is once again confirmed. It is a pity, but understandable, that it was not possible to make a direct study of the children, and that the data are in the main indirect. Attention has already been drawn (page 22) to Kadushin's plea for 'greater respect being accorded to the present and more recent, proximate experiences . . . the present is a countervailing force which exerts a constant pressure, demanding that we live by it . . .'

For this book, therefore, the main interest of Kadushin's work lies in its demonstration that older children with very bad backgrounds and subsequent foster-home changes, selected for a degree of robustness, turn out reasonably well.

CONCLUSIONS

Natural experiments usually involve a multitude of factors over which the scientist has little, if any, influence. He records, often in gross terms, what is happening, or what is thought to have happened in the past. Particularly in the latter case there may be problems of interpretation. In the present section we have turned our attention mainly to studies where children have undergone some major environmental change, but of much less extreme amount than those recorded in the section on 'Studies of Formerly Isolated Children'.

Each of the investigations briefly reviewed at the outset could have been reprinted *in extenso*. We selected for reproduction those more recently published, which are thus less well known, together with a new contribution from Kagan.

Both our review, and the contributions which follow, yield a reasonably consistent picture. One notes first the wide range of individual differences in response to environmental change. These vary from little or no change in the characteristics assessed, to very marked alterations. Nevertheless, actuarially speaking, there is a strong tendency for personal changes to occur following prolonged environmental change, often comparatively late in childhood, adolescence or even young adulthood. Long-term influences may be potent, but even lengthy periods of adversity, if alleviated, have effects which in most cases are modifiable to varying extents, depending both upon constitutional factors and the degree and duration of environmental change, as well as upon the strength of behavioural effects induced earlier.

Only in two studies are findings reported which are to varying extents discrepant with our theme. The first, by Wayne Dennis, is reprinted in full. In our commentary we have suggested alternative hypotheses to account for the data. The second, by Douglas, has been discussed in some detail in this review. This important investigation has some puzzling features, of which the relatively low rate of reported disturbance following hospitalisation is one, and the existence of possible 'sleeper effects' is another. It is also surprising that single effects are related to particular ages of hospital admission and are, within individuals, relatively uncorrelated. These findings, which were unexpected by Douglas, may be correctly interpreted by him. On the other hand, the balance of evidence from other studies might suggest that early hospital admission is an actuarial symptom of present and future disadvantage. These and other problems will receive an overall evaluation in the final section of this book.

CHAPTER SEVEN

Resilience and Continuity in Psychological Development

Jerome Kagan

Each scientific discipline, during successive eras in its growth, is loyal to one member of a set of opposed assumptions that typically form the axioms of the discipline. Holton (1973) has called these polarised premises, *themata*. Debate over whether matter is particulate or wave-like, whether the universe is steady-state or expanding, or whether growth is continuous or discontinuous are among the themes that scientists have debated in the past and will continue to discuss in the future because, as Bohr wisely noted, the propositions are likely to be complementary rather than incompatible.

This chapter considers the evidence bearing on a pair of opposed *themata* that have given direction to the empirical study of human psychological development. One proposition holds that the experiences of infancy produce a set of dispositions that have a continuous influence throughout life, implying that some of the effects of early experience are not malleable to change. The opposed position is that the infant is resilient and the effects of early experience – which can be dramatic – are reversible under proper environmental conditions. The debate centres on the degree of modifiability of psychological structures established early in life. There is unequivocal support for the view that the experiences of the young infant have a powerful contemporary effect on his behaviour, temperament and knowledge. This hypothesis is un-challenged. But it is less clear how stable these early structures are, especially if the environment should change in a serious way. Stated in the interrogative, how resilient – or responsive to change – are the cognitive structures and behavioural dispositions shaped during the first three years of life?

This question is closely related to the usefulness of the concept of critical period. The critical-period hypothesis maintains that, for selected response systems, there is a period of time during which a system is being elaborated most rapidly. Particular environmental events have a strong effect on the system during that special interval, so strong that the resultant dispositions may be difficult or impossible to alter in the future. One of the most impressive supports for this view has come from the work on imprinting (see Hess 1958, 1964; Lorenz 1965), although recently (Hess 1972) contradictory evidence has appeared.

During the early years of this century this theme did not provoke much debate because there was no clearly articulated theoretical position regarding the permanent effects of early encounters. Lines of controversy were drawn when psychoanalytic and behavioural theory appeared, almost simultaneously, as competitors for the ideological loyalty of comparative and developmental psychologists. Freud believed that either extreme nurturance or neglect during infancy would create structures (i.e. fixations in psychoanalytic terminology) that not only would retard the rate at which the child grew into succeeding stages but, more significantly, would predispose him to particular symptoms in adulthood, such as vulnerability to phobias, depression and, in the extreme, psychosis.

The behaviourist's view of early experience was less pessimistic and more flexible, but equally hypothetical. Since every reinforcement strengthened the disposition of any action that preceded it, certain patterns of reinforcement could establish unusually strong habits. But the principle of extinction was potentially as powerful as the principle of reward and, theoretically at least, every adaptive or maladaptive response acquired during the early years could be altered at a later date by changing the pattern of reinforcements. The two theories adopted different stances toward malleability, but a similar attitude toward the contemporary influence of the early environment.

Commitment to a more dogmatic view regarding resilience did not emerge until the comparative psychologists and ethologists alerted the scientific community with demonstrations of dramatic and apparently irreversible effects of early experience. The most impressive examples came from the experiments on imprinting and the production of abnormal behaviour in rhesus monkeys raised with inanimate wire 'mothers' (Harlow and Harlow 1966). These provocative findings made Freud's theoretical position persuasive and strengthened the psychologist's belief that the events of infancy could seriously constrain future functioning.

A different, and far less legitimate, reason for believing in the permanent effect of early experience came from investigations of the academic performance of children. Studies of economically disadvantaged American children, most often black but occasionally Mexican-American, Puerto Rican and white, revealed that children from poverty families performed differently from middle-class children on tests of language, memory, reasoning and problem solving before school entrance. Less adequate, but not wholly unsatisfactory, observations in the homes of poor and middle-class pre-school children revealed that each group was exposed to different patterns of encounters with their parents. This information was interpreted as indicating that the intellectual development of poor children had been impaired by their home experience during the first three years of life. Since the children of the poor consistently remained behind their middle-class peers on standardised tests of academic skills and intelligence, it was suggested that their intellectual retardation (compared with middle-class youngsters) was irreversible.

There is a serious difference, however, between this basis for positing irreversibility and the data derived from the animal work. In the latter case the investigator had some absolute reference for the behaviour of a species reared in the natural environment. If a rhesus monkey raised on a wire surrogate mother did not, after months or years in a rehabilitating context, display any substantial change in self-mutilation, fearfulness, or avoidance of mating behaviour, it was reasonable to entertain the hypothesis of irreversibility. By contrast there is no absolute norm or reference that informs us of the expected level of competence at reading, writing or arithmetic. Those norms change each twenty to fifty years as children acquire more and different words, facts and skills. Half of the words that a Boston first-grader was supposed to know in 1900 would be unfamiliar to a middle-class Boston child in 1976. The poverty child remained behind the middle-class youngster only in relative rank on particular tests. Actually he was acquiring more facts and improving his skills each day. Although the average seven-year-old child of poverty was less proficient than the seven-year-old middle-class child on reading or reasoning skills, the typical fifteen-year-old child of poverty was not less competent than the seven-year-old middle-class youngster.

Although the infant is influenced by his environment from the moment he is born, the equally popular assumption that the effects of those early experiences can extend long into the future does not, at the moment, have unequivocal support. Hence we should ask why many psychologists, parents and educators have been reluctant to examine the validity of that second statement. In addition to the obvious influence of psychoanalytic theory and the persuasive animal data, there are additional reasons, both phenomenological as well as philosophical. Each person feels a compelling sense of continuity and connectedness when he reflects on the experiences of his early childhood. This sense of the past's contribution to the present derives from man's need to regard his life as coherent and his past decisions as part of a rationally causal chain. A second, more speculative, basis for believing in the extended power of early experience could be a derivative of one of the central maxims of western Protestantism – preparation for the future. Application of that maxim to child rearing would lead parents to award validity to the idea that if children are treated optimally during the early years, the healthy attitudes, talents and behaviours established during the first era should provide protection against possible traumas during adolescence and adulthood. Proper early familial treatment, like early vaccination, might inoculate the child against vulnerability to future distress. Finally, faith in the permanent influence of early experience is in accord with the commitment to political egalitarianism that is so strong in western Protestant democracies. If society treats children properly during the opening years there is at least the hope that the distress, incompetence, and hopelessness that prevent full political participation by all adult citizens could be eliminated and a truly egalitarian society established.

One reason why it is difficult to disconfirm that world view is that the vast majority of children remain with their families in similar environmental contexts from birth until late adolescence. As a result differences in intellectual competence, social behaviour, and psychopathology among sixteen-year-olds from different families could just as well be due to events that occurred during the years six to twelve or twelve to sixteen as to experiences during the first two years of life. Consider two sixteen-year-old boys from the same town, one of whom is successful in school and the other failing. There is a strong temptation to attribute primary causality to motivational and intellectual structures established during the first half decade rather than to dispositions that developed later. A Gedanken experiment suggests the potential usefulness of questioning that assumption. Imagine a happy, social, alert, secure, curious, creative and spontaneous three-year-old who is transferred to an environment in which he is punished inconsistently and regularly exposed to violence, cynicism, failure and derogation. If we return ten years later we might not see most of the strengths that were present at age three. This thirteen-year-old might resemble the other children in that family who had been continually exposed to the same regime. Now imagine removing a three-year-old from a toxic environment to a benevolent one and returning ten years later. Intuition suggests that the transferred adolescent will be substantially different from a sibling who had remained in the destructive family context.

The author recently interviewed a fourteen and a half year-old girl who spent most of the first thirty months of her life in a crib in a small bedroom with no toys and a sister one year older than herself. The mother, who felt unable to care for her fourth child, restricted her to the bedroom and instructed her eight-year-old daughter to care for the child. When she was removed to a foster home at two and a half years of age she was severely malnourished, retarded in weight and height, and so retarded psychologically that she was untestable. She has remained with the same foster family for the last twelve years. At the present time her full scale I.Q. is 88; she performs normatively on a wide battery of cognitive tests and her interpersonal behaviour is not seriously different from that of an average rural Ohio adolescent.

Koluchová (1972) has recently reported a similar developmental history for twin Czechoslovakian boys who were placed in total isolation by their stepmother and father from eighteen months to seven years of age. Most of the time the boys were in a small unheated closet but were often locked up for long periods in the cellar of the house. The boys were never allowed outside the house and were inhumanly treated. When the children were removed from the home at age seven they were physically ill, psychologically untestable, and displayed extreme surprise and fear to common events like automobiles and toys. This extreme behavior, which resembled that of Harlow's surrogate-reared monkeys, gradually abated in the hospital environment. The boys were sent to a children's home for six months and then to a foster home. When the boys were tested at eleven years of age – only a few years after their emergence from the isolated environment – their full-scale Wechsler I.Q. scores were 95 and 93, and the physician noted that they appeared about average for their age (see pages 45–66).

We shall deal with this issue later when we compare children growing up in isolated areas and cities. These two cases, many others can be documented, suggest that the psychological structures created by unusual early experience can be changed if the formative environment is altered.

THE CONCEPT OF CONTINUITY

The belief that structures established early in life have an effect that stretches far into the future forms the core of the complicated concept of psychological continuity – a concept with at least three different meanings. The first, rank-order continuity, means that a particular child retains his rank for a particular attribute within a defined cohort over a specified period of time. The respectable stabilities of I.Q., grade point average or reading test score from first grade through high school are popular examples of rank-order continuity. An eight-year-old New York City child who scores in the 30th percentile for reading comprehension would probably remain between the 20th and 40th percentile if he remained in New York City – or any other American urban environment – for the next five years. However if that child were moved to a rural school in western Kenya or north-western Guatemala, his position would probably change from the 30th to the 80th percentile. There would be a discontinuity in his relative ability even though his absolute competence remained unchanged. Statements about continuity based on maintenance of one's rank in a specified cohort are always relative to the reference group with whom the child is being compared.

Ipsative continuity, which is quite different, refers to the child's tendency to display the same hierarchical organisation of behavioural dispositions or competences over time. Imagine a four-year-old boy who consistently withdraws rather than attacks when he is threatened by a child of the same sex and age. We can ask whether this preference to withdraw remains stable over a five- or ten-year period. Although his relative rank for 'disposition to withdraw' might change dramatically if he changed reference groups and became a member of a cohort of children who withdrew even more frequently than he, as long as his tendency to withdraw remained stronger than his tendency to attack, we would be justified in concluding that this organisation of responses displayed ipsative continuity.

The third and most profound meaning of continuity, more commonly referred to as psychological epigenesis, deals with the necessary relations between a set of processes or performances at one time and a successive set at some time in the future. Western psychologists are friendly toward a strong form of epigenesis due, in large part, to the theories of Freud and Piaget. For example, some psychologists believe there is a necessary continuity or relation between fear of parental punishment at age three and an internalised conscience at age ten or a continuity between the opportunity to manipulate objects during infancy and the subsequent appearance of symbolic thought at two years of age. However attractive these epigenetic hypotheses, they are, in the main, neither supported nor disconfirmed by empirical data.

This paper deals primarily with the first two meanings of continuity, with special reference to cognitive development. The major theme of this report is that a slowing or retardation in the emergence of universal psychological competences during the first two years as a result of environmental factors have no important implication for the eventual attainment of universal intellectual competences during pre-adolescence if the environment after infancy is beneficial to growth. Before presenting the data, it will be helpful to examine the various meanings of the concept of 'intelligence' and its dynamic complement 'intellectual development'.

THE CONCEPT OF INTELLIGENCE

There are two independent views of intelligence and intellectual development held by western psychologists. The simplest, and perhaps for that reason the most popular, posits a unitary entity defined as an abstract generalised capacity to acquire new and modify old structures across a wide variety of domains. At the level of process, intelligence is the ability to extract environmental information efficiently, to remember that information, to retrieve appropriate hypotheses, to detect logical inconsistencies, and to give up old ideas and solutions that have ceased to be adaptive. The actualisation of that capacity should improve with age since the more knowledge one possesses the more efficiently one can assimilate new events and activate valid solutions. Additionally some include the extra assumption that improper or depriving experiences early in life can slow the growth of this abstract capacity and prevent the child from attaining his full intellectual potential, the way serious lack of food can prevent a child from attaining the stature his heredity intended.

This model is in partial accord with empirical data, for vocabulary, general knowledge and recall memory – to name a few skills – tend to increase in a linear fashion from the time the child becomes symbolic through young adulthood. The main problem with this model is the relative independence of both levels of functioning at a single age, as well as rate of improvement over time, across a broad array of processes. For this reason many theorists have not liked a unitary concept of intelligence, even though it has provided a rationale for the I.Q. test.

An alternative view posits sets of relatively independent, hierarchically organised cognitive functions and corpora of knowledge characteristic of different stages of development and appropriate to different problems. The developmental aspect of this model, due largely to Piaget (1952), assumes that each stage of development is characterised by a different organisation of abilities with the structures of one stage contributing to those of the succeeding stage. Each child, proceeding at his own pace, passes through an invariant sequence of stages. An appropriate metaphor is the metamorphosis of an insect, for the butterfly is not simply a better caterpillar but a different creature.

A close variation on this theme is less dogmatic about the relation of each stage to the next. Since it is not clear whether the abilities mastered during infancy are necessary for the competences attained by the ten-year-old, and each masters totally different abilities, there is no *a priori* reason to expect either rank-order or ipsative continuity of 'intelligence' from infancy to pre-adolescence. More important, a distinction is made between universal competences natural to the species and culturally specific skills. Each of the universal competences emerges in the context of specific problems. The modal time of appearance of these 'abilities-in-context' will vary with specific environmental opportunities. The age at which each universal competence is attained will not necessarily affect, in a serious way, the eventual mastery of the basic abilities of future stages. The tadpole that is late in metamorphosing will not necessarily be a less-well-adapted frog. For those who have always been friendly to this view of intellectual development, the data to be presented will come as no surprise. For those who believe in a unitary intelligence that can be prevented from complete actualisation by toxic early experience, the data may provoke a temporary feeling of puzzlement.

THE GUATEMALAN STUDY

The author recently observed infants and children living in an isolated, subsistence farming village in the highlands of northwestern Guatemala called San Marcos. As a result of parental treatment, frequent illness, lack of experiential variety and mild malnutrition the one-year-olds were quiet, non-smiling, minimally alert, motorically flaccid and temperamentally passive. This profile of characteristics is in sharp contrast to the modal profile of middle-class American infants who are highly vocal, smiling, alert and active. Experimental and observational procedures designed to assess level of cognitive development among these Indian infants revealed that, relative to the Americans, they were three to twelve months behind the latter depending on the cognitive system studied.

The Guatemalan infants were markedly less attentive than the Americans to visual and auditory events, and this difference was greater at one year than it was at five months (Kagan and Klein 1973). The Guatemalan infants were retarded relative to the Americans in their tendency to reach for an attractive object that they watched being hidden, and not one of a group of twelve infants revealed facial surprise following a sequence in which he watched an object being hidden under a cloth but saw no object when that cloth was removed. These observations suggest a retardation of about four months in the display of behavioural signs diagnostic of what Piaget has called object permanence.

A third source of data came from observations of stranger anxiety. Each of sixteen infants between eight and twenty months was observed following the first exposure to a strange male. The first age at which obvious apprehension or crying occurred was thirteen months, suggesting an approximate lag of five months between the Guatemalan and American infants. Information on non-morphemic babbling and the onset of meaningful speech also supported a diagnosis of slower growth, for there was no marked increase in frequency of babbling or vocalisation between eight and sixteen months among twelve infants observed at home. Comparable observations in American homes reveal a significant increase in babbling and the appearance of morphemic vocalisation for some children. Furthermore, meaningful speech usually appears first at two and a half years of age, about twelve to eighteen months later than the time of average display of initial words in American children. These data, together with the extremely depressed and withdrawn appearance of the Guatemalan infants, suggest that for a small set of universal competences displayed by all children during the first two years of life, the Indians were significantly late in attaining these abilities. Since over 90 per cent of the infants were homogeneously passive, non-alert and quiet, it is unlikely that the recovery of intellectual functioning to be reported was the result of the selective mortality of a small group of severely retarded infants.

The home environments

It is believed that the restricted experience of the Guatemalan infants was responsible for their slower rate of growth. During most of the first year, the infant is tightly clothed and restricted to the inside of a windowless hut about 22 metres square, constructed of bamboo walls and a roof of thatched grass. The dirt floor contains an open fire, some wood, a straw mat, and a few clay receptacles. Ears of corn, cups and pots hang from the walls and roof. The light level inside the hut at noon is low and approximates the level outside at dusk. The infant spends approximately a third of his time on his mother in a sling, a third sitting or lying on a straw mat, and the final third sleeping in his hammock. The infant has no conventional toys with which to play and adults are minimally interactive with him. Time sampled observations of infants in the home revealed that play or vocalisation directed at the baby by others (parents, relatives or older children) occurred less than 10 per cent of the time, in contrast to 25 to 40 per cent of the time in American homes. As a result the babies were generally very quiet.

However by thirteen to sixteen months, when the baby becomes mobile and is allowed to leave the hut, he encounters the greater variety inherent in the outside world. He engages an environment that includes domestic animals, other children, trees, rain, clouds and makes the accommodations those experiences require. The eight- to ten-year-old is assigned tasks and responsibilities, such as helping the father in the field, caring for infants, cooking, cleaning and carrying water. During the post-infancy years the child becomes increasingly alert and active and it is relevant, therefore, to ask if these older Guatemalan children, who were slow in attaining the universal competences of infancy, are different from less isolated Guatemalan or urban western children with respect to some of the universal cognitive competences of pre-adolescence.

The competence of older children

Tests designed to assess cognitive processes believed to be part of the natural competence of growing children were administered to samples of Guatemalan and American children. We tried to create tests that were culturally fair, recognising that this goal is, in the extreme, unattainable. We assumed, along with many psychologists, that perceptual analysis, recall and recognition memory, and inference are among the universal cognitive abilities of children (even though they do not exhaust that set), and our tests were designed to evaluate those processes.

Recall memory for familiar objects

The ability to organise experience for commitment to long-term memory, and to retrieve that information on demand, is a basic cognitive skill. It is generally believed that the form of the organisation contains diagnostic information regarding cognitive maturity for, among western samples, both number of independent units of information as well as the conceptual clustering of that information, increase with age.

A twelve-object recall task was administered to the Indian children of San Marcos and to children from a Ladino village seventeen kilometres from Guatemala City whose infant experience was not as restricted. The eighty subjects from the Ladino village were five and seven years old, equally balanced for age and sex. The fifty-five subjects from San Marcos were between five and twelve years of age (twenty-six boys and twenty-nine girls).

The twelve miniature objects to be recalled were common to village life and belonged to three conceptual categories: animals (pig, dog, horse, cow); kitchen utensils (knife, spoon, fork, glass); and clothing (pants, dress, underpants, hat). Each child was first required to name the objects and if the child was unable to he was given the name. The child was told that after the objects had been randomly arranged on a board he would have ten seconds to inspect them, after which they would be covered with a cloth, and he would be required to say all the objects he could remember.

Table 7.1 contains the average number of objects recalled and the number of pairs of conceptually similar words recalled – an index of clustering – for the first two trials. The maximum clustering score for a single trial was 9 points. All the children showed a level of clustering beyond chance expectation (which is between 1·5 and 2·0 pairs for recall scores of 7 to 8 words); recall scores increased with age for children in both villages (F ranged

	Ladino village			
	trial 1		trial 2	
age	recall	pairs	recall	pairs
5	5·2	2·1	5·4	2·1
7	6·7	3·3	7·8	3·7
	Indian village			
	trial 1		trial 2	
age	recall	pairs	recall	pairs
5–6	7·1	3·4	7·8	3·8
7–8	8·6	3·4	8·3	3·6
9–10	10·3	4·9	10·3	4·3
11–12	9·6	3·4	10·1	3·6

Table 7.1 Mean number of objects and pairs recalled

from 11·2 to 27·7, $p < ·05$), and there was no significant difference in performance between the two samples. Indeed the San Marcos children performed slightly better than the Ladino youngsters.

No five- or six-year-old in either village and only twelve of the forty seven-year-olds in the Ladino village were attending school. School for the others consisted of little more than semi-organised games. Moreover, none of the Indian children from San Marcos had ever left the village, and the five- and six-year-olds typically spent most of the day within a 500 metre radius of their homes. Hence, school attendance and contact with books and a written language do not seem to be prerequisites for clustering in young children.

The recall and cluster scores obtained in Guatemala were remarkably comparable to those reported for middle-class American children. Appel, Cooper, McCarrell, Knight, Yussen and Flavell (1971) presented twelve pictures to Minneapolis children in grade 1 (approximately age seven), and fifteen pictures to children in grade 5 (approximately age eleven) in a single trial recall task similar to the one described here. The recall scores were 66 per cent for the seven-year-olds and 80 per cent for the eleven-year-olds. These values are almost identical to those obtained in both Guatemalan villages. The cluster indices were also comparable. The American seven-year-olds had a cluster ratio of 0·25; the Indian five- and six-year-olds had a ratio of 0·39.*

Recognition memory

The robust performance on recall was also found on a recognition memory task for thirty-two photos of faces, balanced for sex, child versus adult and Indian versus Caucasian, administered to thirty-five American and thirty-eight San Marcos children aged eight to eleven. Each child initially inspected thirty-two chromatic photographs of faces, one at a time, in a self-paced procedure. Each child's recognition memory was tested by showing him thirty-two pairs of photographs (each pair was of the same sex, age and ethnicity), one of which was old and the other new. The

---

* The cluster index is the ratio of the number of pairs recalled to the product of the number of categories in the list times one less than the number of words in each category.

child had to state which photograph he had seen during the inspection phase. Although the American eight- and nine-year-olds performed slightly better than the Guatemalans (82 versus 70 per cent) there was no significant cultural difference among the ten- and eleven-year-olds (91 versus 87 per cent). Moreover, there was no cultural difference at any age for the highest performance attained by a single child. These data are in accord with those of Kagan, Klein, Haith and Morrison (1973) and Scott (1973).

The favoured interpretation of the poorer performance of the younger children in both recognition memory studies is that some of them did not completely understand the task, and others did not activate the proper problem-solving strategies during the registration and retrieval phases of the task.

It appears that recall and recognition memory are basic cognitive functions that seem to mature in a regular way in a natural environment. The cognitive retardation observed during the first year does not have any serious predictive validity for these two important aspects of cognitive functioning for children ten to eleven years of age.

Perceptual analysis

The Guatemalan children were also capable of solving difficult Embedded Figures Test items. The test consisted of twelve colour drawings of familiar objects in which a triangle had been embedded as part of the object. The child had to locate the hidden triangle. The test was administered to the rural Indian children of San Marcos, as well as to less-isolated Indians living close to Guatemala City (labelled Indian in figure 7.1), Ladino villages and two groups from Guatemala City (see figure 7.1).

The Guatemala City middle-class children had the highest scores and, except for San Marcos, the rural children the poorest. The surprisingly competent performance of the San Marcos children is due, we believe, to the more friendly conditions of testing. This suggestion is affirmed by an independent study in which a special attempt was made to maximise rapport and comprehension of instructions with a group of rural isolated children before administering a large battery of tests. Although all test performances were not facilitated by this rapport-raising procedure, performance on the Embedded Figures Test was improved considerably. It is important to note that no five- or six-year-old was completely incapable of solving some of these problems. The village differences in mean score reflect the fact that the rural children had difficulty with three or four of the harder items. This was the first time

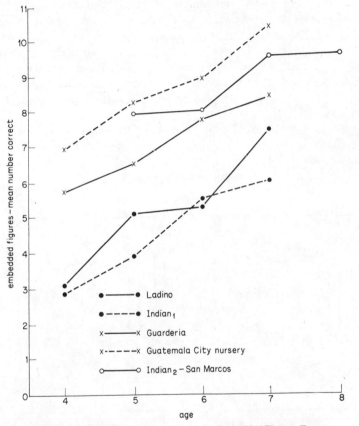

Figure 7.1   Mean number correct on the Embedded Figures Test

that many rural children had ever seen a two-dimensional drawing and most of the five-, six- and seven-year-olds in San Marcos had no opportunity to play with books, paper, pictures or crayons. None the less these children solved seven or eight of the test items. As with recall and recognition memory, the performance of the San Marcos child was comparable to that of his age peer in a modern urban setting.

Perceptual inference

The competence of the San Marcos children on the Embedded Figures Test is affirmed by their performance on a test administered only in San Marcos and Cambridge and called Perceptual Inference. The children (sixty American and fifty-five Guatemalan, five to twelve years of age) were shown a schematic drawing of an object and asked to guess what that object might be if the drawing were completed. The child was given a total of four clues for each of the thirteen items, where each clue added more information. The child had to guess an object from an incomplete illustration, to make an inference from minimal information (see figures 7.2 and 3).

There was no significant cultural difference for the children seven to twelve years of age, although the American five- and six-year-olds did perform significantly better than the Indian children. In San Marcos performance improved from 62 per cent

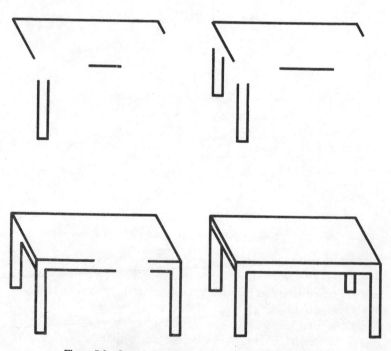

Figure 7.2   Sample item from the Perceptual Inference Test

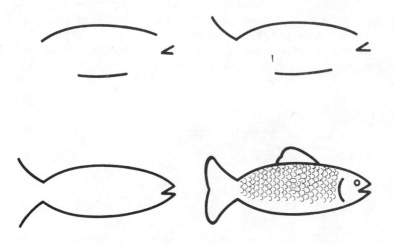

Figure 7.3   Sample item from the Perceptual Inference Test

correct on one of the first two clues for the five- and six-year-olds to 77 per cent correct for the nine- to twelve-year-olds. The comparable changes for the American children were from 77 to 84 per cent (see figure 7.4).

Familiarity with the test objects was critical for success. All the San Marcos children had seen hats, fish and corn and these items were rarely missed. By contrast many American children failed these items. No San Marcos child not attending school, and therefore unfamiliar with books, correctly passed the book item; whereas, most of those in school passed it correctly. As with memory and perceptual analysis, the retardation seen during infancy did not predict comparable retardation in the ability of the eleven-year-old to make difficult perceptual inferences.

Conceptual inference

The San Marcos child also performed well on questions requiring conceptual inference. In this test the child was told verbally three characteristics of an object and required to guess the object. Some of the examples included: what has wings, eats chickens and lives in a tree; what moves trees, cannot be seen and makes one cold; what is made of wood, is used to carry things and allows one to make journeys. There was improved performance with age; the five- and six-year-olds obtained an average of 9 out of 14 correct, and the eleven- and twelve-year-olds obtained 12 out of 14 correct. The San Marcos child was capable of making inferences from both visual and verbal information.

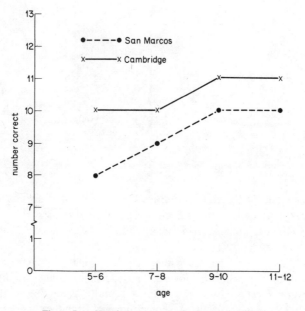

Figure 7.4   Number correct on the Perceptual Test

This corpus of data implies that slower attainment of selected universal competences of infancy does not have any important implications for the competences of the pre-adolescents with respect to perceptual analysis, perceptual inference, recall and recognition memory. Indeed the Guatemalan ten-year-olds performed at a level comparable to those of American middle-class children.

OTHER STUDIES

Although the isolated Indian eleven-year-old children seemed to possess some of the competences that develop in any natural environment, they were grossly incompetent at culturally specific skills like reading, writing and arithmetic. That fact has a parallel in a recent comparison of seven- to nine-year-old Norwegian children from isolated farms, villages or towns (Hollos and Cowan 1973). The isolated farm families, part of a rural community of about three hundred people, were so separated from one another that daily interaction among them was minimal. As in San Marcos the children spent most of their time in solitary play and rarely left the family farm before eight years of age when they went to school. There were few commercial games or toys and most interaction between adults and children or between children was non-verbal. As in San Marcos mothers did not talk very much to their children and most information was communicated by gesture. A sample of forty-eight of these farm children was compared with equal numbers from a village of fourteen hundred, which was far less isolated, and a town of six thousand, which was a tourist centre with developed industry. There was much more verbal interaction and greater variety of experience in the two larger settings than in the isolated farm contexts.

The children were administered two classes of problems. The first included Piaget's classification and conservation tasks, which reflects competences most children develop in a natural environment. The second set included role taking and verbal skills that required the child to tell stories to a person whom the child was led to believe was naïve about the content. There was no difference among the three groups of children on the classification and conservation tasks; but the isolated farm children scored markedly below the two less-isolated groups on the role taking–verbalisation problems. In both San Marcos and rural Norway extreme isolation and a predominantly non-verbal environment do not prevent children from developing those cognitive competences that seem to be universal, but do impair the acquisition of culturally specific abilities.

Haggard (1973), studying similar populations in Norway, compared forty children, seven to fourteen years of age, living on isolated farms with twenty-eight children of the same age who lived in an urban city of seven thousand people. The children were matched on sex, family education and paternal occupation. One of the tests administered was the Wechsler Intelligence Scale for Children, which contains ten subscales, differing in reliance on acquired knowledge. The urban children were significantly better than the isolated ones on four scales – picture arrangement, comprehension, vocabulary and coding. The first three are the most subject to specific cultural experience. In order to solve the picture arrangement test, for example, the child must be familiar with story sequences involving umbrellas and other objects that are likely to occur in the city, but not on the isolated farms. In addition the coding and picture-arrangement tests give bonus scores for fast performance. The differences between the two groups were minimal for object assembly (a puzzle), picture completion (involving perceptual analysis), and short-term memory for digits. The last two are comparable to tests given to the San Marcos children.

Haggard concluded: 'The isolates appear to do relatively better when accurate perception, memory and non-fantasy reasoning is called for; whereas, the control children appear to do relatively better when speed, verbal skills and tests based on familiarity with social norms are involved' (Haggard 1973, p. 130).

As in San Marcos, the isolated children improved markedly between seven and fourteen years of age. Moreover, as in San Marcos, no differences between isolated and urban children appeared on the Embedded Figures Test (see Karp and Konstadt 1963) or on explanations of natural phenomena (e.g. why do clouds move across the sky? why does rain fall more often in summer?).

The suggestion that basic cognitive competences emerge at different times and that the child retains the capacity for actualisation of the basic human competences until a late age is not substantially different from the earlier conclusions of Dennis and Najarian (1957). Although the forty-nine infants two to twelve months of age living in poorly staffed Lebanese institutions were seriously retarded on the Cattell Developmental Scale (mean developmental quotient of 68 compared with a quotient of 102 for a comparison group), the four and a half- to six-year-olds who had resided in the same institution all their lives performed at a level comparable to American norms on a memory test (Knox Cubes) as well as on Porteus Mazes and the Goodenough Draw-a-Man-Test.

Of more direct relevance is Dennis's recent follow-up study of sixteen children who were adopted out of the same Lebanese institution between twelve and twenty-four months of age – the period during which the San Marcos infant leaves the unstimulating environment of the dark hut – with an average developmental quotient of 50 on the Cattell Infant Scale. Even though the assessment of later intellectual ability was based on the culturally biased Stanford-Binet I.Q. Test, the average I.Q., obtained when the children were between four and twelve years of age, was 101, and thirteen of the sixteen children had I.Q. scores of 90 or above.*

This finding is in substantial agreement with a recent follow-up study of sixty-five four and a half-year-old children who had spent their first two to four years in an institution in which an exclusive relation between an infant and one caretaker was actively discouraged. Of the original group of sixty-five, fifteen were now living with their natural mothers, twenty-four had been adopted, and twenty-six were still living in the institution. There was no difference among the three groups at four and a half years of age on Wechsler I.Q. scores (the I.Q. means ranged from 100 to 115). Although the institutionalised children had been retarded in language development when they were two years old, they were not retarded with respect to British norms at four and a half years.

No evidence of cognitive retardation, verbal or otherwise, was found in a group of four year old children institutionalized since early infancy . . . As far as reversibility of the ill effects of institutionalization is concerned, cognitive retardation was reversed even within the institution between ages 2 and 4. (Tizard and Rees 1974, p. 97 and 98; see also Rheingold and Bayley 1959)

Animal investigations

More dramatic support for the notion that psychological development is resilient comes from recent experimental studies with animals. Several years ago Harlow's group demonstrated that although monkeys reared in isolation for the first six months displayed abnormal and often bizarre social behaviours they could, if the experimenter were patient, solve the complex learning problems normally administered to feral born monkeys. The prolonged isolation did not destroy their cognitive competence (Harlow, Schiltz and Harlow 1969). More recently Suomi and Harlow (1972) have shown that even the stereotyped and bizarre social behaviour shown by six-month isolates can be altered by placing them with female monkeys three months younger than themselves over a twenty-six-week therapeutic period. 'By the end of the therapy

* Editorial note: the next chapter includes these and other results of the Dennis study.

period the behavioural levels were virtually indistinguishable from those of the socially competent therapist monkeys' (Soumi and Harlow 1972, p. 491; see Gomber and Mitchell for a similar result).

Even imprinting toward a non-natural object in a laboratory context seems to be reversible. In a laboratory context Hess attempted to imprint ducklings to human beings. For twenty continuous hours newly hatched ducklings were exposed to adults and, before long, followed the adults. The ducks were then given a female mallard that had hatched a clutch of several ducklings several hours before. After only an hour and a half of exposure to the female, the human imprinted ducklings followed the female on her first exodus from the nest. The laboratory imprinting had been reversed (Hess 1972). This phenomenon is analogous to changes in the object of primary attachment among primates. Rhesus monkeys were raised from birth with cloth surrogates, their mothers or a peer monkey for three to ten months. Then all the monkeys were separated from these objects of primary attachment and gradually exposed to spayed, adult female dogs. Initially most of the monkeys were fearful, but this behaviour disappeared quickly and after seven hours all monkeys approached the dogs and eventually clung to them. Soon the monkeys displayed the classic signs of attachment – clinging and following. The initial attachment had been changed (Mason and Kenney 1974).

These dramatic alterations in molar behaviour are in accord with replicated reports of recovery of visual function in monkeys and cats deprived of patterned light soon after birth (Wilson and Riesen 1966; Baxter 1966; Chow and Stewart 1972). Kittens deprived of light for one year recovered basic visual functions after only ten days in the experimenter's home (Baxter 1966); kittens who had one or both eyes sutured for close to two years were able to learn pattern discriminations with the deprived eye only after moderate training (Chow and Stewart 1972). Even complex cognitive functions can recover following removal of frontal cortex in young monkeys. In a recent dramatic study rhesus monkeys were given bilateral, orbital prefrontal lesions during the first, fourth or eighth week of life compared with age-matched, unoperated controls at one to one and a half years and again at two years of age. The monkeys were tested on spatial delayed response, visual pattern discrimination, spatial delayed alternation and object discrimination reversal. The task most sensitive to the lesion, spatial delayed alternation, requires the animal to alternate his responses to the right and left food wells on succeeding trials with a five-second delay between trials. The operated monkeys were seriously impaired when tested at one to one and a half years of age, regardless of when the operation had been performed (one, four or eight weeks). But when they were two years of age, they had recovered that competence and were not significantly different from the unoperated controls. The investigators suggested that this result was due to maturation of other cortical regions during the second year of life (Miller, Goldman and Rosvold 1973).

If the extreme behavioural and perceptual sequelae of isolation and brain ablation in monkeys and cats can be altered by such brief periods of rehabilitative experience or time for recovery, it is not difficult to believe that the rural Guatemalan infant is capable of as dramatic a recovery over a period of nine years. These data do not indicate the impotence of early environments, but rather the potency of the environment in which the organism is functioning. There is no question that early experience seriously affects kittens, monkeys and children. If the first environment does not permit the full actualisation of psychological competences, the organism will function below his ability as long as he remains in that context. But if he is transferred to an environment that presents greater variety and requires more accommodations, he seems more capable of exploiting that experience and repairing the damage wrought by the first environment than some theorists have implied.

LONGITUDINAL STUDIES OF AMERICAN CHILDREN

Longitudinal studies of American children also fail to provide convincing support for the view that a mother's treatment of her child during the first three years of life is strongly predictive of adult behaviour. In a longitudinal study of the Fels population, Caucasian and middle class (Kagan and Moss 1962), ratings of direct observations of mothers and children in the home and of the children in the nursery school were made during successive three- to four-year periods (0–3, 3–6, 6–10, 10–14 years of age). These ratings, based on naturalistic observations, were correlated with ratings of adolescent and adult behaviour and personality based on extensive interviews. There was little relation between important aspects of the mother's treatment of the child during the first three years of life and a variety of psychological dispositions displayed during adolescence or adulthood. There was, for example, no consistent relation between maternal hostility toward the child and variables concerned with anger arousal or aggressive behaviour; no relation between early maternal over-protection or restriction and the adult's dependency on various targets (either parents or friends), or the adult tendency to withdraw in times of stress.

There was a moderately positive relation between maternal acceleration of intellectual skills and adult concern with intellectual achievement in women, although not in men. However these correlations were low (approximately 0.3), and if one examined only the educational level of each parent (an index of familial social class) rather than the mother's specific behaviors, the correlations with adult behavior were stronger (about 0.5 and 0.6). Since social class represents a complex and continuing set of experiences that influences beliefs about the self throughout the life span, it is possible that the experiences during later childhood were as, or more, influential than the maternal treatments experienced during the first three years.

Moreover, with the exception of infant passivity, there was little relation between the infant's behaviour during the first three years and his adult profile. Occurrence of temper tantrums during infancy was unrelated to aggressive behaviour in adulthood; mastery attempts during the first three years were unrelated to achievement or fear of failure in adulthood; anxiety to strangers was unrelated to adult social anxiety or spontaneity. The sole support for long-term continuity (in the rank-order meaning of the word) was the tendency for passive infant males to be more dependent as adults on their wives or sweethearts than less passive infants. Generally, a moderately strong predictive relation between child and adult behaviour did not emerge until the child was between six and ten years old. The dispositions displayed during the first three years did not seem seriously to constrain the profile of adult behavior.

The author recently completed a more focused and methodologically more rigorous longitudinal investigation of first-born white children over the period four to twenty-seven months of age (Kagan 1971). One might have expected stronger instances of continuity over this short interval. But there was minimal rank-order continuity for most variables from four or eight months to twenty-seven months of age. Very active eight-month-old babies were not highly motoric twenty months later; extremely fretful four-month-olds were not the most irritable two-year-olds. The transient quality of spontaneous behaviors displayed during the first year is also characteristic of responses that are deliberately shaped. An eight-week experimental intervention with six-month-old institutionalised infants made them significantly more responsive than controls. However, when the infants were visited one year later in a home setting, the effects of the intervention had vanished (Rheingold and Bayley 1959).

CONCLUSIONS

The total corpus of information implies that the young animal retains an enormous capacity for change in early patterns of behaviour and cognitive competence, especially if the initial environment is seriously altered. The data offer no firm support for the popular belief that certain events during the first year can produce irreversible consequences in either human or infrahuman infants. If one limits the discussion to universal cognitive competences, in contrast to culturally specific skills, it appears that a slower rate of mastery of the universal abilities during the first two years places no serious constraints on the eventual attainment of many of the competences of pre-adolescence. For most of this century developmental psychology has been friendly toward the pole of the irreversibility—reversibility theme that posited irreversible effects of early experience. The extreme form of that position is as unlikely as the opposite pole that assumes complete capacity for resilience of all dispositions at any age. The purpose of this paper has been to persuade the receptive reader to move just a little closer toward the latter view. The first messages written on the *tabula rasa* may not necessarily be the most difficult to erase.

This research was supported in part by grant number HD-04299, and contract number Ph 43-65-640 from the National Institute of Child Health and Human Development, grant number GS-33048, Collaborative Research on Uniform Measures of Social Competence, National Science Foundation, and a grant from the Spencer Foundation, Chicago, Illinois.

CHAPTER EIGHT

Children of the Crèche: Conclusions and Implications

Wayne Dennis

A BRIEF REVIEW OF FINDINGS

Our study of the role of environment in the development of human behavior took advantage of a 'natural experiment' brought about by cultural change. This 'experiment' was performed by the Crèche, a Lebanese social agency devoted to the care of foundlings which had for years institutionalized its charges from birth to sixteen years. In 1956 it began to substitute for this practice the placement of foundlings in adoptive homes, and within a few years adoption became a matter of general policy. This report has dealt in detail with the results of this change upon the I.Q. of the foundlings and other aspects of their behavior.

Before adoption was introduced, all foundlings received by the Crèche were kept in that institution until they were about six years of age. In this period there was no significant difference between the mean D.Q.s and I.Q.s of boys and girls: the mean in both sexes after the first year was slightly above 50.

After their transfer to another institution (Zouk), the mental growth of the girls continued at the same rate. The average foundling girl at sixteen years (and later) had a mean I.Q. of approximately 50. Most of the scores were between 30 and 60; none reached 100.

The boys, who were sent to a separate institution (Brumana) fared better, because the institutional program was better. They attained in the institution a mean I.Q. of about 80.

Soon after adoption was introduced by the Crèche, all the foundlings, except a few physically handicapped cases, were made

Reprinted from Dennis, W. (1973) *Children of the Crèche* (New York: Appleton-Century-Crofts)

available for adoption. Thus in the early years of adoption the ages of the children who were adopted ranged from birth to six years. A few were older than six years when they left the Crèche. After the policy of placing all foundlings in adoptive homes had been in effect for a few years, no older foundling remained in the Crèche, and only foundlings between birth and two years were available for adoption.

It was found that, as a group, children adopted from the Crèche within the first two years of life overcame their initial retardation and soon reached a mean I.Q. of approximately 100, which was maintained. In other words children adopted prior to age two, who, if they had remained in institutions as had their predecessors would have had very low I.Q.s, in adoptive homes reached normality.

It was found that, on the average, the children who were adopted after the age of two years developed intellectually at a normal rate; that is, typically in one chronological year they gained one year of M.A. But unlike those who were adopted at two years or under, they did not overcome their pre-adoption retardation. Those adopted at four years of age who were retarded to the extent of two years in mean M.A., when tested subsequently at ages ten or fourteen, were found, as a group, still to be retarded by two years, although during the adoptive period they underwent gains in years of M.A. equivalent numerically to the years of adoption.

During adoption they increased in I.Q., because their fixed amount of retardation in M.A. became smaller and smaller in relation to chronological age as time passed. Because of their residual retardation, no subgroup of foundlings adopted after age two attained a mean I.Q. of 100. Furthermore, the greater the age of adoption, the lower the eventual mean I.Q. attained. For example, cases adopted at age six were retarded approximately three years at age sixteen.

In addition to these findings on the comparative intellectual development of foundlings during periods of institutionalization and periods of adoption, the preceding chapters [of *Children of the Crèche*] have also reported upon the intelligence of groups of children who were family-reared in Lebanon and tested at various ages. In general their mean scores approximated those of comparable American groups.

While the test scores have received the greatest emphasis in this report, the data, fewer in quantity, on school progress, social, marital and vocational adjustment, and psychiatric referrals are probably of equal importance. It has been shown that the two kinds of data are closely related. Those who were in experientially deprived institutions throughout childhood were not only of low intelligence but also evinced more signs of social maladjustment and personality disorder than did the adoptees.

THE GENETIC POTENTIAL INTELLIGENCE OF ADOPTED CHILDREN

We have proposed that the mean genetic potential of Crèche foundlings for intellectual development in a modern middle-class environment was approximately 100. We base this estimate upon the fact that those adopted from the Crèche within the first two years of age reached a mean I.Q. of only slightly less than 100 after only a few years of adoption, and can be assumed to have reached a mean of 100 sometime later.

That children available for adoption at an early age are potentially normal in intelligence is not a new finding, as we shall now show. In our review of several earlier investigations, which follows, we shall deal only with the point at issue, ignoring other voluminous data which these studies have supplied.

A series of investigations dealing with the intelligence of adopted children began to be published in 1928. Two were published in that year, one by Burks and one by Freeman, Holzinger and Mitchell. These were followed by Leahy's report (1935) and by studies by Skodak and Skeels and their associates published between 1935 and 1966. These varied and extensive reports form the core of our knowledge of the effects of heredity and environment upon intelligence at the present time. They have been reviewed and interpreted many times and are fundamental to the recent discussions by Jensen (1969) and his adversaries. Since the planners of these studies wished to study the development of adopted children who had been reared in normal environments from an early age, they chose for study primarily children who had been placed in adoptive homes before they were two years of age, in many cases before they were six months of age. Selection on this basis served to rule out most adoptions occasioned by the mother's or father's illness and death. The adoptees in these investigations, as in the present one, were in the main children of unwed mothers who, when the babies were born, turned them over to the care of others.

Burks (1928) reported on the intelligence of 214 children adopted at the mean age of three months (none was over one year when adopted) and on 105 'own' children who were matched with the controls in age, sex and the locality in which they lived. In addition the foster fathers of the adoptees and the fathers of the controls were matched in occupational level. Intelligence tests were administered at various times between the ages of five and fourteen years. The mean I.Q. of the adopted children was 107, that of the 'own' children 115. While the own children tested higher than the adopted ones, the mean of the latter was above the norm of 100.

In the Freeman, Holzinger and Mitchell report (1928) the subgroup, which closely resembles the early-adopted foundlings of the present study, consisted of 111 illegitimate children who were placed in foster homes before they were two years of age. When tested several years after adoption, their mean I.Q. was 106. Classified according to the rated excellence of their foster homes, those placed in 'good' homes averaged 112, those in average homes 105, those in poor homes 96.

The Leahy study (1935) was similar to that of Burks. The 194 adoptees were in all cases illegitimate and were adopted at six months or earlier. An equal number of 'own' children chosen for comparison were matched with the foster children so that the two sets of homes were approximately equal in several respects. There was evidence which indicated that in both groups of subjects the parents and the homes were somewhat above average. The members of each matched pair were tested at about the same age. The testing occurred between five and fourteen years of age; the mean I.Q. of each group was 110.

The studies by Skodak, Skeels and their associates at the State University of Iowa constitute a complex series of investigations which it is not feasible to review in detail. We shall refer only to those studies which contain data concerning the intelligence of adopted children.

We shall mention first a study which was reported by Skodak in 1939, again by Skeels in 1940 and summarized by Skeels in 1942. This investigation dealt with 154 children, 140 of whom were illegitimate, who were adopted under six months of age. Their average age when they were first tested was two years seven months. They were retested at the average age of four years four months. In this study the Kuhlmann Test was used for those under three and a half years; the S–B was administered to older subjects. The mean I.Q. in Test 1 was 116; on Test 2 it was 112. Twenty-eight of the cases were tested at age five years or later and averaged 111.

Additional follow-up studies of 100 of these children when they were between the ages of eleven and seventeen years were reported in 1945 and 1949 by Skodak and Skeels. These studies involved additional administrations of the S–B, which yielded essentially the same results as had earlier tests; that is, a mean level of intelligence of above 100 was maintained at later age levels.

The studies just reviewed are in agreement with our findings that, if children, most of them illegitimate, are adopted before the age of two years, their mean I.Q. is usually 100 or above. In other words, as a group, the children who soon after birth become available for adoption, and are adopted, have the genetic capabilities for becoming normal in intelligence. That some groups of adopted children have mean I.Q.s several points above 100 may be due to their having been placed in better-than-average homes, or it may be that children of superior genetic potential were chosen for adoption.

CAUSES OF THE RETARDATION OF CRÈCHE FOUNDLINGS

We believe that it has now been established that the *potential mean I.Q.* of foundlings who entered the Crèche, including those who later entered the institutions at Zouk and Brumana prior to 1956 and those adopted after 1956, was in the neighborhood of 100. But the *functional mean I.Q.* obtained from fifty foundlings in the Crèche between ages one and seven was 53. For thirty-five older foundlings tested at Zouk or elsewhere at ages beyond 12–0 the mean I.Q. was 54. The mean of foundling boys at Brumana was 81.

It is our conviction that the difference between these means and the post-adoptive mean of about 100 of those who were adopted within their first two years of age was due to the deprivation of cognitive experiences in the institutional environments.

What are the alternative hypotheses? Some sort of selection of the 'best' cases for adoption and the retention by the institutions of the 'worst' cases is the obvious possibility. But on what basis could the 'best' have been chosen for adoption in the first two years of life? No test or other measure of behavior made in the first two years of life has been shown to have more than a slight relationship to later I.Q.s. There *is* a relationship between later intelligence of the child and the intelligence of the biological parents, but we doubt that the adoptive parents were given any information about the biological mother, and we doubt that the nuns knew who, or what kind of man, was the biological father. But if the natural parents had been known by the nuns, how could selection on the basis of potential intelligence have occurred? Most of the older Zouk girls and Brumana boys who became our subjects left the Crèche before the practice of adoption began at the Crèche. And at the time that they left, *all* foundlings, with the exception of a few physical defectives and some children reclaimed by relatives, were being sent to Zouk and Brumana. In contrast, in the years during which our *adopted* subjects left the Crèche nearly *all* foundlings were being adopted. How could massive selection have occurred?

An additional problem is the following: How could a nun, or a prospective foster parent, even given omniscience, select from a population in which no scores of 100 occur a group of adoptees whose mean is 100? Even if some slight selection on the basis of someone's knowledge of parentage had taken place, it could have taken place only within a period of two or three years, when only some of the foundlings were being adopted. Only a small proportion of our subjects left the Crèche during that period.

We have examined every possibility of which we can conceive which might explain an eventual mean I.Q. of roughly 50 for Crèche foundling girls who were tested in the Crèche and at Zouk, of 81 at Brumana, and an eventual mean of approximately 100 for foundling girls and boys who were adopted from the Crèche during the first two years of life. The only explanation possible appears to be that the institutionally reared girls were environmentally deprived to a great extent in respect to cognitive experience, the Brumana boys to a lesser extent, and that both the boys and the girls after adoption in the first two years received normal childhood experiences in a family situation similar to the experiences of those on whom test norms are based. Furthermore it appears that experiential deprivation which occurs before the age of two does not have lasting intellectual consequences if followed by normal everyday cognitive experience.

RESIDUAL RETARDATION AND RATE OF MENTAL DEVELOPMENT

It is scarcely necessary to remind the reader that the adoptees and the Brumana boys improved in I.Q. after leaving the Crèche. But this improvement, within the upper limits of the ages covered by our investigations, did not enable them to attain a mean I.Q. of 100. The evidence indicates that, after being placed in an ameliorative environment at ages beyond two, despite I.Q. gains, a deficit in M.A. remained and was probably permanent.

In earlier chapters evidence has been adduced to show that if the intellectual deficit of Crèche foundlings is stated in terms of retardation in M.A., the mean deficit after leaving the Crèche and being placed in Brumana or being adopted remained the same as it was on their departure. It has also been shown that these two groups of subjects, after leaving the Crèche and entering other environments, had a mean R.M.D.* of 100. It does not seem possible to propose a sensible cause for the improvement in the intellectual progress of these two groups of subjects except to attribute it to the enrichment of cognitive experience provided by their new environments. Yet these subjects appeared to have an intellectual limitation which prevented their mean initial retardation from being reduced by more than a few months of M.A. and their mean R.M.D. from rising but slightly above 100.

We should like to propose here that the R.M.D. which occurs in experientially handicapped children when they are placed in a normal environment is comparable to the I.Q. which would have been characteristic of them if they had been in an intellectually favorable environment from birth. In other words, for those who suffer experiential deprivation which lasts beyond age two and who are later placed in an ameliorative environment, the R.M.D. in the ameliorative environment may be an indicator of genetic potential intelligence. To put it another way, the way to measure

* Editorial note: the increase in mental age during adoption, divided by the number of years of adoption, times 100 is the R.M.D. (rate of mental development).

the genetic potential of a child intellectually handicapped by his environment is to put him in a cognitively normal environment and measure his R.M.D. The index of his potential is not his earlier I.Q., or even his improved I.Q., but his R.M.D. in his new situation. At this time we are unable to suggest how additional tests of this hypothesis can be made, but it is likely that they will be forthcoming.

The corollary arising from this view is that if the R.M.D. in a 'good' environment is to quite an extent limited by genes, a complete recovery from the effects of earlier environmental handicap which has extended beyond the age of two will not occur, unless a method of remediation more effective than normal family life can be developed. It is our belief that, for a child who has been mentally retarded by experiential deprivation, no more effective and dependable program of remediation is available today than placement in a home with two adoptive parents, concerned, intelligent and educated, who will spend several hours a day in cognitive interaction with him, in addition to providing him with classroom schooling and child contacts. It remains to be seen whether or not a better scheme can be devised.

Our own data on the R.M.D. of foundlings at Brumana may be cited as refuting the opinion we have just espoused, because at Brumana an R.M.D. of 100 prevailed. Our answer is that the families which adopt foundlings are not, in the main, extraordinary families, and are not difficult to find. On the other hand the cognitive possibilities available to Brumana boys were unusual, and the presence of a Mother Superior who could take full advantage of them was even more extraordinary. One cannot expect that many parochial institutions, government projects or volunteer agencies will equal the record of the institution at Brumana, just as not many hungry animals can count upon being fed by St. Francis. Only a very unusual institution can equal an adoptive family, and probably few exist which provide advantages *superior* to adoption.

THE IMPLICATIONS OF OUR FINDINGS FOR INSTITUTIONS AND FOR ADOPTION

The implications of our findings for those persons connected with institutions and for those playing a role in adoptions may be obvious, but nevertheless we have an obligation to express our conception of them.

We have visited a considerable number of institutions other than those on which we have reported here. We believe it possible for an institution to be 'good'. We are able to cite Brumana as a case in point, and we could cite a few others in which we believe cognitive growth and personality development are not harmed. Institutionalization, and it sometimes is necessary, *can* produce normal development; that is, institutionalization can be made acceptable – but it seldom is. There seem to be few if any reasons why children should be retained in an institution if they can be adopted. Unfortunately, even today some institutions refuse to offer their children for adoption, even though many people want them. Some of these institutions are transforming children who are potentially normal in intelligence into adults of permanent feeble-mindedness.

In our opinion it would be a reasonable requirement that each institution which receives abandoned or neglected children be required to submit to its governing board, annually, for each child the result of a mental test given by a qualified person. Such reports could well be the basis for remedial action with respect to the institutional regime and should serve to show whether or not adoption at an early age rather than retention in an institution should be introduced, at least on a trial basis.

If children are placed in an institution while awaiting adoption, it appears from our data, that unless the institution can show itself to be as favorable for mental development as are adoptive families, the children, if possible, should be placed in adoptive homes before they are two years of age. This is the current policy of enlightened placement agencies.

THE PREVALENCE OF EXPERIENTIAL DEPRIVATION

Throughout this paper we have been concerned almost entirely with the development of institutional children, adoptees and their comparison groups. But our concern would be very restricted if it were limited to such groups. They serve to demonstrate that experiential deprivation can have severe and enduring consequences, but social and developmental impairment occurs not only in institutions but in much larger populations which will be affected but slightly if at all by a wider acceptance of adoption. We would be remiss if we ended an account of the effects of the poverty of experience which occur within institutions without indicating the extent to which they occur in much more populous settings.

In recent decades, child psychiatrists and psychologists have focused much of their attention upon early childhood with a stress upon the consequences of maternal deprivation and other kinds of restriction or neglect in infancy (Spitz 1945 and 1946, Bowlby 1957, Goldfarb 1955, Casler 1961, and Ainsworth 1962a and 1962b). Among these consequences are sometimes low I.Q.s.

However, these publications have usually failed to mention that other investigators have shown that many groups of children, all of whom were living with their mothers and fathers, have also been found to have low I.Q.s and that environmental depression of intelligence is not limited to early childhood. To provide a wider perspective for the present study, we present a brief review of some of these other studies, most of which were conducted in the 1920s and 1930s.

An early and famous report of low intelligence among underprivileged children who remained with their parents was that concerning English canal boat children and gypsy children by Gordon (1923). The parents of both groups were not only poor and illiterate, but they were also itinerants who almost continually moved about, the gypsies by land and the boatmen by canals. As a consequence the children remained in a given school only a short time and often were not in school at all. Their total days of formal schooling in a year were few. The intellectual background of their parents provided only the limited requirements of their occupations, which did not include reading, writing, or extensive vocabularies.

Gordon, one of His Majesty's Inspectors of Schools, conducted a remarkably good study. He was one of the first in England to use the Terman's 1916 revision of the Binet-Simon Tests in a research study. His original monograph is difficult to find, but excerpts from it have been reprinted by Al-Issa and Dennis (1970) and by Dennis (1972).

Gordon found among the canal boat children a correlation of —0.76 between age and I.Q., that is, the older the child the lower the I.Q. The average I.Q. at about six years of age was 87; at about age twelve it was 60, which is nearly as low as that of the Zouk girls. Apparently the cognitive environment of the canal boat homes was almost adequate for normal development at the six-year level but not for twelve-year-olds.

The gypsies were more in contact with the English communities among whom they moved than were the canal boat people. Their children attended school more frequently, were not as low in I.Q. as the canal boat children, but showed the same downward trend in I.Q. with age. The numbers at various age levels are not sufficient to yield reliable averages at each age, but the mean for the gypsies at ages five and six was about 95 and at ages eleven and twelve about 75.

The situation of the Virginia mountain children studied by Sherman and Key (1932) was similar to that of Gordon's subjects except that the mountain children were not mobile. The social, cultural and educational isolation of the mountain children was due to geography rather than to the transient residence of their parents. The isolation of the mountain families at that time was attributable largely to the sparseness and scattered nature of the population and the absence or bad condition of roads. These two conditions made it impossible to provide transportation to schools (in some communities all transportation was by foot only). Isolation also prevented or reduced outside employment in, and social and cultural contacts with, the nearby towns and cities.

The mountain homes provided little cognitive stimulation. Since parents could not read, the homes contained no printed matter. In 1929–30 radios were not present in mountain homes. The book of reminiscences by Pollock (1960) provides a much fuller picture of primitive life in the isolated portions of the Blue Ridge mountains in 1930–2 than does the article by Sherman and Key and the subsequent book by Sherman and Henry (1933).

Sherman and Key obtained S-B scores on thirty-two children in four mountain valleys. These scores are not reported by age. The mean I.Q. was 72. The Pintner-Cunningham Test, the National Intelligence Test, the Draw-a-Man Test and a Performance Scale were given to a larger number of mountain subjects. Among the twelve or thirteen subjects at ages six to eight, the mean I.Q.s in the various tests ranged from 80 to 91. At ages twelve to sixteen, the total number of subjects given each test ranged from fifteen to twenty-seven. The means were much lower than those for the younger children, the mid-average being 68. The corresponding averages for the nearby town of Briarsville were somewhat higher but also declined with age on each test. For example the average on the Draw-a-Man Test declined from 93 at ages six to eight to 70 at ages fourteen to sixteen.

Skeels and Fillmore (1937) studied the I.Q.s upon admission to an orphanage of children who had previously been in underprivileged homes. Those entering at ages two to four years had a mean I.Q. of 93. Those entering later had progressively lower I.Q.s on admission, reaching the low mean of 80 for those admitted at ages thirteen and fourteen. Similar reports of the low I.Q.s of underprivileged children have been reported by Asher (1935), Edwards and Jones (1938), and Wheeler (1932, 1942).

While the studies of U.S. groups just reviewed do not tend to show early retardation, low mean I.Q.s do occur in many groups before the age of six years. We have reported (Dennis 1966) results obtained from forty groups of children to whom the Goodenough Draw-a-Man Test was administered at about six years of age. The Draw-a-Man Test was employed because it does not require verbal responses and is acceptable to almost any group. The mean scores among these groups ranged from a top mean of 125 to a low mean of 53. The two lowest means were obtained from children of two illiterate groups, one consisting of Bedouins in Syria and one of Shilluk Negroes in Sudan. Neither attended school. The respective means were 56 and 53. The means of six other groups, three of them in the United States, were below 80.

No concerted effort has been made by anyone to estimate the number of persons below specified levels of intelligence among various groups, including groups in non-modernized countries. Our own efforts in that direction have consisted in finding the means, below which 50 per cent lie, in a miscellany of groups on the Draw-a-Man Test. Results have been obtained in approximately sixty communities but are not as yet ready for presentation. We may say, however, that the information at hand warrants the prediction that there are millions of children with Draw-a-Man I.Q.s below 70, and that the low values of these scores are due, in the main, to experiential deprivation. The moral, if one may call it a moral, is that many homes and communities in the world today are as intellectually vacuous as the life space of the foundlings of the Crèche and of Zouk.

The areas of lowest intelligence are those not as yet transformed by modern civilization. In these areas there are no tractors and trucks, in some regions not even mules. Man is the beast of burden, and the only source of power is human muscle. Under such conditions the need for food and shelter and escape from disease are uppermost in the mind, and there is little concern for learning, schooling, reading or interchange of information, even with regard to the immediate environment.

For these millions of children, adoption cannot provide the solution which it has provided to the children of the Crèche. Only the promotion of massive social changes, such as have occurred in 'modern countries', can do it. Modernization is required to transform genetic potential into functional adequacy. Until this happens, children and adults in uncounted numbers around the world, be it Appalachia, India, Brazil, or elsewhere, living in stultifying and intellectually depressing environments, will have a mentality not much above that of the foundlings at Zouk.

CHAPTER NINE

A Comparison of the Effects of Adoption, Restoration to the Natural Mother, and Continued Institutionalization on the Cognitive Development of Four-Year-Old Children

Barbara Tizard and Judith Rees

The influential publications of Bowlby (1951), Goldfarb (1945), and Spitz (1949) characterized children brought up in institutions as intellectually retarded with specific difficulties in language development and the ability to concentrate. In early childhood they were said to show an indiscriminate demand for affection and excessive attention seeking, followed later by a lasting inability to form deep emotional relationships. These abnormalities were said to be irreversible; they were attributed to the absence of a warm continuous relationship with a mother figure during the critical years of infancy.

Current opinion is increasingly skeptical of these views (Caldwell 1970; Rutter 1972). As institutions improve, abnormalities in development appear less marked. The concepts of critical periods, irreversible effects, and the key role of affectional bonds on cognitive development, invoked to explain institutional deprivation, are today less widely accepted (Clarke 1968; Stein and Susser 1970). The institution as an environment for development is due for reappraisal. There is still, however, inadequate evidence on many points: (1) Which aspects of the institutional environment are likely to have an adverse effect on development? (Most studies have been concerned with children in residential institutions which combine a number of potentially adverse features, e.g. multiple caretaking, poor stimulation, and poor staff—child ratios.) (2) What kinds of change must be made in the child's environment in order to reverse these adverse effects? (It is usually tacitly assumed that transfer to a private family is both a necessary and sufficient change.)

Reprinted from *Child Development* 45 (1974), 92–9

(3) What is the upper age limit, if any, at which these effects can be reversed? (The two most widely quoted studies claiming reversibility concern infants transferred from institutions before the age of two [Rheingold and Bayley 1959; Skeels 1966].)

The authors attempted to answer these questions in the setting of a group of British residential nurseries run by three voluntary societies. In these nurseries a high staff—child ratio and generous provision of toys, books and outings were combined with multiple caretaking, constant staff changes, and official disapproval of close personal relationships. It was therefore possible to assess the effect on development of an environment which denied the child a close or continuous relationship with a mother figure but was otherwise rich in stimulation. Further, since it was the custom to place many children for adoption or to restore them to their mothers between the ages of two and four years, it was possible to compare the development of children remaining in institutions with those transferred to private families in widely differing social circumstances.

In an earlier study the development of thirty children in these nurseries had been assessed at the age of twenty-four months (Tizard and Joseph 1970a; Tizard and Tizard 1971). Their mean Cattell mental age was then twenty-two months. They were retarded in language development, but compared with a group of London working-class children living at home showed no gross behavioral disturbance. In the present study these children, together with an additional group, were reassessed at the age of four and a half years. Those who had been adopted or restored to their mothers in the interim were compared with those who remained in the institution. Only the findings regarding cognitive behaviors are reported below.

METHOD

Selection of group

By the age of four and a half only twenty-six of the original group of thirty could be reassessed. (One had died, one was seriously ill with leukemia, one had emigrated with her mother, and the mother of another child refused permission.) Five of the remaining children were in institutions, ten had been adopted, nine had been restored to their mothers, and two had recently been fostered. These two children were excluded from the present study. In order to get adequate numbers new children were added, who fulfilled the same criteria as the original group. These were that they had been healthy full-term babies, that they had been admitted to one of the societies' residential nurseries before the age of four months, that they had remained there without interruption until at least the age of two years, and that at the age of four and a half they were either still in the institution or at least six months previously (i.e. between the ages of two and four years) they had been adopted or restored to their mothers. In the first study sex and color limitations were imposed: equal numbers of boys and girls were selected; two-thirds of the children chosen were white and one-third non-white. When the group was expanded these limitations could not be imposed because of the difficulty of finding enough girls. (Girls tend to have left these residential nurseries before the age of two.) The final group of sixty-five was composed of twenty-four white boys, twenty-one non-white boys, thirteen white girls, and seven non-white girls. Since boys, and especially non-white boys, tend to remain in institutions (Tizard and Joseph 1970b), the largest group of children, twenty-six, was found in institutions. A further twenty-four had been adopted, and fifteen had been restored to their mothers. The mean age of leaving the institutions was 3·11 years, S.D. 0·69, for the adopted children, and 3·50 years, S.D. 0·58, for the restored children ($t = 1·88$, N.S.).

Selection for adoption, restoration and institutional care

To make valid comparisons between the groups of children it is crucial to rule out the possibility of selective allocation, for example, a tendency for the most intelligent children to be adopted and for the 'rejects' to remain in the institution. Of the sixty-five children in the study all but two were illegitimate, and all had been admitted to nurseries as infants either because their mothers hoped to care for them later or because they wished for adoption. Between the ages of two and four, adoptive homes had been found for twenty-four of the sixty-five children. There were usually multiple reasons why adoption was not carried out before two years – the child might be of mixed race and have a family history of epilepsy. The most frequent named reasons for delay were a family history of epilepsy or psychiatric illness, the indecisiveness of the mother and the mixed race of the child. In four cases the mental retardation of a parent, in three cases the health of the child, and in three cases the slow development of the child were mentioned.

A further fifteen children had been restored to their mothers by the age of four and a half. In seven cases the child's mother had reclaimed him after marriage, usually not to the putative father. The material circumstances of the eight single mothers were poor; in four cases the mother had four to six other children to support.

Of the twenty-six children who remained in institutions, seventeen were there because the mother or putative father still planned to reclaim the child. In two further cases adoption had not been arranged because the natural mother could not be traced; of the remaining seven, four were black children for whom adoptive parents could not be found and three were considered unsuitable for adoption, in one case because of the subnormal intelligence of the mother, in the second because of the slow development of the child, and in the third because of a possible (later unconfirmed) heart defect. Thus only two of the twenty-six children could be considered adoption 'rejects' on intellectual grounds: their full-scale W.P.P.S.I. I.Q.s at four and a half years were 88 and 87.

Evidence on the occupation and education of the natural parents was incomplete but did not suggest that selective placement by I.Q. had occurred. One or both natural parents of six institutional children, four adopted children and two restored children were known to have received more than the legal minimum of schooling. The occupations of the natural fathers of eighteen institutional, twenty adopted, and eleven restored children were known; 50 per cent of the fathers of the adopted children but only 18 per cent of the fathers of the restored children and 28 per cent of the fathers of the institutional children were known to be in semi-skilled or unskilled occupations, $x^2(2) = 3.76$, N.S.

The assessment at two years also provided little evidence of selective placement by I.Q. The mean Cattell mental age at twenty-four months of the five children still in institutions at four and a half years was 21.1 months; of the nine children subsequently restored, 22.2 months; and of the ten children subsequently adopted, 22.8 months, F = 1.68, N.S.

The child's placement at four and a half years therefore depended mainly on his mother's wishes and his racial origin. The proportions of white children and children of mixed race were about the same in the adopted and restored groups, but there were significantly fewer white children and significantly more children with two West Indian or African parents in the institutions than in the other groups. Eight were in institutions, one was restored, and none was adopted, $x^2(2) = 10\cdot74, p < \cdot01$.

Adoptive parents

The adoptive parents differed from the three groups of natural parents in age, color and social class. The mean ages of the four groups of mothers at the time of the children's birth were: adoptive mothers, $32\cdot17$ years; natural mothers of adopted children, $21\cdot81$ years; mothers of restored children, $22\cdot47$ years; mothers of institutional children, $23\cdot19$ years, $F = 23\cdot92, p < \cdot001$. All the adoptive parents were white. The social-class distribution of the adoptive fathers differed from that of the other groups: a larger proportion were professional and business men (social class 1 and 2) and none was a semi-skilled or unskilled worker, $x^2(4) = 9\cdot96, p < \cdot05$.

London working-class children

All the London children living at home with their parents who had been tested at two as a contrast group were traced and retested. The fathers of all the children were working class, and the proportions of skilled, semi-skilled, and unskilled workers corresponded to those in the South-East England census; only one parent had received more than the legal minimum of schooling. However it is not claimed that these families are a representative sample. All had agreed to take part in the study, all had small families, and none of the mothers worked full time.

Size of families

The mean number of children per family was small in all groups (adopted children, $1\cdot96$, S.D. $1\cdot0$; restored children, $2\cdot40$, S.D. $1\cdot8$; London working-class group, $2\cdot33$, S.D. $0\cdot71$), and the differences were not significant. Four of the restored children, but no child in any other group, were living in families of five or more children.

The nursery environment

This has been described more fully elsewhere (Tizard and Tizard 1971). The average ratio of children to nurses was $1\cdot37$, S.D.

0·20. The children lived in mixed-age 'family groups' of six children, each with its own suite of rooms and two assigned nurses, and were well supplied with toys and books. Considerable efforts were made to broaden their experience, for example, by outings and weekend visits to the homes of staff members. However because the nurseries were training centers for nursery nurses, staff changes were very frequent; on an average twenty-four different nurses were found to have worked with each child for at least a week during the course of two years, and close personal relationships between nurses and children were strongly discouraged.

Assessment procedure

The children were visited by one investigator (J.R.) within a month either way of attaining the age of four and a half. The investigator knew to which group the child belonged, but was not informed of the senior author's expectations. The mean age of the children in each group on testing ranged from 4·56 to 4·60 years. The institutional children were in nineteen different institutions, and the restored and adopted children were scattered throughout Great Britain. Several hours were spent by the investigator in the child's home or institution, interviewing the adults and collecting information. Only the cognitive assessment and the child's behavior in the test situation are reported here.

RESPONSE TO STRANGERS

This was included because of its possible relevance to test interpretation in young children. After an initial short conversation with mother or nurse in the child's presence, the investigator made two standardized overtures to the child and rated his response. The scale was adapted from one devised by Rheingold (Rheingold and Bayley 1959) for babies. First she turned to the child, smiled, and said, 'Hullo', addressing him by name. She rated the child's response to her on a seven-point scale, ranging from 1 (cries and/or runs away) to 7 (smiles and/or responds verbally and then talks spontaneously).

Next the investigator took some toys from her test box, smiled, and said; 'Would you like to come and look at these?' She then rated the child's response on a seven-point scale ranging from

.1 (cries and /or runs away) to 7 (approaches straightaway, talking). The rank-order correlation between the scores of the two investigators when assessing a pilot sample of twenty children with the combined scale was 0·91 on one occasion and 0·94 on another occasion with a different twenty children.

PSYCHOLOGICAL TESTING

The child was then tested with the Wechsler Pre-school and Primary Scale of Intelligence, while the mother or nurse remained in the room.

BEHAVIOR DURING TESTING

After testing the investigator rated noncognitive aspects of the child's behavior during the test on four five-point scales, inspired by the Bayley Infant Behavior Profile (Bayley 1966). Each scale measured a different aspect of the child's response to the demands of the test, and an attempt was made to anchor each point on the scale to specific behavioral acts. Thus the score for cooperativeness depended on the number of times the child refused or resisted a test item, the score for restlessness on the frequency with which the child got out of his chair, the score for concentration on the frequency with which the child had to be checked from various distractions, and the score for talkativeness on the amount of speech and whether it was spontaneous. These ratings were made because of their possible relevance to the interpretation of test results, as well as forming part of the noncognitive assessment of the children.

ASSESSMENT OF BREADTH OF EXPERIENCES

The mother or nurse was then asked how frequently the child had certain experiences, and she was asked to show what toys and books were available to him. The experiences included two 'literary' experiences (i.e. being read to, being taken to a children's library), ten everyday experiences in the adult world (e.g. shopping, going for walks), and ten less frequent 'treat' experiences (e.g. holidays away from home, visits to the cinema and zoo).

This scale was included as an index of the variety of stimulation in the child's environment, which, although crude, was expected

	adopted (%)	restored (%)	institutional (%)	London children (%)	x^2	d.f.	p
Response to a stranger:							
smiled on being greeted	54	47	23	23	8·2	3	<·05
approached when asked, smiling and/or talking	67	53	35	27	10·1	3	<·02
Behavior during testing:							
refusing no test items	50	33	27	15	7·4	3	N.S.
talked spontaneously throughout	38	47	13	16	8·9	3	<·05
checked from distracting activities	33	87	73	72	15·1	3	<·01
left the table several times	17	27	40	20	4·2	3	N.S.
Books and toys:							
read to daily	67	25	69	50	8·2	3	<·05
owning 13 out of 15 types of toy	75	20	100	70	30·1	3	<·001

Table 9.1   Behavioral ratings, books and toys

to relate to his test achievements. Some items were taken from Caldwell's 'Inventory of home stimulation', which covers much wider aspects of experience (Caldwell, Heider and Kaplan 1966).

Results

RESPONSE TO STRANGERS

The adopted and restored children were significantly more friendly at the initial encounter than the other groups (table 9.1). One very shy institutional child could not be tested even after a second visit a few weeks later, hence the I.Q. results are derived from only twenty-five institutional children.

WECHSLER INTELLIGENCE SCALE

Tables 9.2 and 9.3 show that, as expected, the mean scores of all the groups were at least average and that there was no evidence of language retardation in the institutional children. The scores

group	full-scale	verbal	performance
adopted (24)*			
M	114·92	115·92	110·67
SD	11·21	9·13	12·67
institutional (25)			
M	104·88	105·41	102·64
SD	10·11	10·07	10·92
restored (15)			
M	100·07	103·47	96·53
SD	10·77	11·61	10·14
London contrast group (30)			
M	111·47	112·83	107·56
SD	11·63	10·59	12·54

* Ns in parentheses

Table 9.2   W.P.P.S.I. I.Q.s

of the adopted children were higher than those of any other group and significantly higher than all groups except the London working-class group. The mean test scores of the restored children were lower, though not significantly so, than those of the institutional group. There was no significant difference between the mean scores of the girls and boys, or the white and non-white children. For the restored and adopted children the correlation between their age on leaving the institution and their W.P.P.S.I. full-scale I.Q.s was very low and not significant. (All the children had been in their new homes at least six months.)

source	d.f.	MS	F
between groups	3	879·81	7·27*
within groups	90	121·01	—
total	93	—	—

* $p < ·001$

Table 9.3   Analysis of variance of full-scale W.P.P.S.I. I.Q.s

BEHAVIOR DURING TESTING

Not only were the adopted and the restored children initially more friendly than the other groups, but they also tended to be more cooperative during testing, and more of them talked spontaneously throughout the test (table 9.1). The adopted children were also the least frequently distracted and the least restless, while the institutional children were the most restless.

BREADTH OF EXPERIENCE

Each child was given three scores, one for 'frequency of experiences in the adult world', one for 'frequency of special treats and excursions', and one for 'literary experiences'. The first two scores were derived by assigning a score of 3, 2 or 1 to each item, depending on the frequency with which it was reported. Each treat (e.g. a visit to the zoo) was given a score of 3 if it had occurred at least twice in the last year, 2 if it had occurred once in the last year, and 1 if it had not occurred in the last year. The more ordinary experiences of the adult world (e.g. shopping) were given a score of 3 if they occurred at least three times a week, 2 if they occurred at least once a week, and 1 if they occurred less often. The two items constituting literary experience (i.e. being read to and being taken to a children's library) were each given scores of 7–1, depending on the frequency of occurrence.

The mean scores of the four groups are listed in table 9.4. The adopted children had significantly more treats and literary experiences than any other group, while the restored children had significantly fewer literary experiences than the institutional children but significantly more everyday experiences in the adult world. The institutional children were, in fact, read to as often as the adopted children, and the institutions were better equipped with toys and books than any group of private families (table 9.1).

	adopted children	restored children	institu- tional children	London group	F	p
common events	24·00	21·73	19·35	24·80	19·12	<·001
literary experiences	10·17	6·13	8·08	8·17	5·73	<·001
special treats	18·25	14·53	14·73	15·97	7·95	<·001

Table 9.4   Breadth of experience (mean scores)

RELATIONSHIP BETWEEN SCORES

As expected, significant if small relationships were found between W.P.P.S.I. I.Q.s and scores for breadth of experience. The product-moment correlation between W.P.P.S.I. full-scale I.Q. and frequency of treats was $r(92) = ·26$, $p < ·02$; between W.P.P.S.I. full-scale I.Q. and frequency of everyday experiences, $r(92) = ·21$, $p < ·05$. The distribution of frequency of literary experiences was bimodal — children tended to be read to and taken to libraries frequently or not at all. No child with a W.P.P.S.I. I.Q. below 110 was both read to at least three times a week and taken to a children's library at least once a month, while 42 per cent of children with I.Q.s of 110 or more had these experiences, $x^2(2) = 20·92$, $p < ·001$. Most of the noncognitive aspects of the children's behavior during testing, except talkativeness, were also related to I.Q. The product-moment correlation between W.P.P.S.I. full-scale I.Q. and rating of initial friendliness was $r(92) = ·26$, $p < ·02$. Children with I.Q.s below 110 more often refused or resisted one or more test items, $x^2(2) = 9·90$, $p < ·02$; more often got up from their chairs during the test, $x^2(2) = 13·83$, $p < ·001$; and more often had to be restrained from distracting activities, $x^2(2) = 27\cdot82$, $p < \cdot001$. With the exception of the last two findings, significant relationships were not found within each group, but only within the total group of ninety-four children.

BREADTH OF EXPERIENCE AT TWO AND FOUR YEARS

Seven items from the breadth-of-experience scales had also been asked in the assessment of two-year-olds. The mean score of the thirty London working-class children for these items was almost identical at two and four years, but the mean score of the institutional children was significantly higher at four years (mean at 2, 14·66, S.D. 1·73; mean at 4, 17·00, S.D. 2·38; $t = 4\cdot28$, $p < \cdot001$). While both two- and four-year-olds living at home were exposed to a wide variety of experiences as their mothers' constant companions, such experiences had to be deliberately planned for institutional children, and there was a tendency to omit two-year-olds from the plans.

Discussion

No evidence of cognitive retardation, verbal or otherwise, was found in a group of four-year-old children, institutionalized since early infancy. This finding is in accord with an earlier study of the senior author's using a different tester, test and children (Tizard, Cooperman, Joseph and Tizard 1972). In all the institutions concerned, close personal relationships between staff and children were discouraged, and the care of the children had passed through many different hands. The findings of the two studies constitute strong evidence that a good staff-child ratio, together with a generous provision of toys, books and outings, will promote an average level of cognitive development at four years, in the absence of any close and/or continuous relationship with a mother substitute.

At the age of two we found these same children to be somewhat retarded in language development; by four and a half years, whether still institutionalized or not, this retardation had disappeared. During the intervening period the institutional children had been cared for by a continuously changing roster of staff, but two measured aspects of the environment had improved: the children were spoken to with increasing frequency as they grew older (Tizard and others 1972), and a more varied range of experiences was offered them. As far as cognitive development is concerned, institutional life is clearly not inevitably depriving; indeed, many of the children must have developed faster than they would have done at home. All the evidence from this and other studies suggests that children who are not often talked to or read to and are not given a variety of stimulation tend to be retarded whatever the social setting; institutional retardation, when it occurs, derives from the same poverty of experience as other environmentally produced retardations.

In support of this conclusion, we found the mean test results of the children restored to their mothers a year previously, at an average age of three and a half, were lower, although not significantly so, than those of the institutional children. In exchange for acquiring a mother they had lost some environmental advantages (e.g. they had many fewer toys and books and were read to less often). An alternative explanation for the results, that it was 'too late' for a transfer from the institution to affect cognitive development, is not supported by the finding of a significantly higher mean I.Q. in the adopted group. These children had acquired not only a mother, but a much richer environment than was provided by the institution: on all our measures of breadth of experience the adopted children scored highest. The relative poverty of experience offered to the restored children probably has complex determinants; not only were the adoptive mothers older and of a higher social class than the mothers of the restored children, but their relationships with their children were much easier and happier. (This evidence will be discussed more fully elsewhere in relation to the noncognitive development of the children.)

The adopted children were not only intellectually more advanced, but also friendlier, more talkative, and more cooperative than the institutional children. The unusual degree of ease shown by the adopted children with strangers is an interesting phenomenon which will be discussed with the noncognitive findings: it cannot account for their test superiority since the restored children, who were equally friendly, scored lowest while the London working-class children who were by comparison shy, silent, and uncooperative, had mean I.Q.s not significantly lower than the adopted children.

As far as reversibility of the ill-effects of institutionalization is concerned, cognitive retardation was reversed even within the institution between the ages of two and four. Nor was it too late at three for a marked acceleration to occur in children transferred to the very favorable environment of the adoptive homes. These findings would appear to imply that improvement within the institution could produce the same acceleration as adoption, and indeed in a study of a variety of residential nurseries we found the same differences in language development between children in the most- and the least-stimulating nurseries as between institutional and adopted children in the present study (Tizard and others 1972). Of course these findings cannot be generalized to noncognitive aspects of the children's development, which will be reported subsequently.

FURTHER NOTE: DECEMBER 1975

At about the age of eight and a quarter years all the children were traced, and where possible reassessed by Jill Hodges. A full account of this study will be published later. Only fifty-one of the sixty-five institutional and ex-institutional children tested at four and a half years could be visited. Six families had gone abroad (in four cases one parent was not British) and eight families refused to see us. These refusals were not unexpected: many families were anxious to forget, or did not want their neighbours to find out about, the early history of the child. However, a comparison of the mean W.P.P.S.I. I.Q.s at four and a half years of the original groups (table 9.2) and the depleted groups (table 9.5) suggests that the children we failed to test did not differ in I.Q. from the rest.

Table 9.5 shows that the mean I.Q.s of three of the original groups of children (London contrast group, children adopted between two and four years, children restored between two and four years) changed very little between four and a half and eight years. However all but one of the institutional children's I.Q.s decreased. The significance of this finding will be discussed elsewhere. Nevertheless it should be noted that the mean I.Q. of the institutional children is still average; table 9.5 shows that it was not the case that the brighter children were fostered or adopted after four and a half years, leaving the duller children in the institutions. As explained in the main article all our evidence suggests that placement was determined by the mother's wishes and the child's colour.

The mean I.Q. of the eight children adopted or fostered after the age of four and a half years is much lower than that of the children adopted between two to four years. The numbers are too small for any conclusions to be drawn, but it is certainly the case that only one of these children had increased in I.Q. The three most likely explanations for the finding would appear to be (1) that there were differences in the intellectual potential of the early and late adopted children, the brighter children being selected for adoption first; (2) that there were differences in the I.Q. of the adoptive parents of the two groups of children, the adoptive and foster families which took the older children being less intellectual; (3) that whether or not there were differences in the two groups of children and adoptive parents, I.Q. increases occur less rapidly over the age of four.

As argued in the main article there is little evidence to support the first hypothesis, but our data do suggest that the adoptive and foster parents who took the older children were of lower social class and less highly educated than the adoptive parents of the younger children. For this reason our data are not suitable for testing the third hypothesis, which none the less merits consideration. We have presented evidence elsewhere (Tizard and others 1972) that the test scores of children in different settings are influenced by the number and quality of interactions they have with adults. From this point of view it may well be more difficult to increase the I.Q. of an older child from average to above average by adoption or fostering, not because he has passed a 'critical period' in his development, but simply because he is likely to have fewer occasions to interact with his new parents than a younger child. A child placed for adoption or fostering in Britain after the age of four and three-quarters years is likely to be in school all day, and even when out of school to be more oriented towards his peers than a younger child, and more able and used to amusing himself. Even in the limited time that he spends with his adoptive parents, therefore, he is likely to turn to them less often than would a younger child, and because of his greater resourcefulness his adoptive parents in their turn are likely to initiate fewer interactions.

The possible role of other factors, such as the marked inability to concentrate of many institutional children by the age of five, will be discussed in the fuller presentation of results.

group	N	full-scale W.P.P.S.I. at 4½ years		age at leaving institution	W.I.S.C.						Neale reading age	age at re-test
					full-scale (8 years)		verbal I.Q. (8 years)		performance I.Q. (8 years)			
		mean	S.D.		mean	S.D.	mean	S.D.	mean	S.D.	mean	mean
London working-class children	29	112·0	11·7	—	mean 110·4	S.D. 13·8	mean 110·7	S.D. 13·2	mean 108·2	S.D. 13·7	mean 8-6	mean 8-3
children adopted between 2 and 4½ years	20	116·1	11·6	mean 3-1	115·0	12·0	112·9	9·9	114·1	15·2	8-9	8-3
children restored to parents between 2 and 4½ years	9	mean 98·2	S.D. 10·4	mean 3-8	mean 103·4	S.D. 16·6	mean 101·8	S.D. 15·7	mean 104·7	S.D. 17·8	mean 8-1	mean 8-4
		individual scores										
		108		4-1	119		121		113		8-1	8-3
		101		3-3	107		100		114		6-7	8-2
		106		4-0	114		99		128		8-10	8-4
		114		3-9	117		124		107		9-7	8-5
		88		3-0	91		96		87		6-11	8-3
		88		3-9	105		100		110		7-10	8-6
		93		4-3	83		86		83		8-11	8-4
		84		4-1	75		76		78		6-6	8-3
		102		3-1	120		114		122		9-5	8-7
children still in institutions at 8 years	7	mean 105·1	S.D. 10·4		mean 98·6	S.D. 10·0	mean 97·0	S.D. 12·1	mean 100·7	S.D. 8·6	mean 8-2	mean 8-4
		individual scores										

individual scores

Group	IQ	age	IQ	IQ	IQ	age	age
children adopted after 4½ years 5	111	—	93	85	103	7–11	8–7
	114	—	113	113	111	7–8	8–5
	101	—	91	87	97	6–6	8–4
	89	—	92	89	97	10–0	8–4
	94	—	88	92	86	7–6	8–4
	113	—	109	114	101	8–4	8–2
	114	—	104	99	110	9–7	8–3
(child too fearful to test)	114	7–4	107	106	106	8–0	8–4
	87	7–1	83	77	93	8–11	8–4
	—	5–2	84	74	99	6–4	8–6
	107	4–6	125	121	124	9–1	8–2
	111	4–11	104	97	111	8–7	8–5
children fostered from institutions after 4½ years 3	106	6–7	92	89	97	7–7	8–7
	93	5–3	90	101	79	6–6	8–3
	109	5–10	96	108	85	8–5	8–6
children restored from institutions to parents after 4½ years 4	111	4–9	114	119	106	8–9	8–6
	95	4–10	99	85	115	8–11	8–11
	88	7–2	69	76	67	7–10	8–6
	101	4–7	90	92	89	6–3	8–5
children restored or fostered and then returned to institution 3	96	3–0	98	96	100	8–5	8–5
	109	5–1	106	110	100	6–8	8–1
	89	4–6	88	85	93	6–6	8–11

Table 9.5   Test scores at 4½ and 8 years

This research was supported by grants from Dr Barnado's Society and depended on the generous cooperation of the staff of Dr Barnado's Society, the Church of England Children's Society, the National Children's Home, and the many natural and adoptive parents.

CHAPTER TEN

Parent–Child Separation: Psychological Effects on the Children

Michael Rutter

INTRODUCTION

The importance of the family as a formative influence on a child's personality growth needs no arguing. Particularly in early childhood it is the matrix within which the child develops, the area where his strongest emotional ties are formed and the background against which his most intense personal life is enacted (Lewis 1956). The family is the most intimate, one of the most important and most studied of all human groups and yet our knowledge of it remains rudimentary (Anthony and Koupernik 1970).

Misconceptions, myths and false knowledge on the effects of different patterns of child rearing are rife. Generations of doctors, psychologists, nurses and educators have pontificated on what parents need to do in order to bring up their children to be healthy and well-adjusted adults. Over the last fifty years we have been exhorted in the name of mental health to suppress masturbation, to feed children by the clock and then to let them gratify their impulses in whatever way they wish (Stendler 1950; Wolfenstein 1953). However the claims that these policies were necessary for normal emotional development were made in the absence of supporting evidence. Research findings have failed to show any significant effects stemming from patterns of feeding, time of weaning, type of toilet-training and the like (Caldwell 1964) and the consequences of different patterns of discipline appear surprisingly slight (Becker 1964).

Uninterrupted mother–child contact has also been the subject of firm claims. Bowlby (1946) suggested that 'prolonged separation of a child from his mother (or mother substitute) during the first

Reprinted from *Journal of Child Psychology and Psychiatry* 12 (1971), 233–60 five years of his life stands foremost among the causes of delinquent character development and persistent misbehaviour'. More recently, he reiterated that because of its long-term consequences a child should be separated from his parents only in exceptional circumstances (Bowlby 1958a, 1958b). These statements are arguable (O'Connor 1956) but are cautious compared with those of some other writers. For example Baers (1954) claimed that the normal growth of children is dependent on the mother's *full-time* occupation in the role of child rearing and that 'anything that hinders women in the fulfilment of this mission must be regarded as contrary to human progress'. Similarly a W.H.O. Expert Committee (W.H.O. 1951) concluded that the use of day nurseries and crèches inevitably caused 'permanent damage to the emotional health of a future generation'. It is, perhaps, noteworthy that assertions of this kind have mostly been made by men and from the tenor of their comments we might well agree with Margaret Mead (1954) when she suggests that the campaign on the evils of mother–child separation is just another attempt by men to shackle women to the home. Nevertheless it would be wrong to dismiss the argument on these grounds. If mother–child separation actually does lead to delinquent character formations and if care by fathers cannot compensate, then, however much the Women's Liberation Movement may protest, it is necessary for women to be tied to their children during the growing years.

But, first, we must know the facts. We are still not sufficiently in the habit of critically examining the facts about a question before arriving at our conclusions about it (Fletcher 1966). Many of the statements I have quoted imply that we understand exactly what sort of upbringing a child needs and precisely which factors cause psychiatric disorder in children. But we do not, and it is our failure to *recognize* our ignorance which has led to these confident but contradictory claims. It is not the ignorance as such which is harmful but rather our 'knowing' so many things that are not true. Our theories on the importance of the family have multiplied and become increasingly certain long before we know what are the facts the theories have to explain.

Of course it would be quite futile to collect facts without a purpose. As Medawar (1967, 1969) has described so well, science consists of both discovery and proof, hypothesis and then careful testing to discriminate between alternative hypotheses.

My purpose in this paper is to illustrate this process with respect to family studies. In order to emphasise that research is the *act* of scientific inquiry, the *search* for truth and not the *statement* of knowledge, I am going to describe how my colleagues and I set out to answer just one simple question on the psychological effects of a child's separation from his mother. This question was chosen as one which has aroused great interest, which carries with it wide-ranging implications for community policies and which, as my introduction showed, has been the subject of very strong claims concerning its consequences.

The research method I will use is that of epidemiology. Epidemiology is simply the study of the distribution of disorders in a community together with an examination of how the distribution varies with particular environmental circumstances. Originally this was a technique used with great success in the study of the cause of infectious diseases and other medical conditions (Morris 1957; Terris 1964). On the other hand it can also be used to study the social causes of psychiatric disorder (Lin and Standley 1962; Shepherd and Cooper 1964) and the psychological effects of family influences (Christensen 1969). That is the way I shall be using it here.

In order to give some 'feel' of the successive steps of research I will confine more detailed descriptions to the work carried out over the last ten years by my collaborators and myself. In doing this I should emphasise that I am speaking as the representative of a research team, or more accurately several research teams, and many of the ideas I express stem as much from them as from me.

However, the validity of any observation is upheld only when it is repeated in other dependent investigations. There are now many family studies using a variety of methods (Christensen 1964; Handel 1967; Anthony and Koupernik 1970) and I will try to point out which of our findings have been supported by other research.

MEASUREMENT OF FAMILY CHARACTERISTICS

The first task that faced us in our family studies was how to measure the family characteristics in which we were interested and how to assess children's psychological development. We wanted to determine what actually happened in the home with regard to different aspects of family life, and interview methods were developed for this purpose (Brown and Rutter 1966; Rutter and Brown 1966).

The interview served two quite distinct functions: (1) to obtain an accurate account of various events and happenings in the family (who put the children to bed, how often the parents played or talked with the children, how often they quarrelled and so forth), and (2) to provide a standard stimulus for eliciting emotions and attitudes (warmth, criticism, hostility, dissatisfaction and the like). Different techniques were necessary for these two aspects of the interview.

As our interviewing techniques have been outlined previously (Brown and Rutter 1966; Rutter and Brown 1966), I will merely state that some three years were spent in devising methods which could differentiate successfully between different aspects of family life. In particular it was found essential to distinguish between what people did in the home and what they felt about it – between the acts and the emotions accompanying the acts. It was also necessary to measure emotions separately in relation to different members of the family. Quite often parents may be very warm towards one child and yet rejecting another. Finally, it was important to consider negative and positive feelings separately. Frequently, people have 'mixed' feelings, both loving and hating someone at the same time. Making these distinctions it proved possible to devise reasonably accurate measures of the central features of family life. Systematic investigation showed that the ratings had a satisfactory level of reliability and validity.

MEASUREMENT OF PSYCHIATRIC STATE

Similar care had to be taken in the measurement of the children's emotional and behavioural state. For this purpose we used both questionnaire and interview measures of behaviour in different situations. As with the family measures, the reliability and, as far as possible, the validity of the ratings were tested and found adequate (Rutter and Graham 1968; Graham and Rutter 1968; Rutter 1967; Rutter, Tizard and Whitmore 1970).

SAMPLES

The effects of different family influences on children's psychological development have been examined in several populations. For the purpose of this paper I will refer to only two – both of which, as it happens, were being studied primarily for other reasons. This has the advantage that we have a lot of information on additional aspects of children's circumstances and development which help to put the family findings into perspective.

The first group studied consisted of the families of nine-to-twelve-year-old children living in a community of small towns – namely the Isle of Wight. This study* investigated the educational, physical and psychiatric handicaps in school-age children (Rutter, Tizard and Whitmore 1970; Rutter, Graham and Yule 1970). The second sample was a representative group of London families, in which one or both parents had been under psychiatric care (Rutter 1970b). The study† was designed to investigate the difficulties faced by families when one parent became sick, with the aim of determining to what extent their needs were being met by the current provision of services. In both cases we have been extremely fortunate in the cooperation we have received and we are most grateful to the many families who have helped us in this work.

PARENT–CHILD SEPARATION

So much for the background. Let me now consider the findings on the effects of parent–child separation. If separation is such a serious hazard to mental health as claimed, there are vital implications for public health policy and important opportunities for the prevention of psychiatric disorder. But are the claims true?

In order to answer that question we have first got to pose it more precisely. All children must separate from their parents at some time if they are to develop independent personalities. Furthermore, most youngsters experience some form of temporary separation from their parents during childhood. For example, Douglas and others (1966) found that one in three children were separated from their parents for at least one week before the age of four and a half years. Obviously most of these turn out to

* This study was carried out in collaboration with Professor J. Tizard, Dr K. Whitmore, Dr P. Graham, Mr W. Yule and Mr L. Rigley.
† This study was undertaken together with Mrs S. George, Dr P. Graham, Miss B. Osborn, Mr D. Quinton, Miss O. Rowlands, Miss C. Tupling and Mr P. Ziffo.

be quite normal boys and girls so the question is not 'should separation be allowed' but rather 'what sort of separation, at what age, for how long, and for what reason leads to psychological disturbance?' Also, we need to specify separation from which parent? Most emphasis has been placed on *mother*—child separation, the father being regarded as a relatively insignificant figure with respect to a child's personality development. Is this so? Finally, it has been suggested that it is necessary for children to have a relationship with a *single* mother figure and that harm will come if mothering is divided among several people. So the apparently simple question 'Is separation from their parents bad for children?' turns out to be quite complicated.

SHORT-TERM EFFECTS

In attempting to provide a solution to the problem it may be appropriate to begin with the short-term effects of parent–child separation. This has been most studied in children admitted to hospital. Bowlby and his colleagues noted the frequency with which children were upset after admission and described three phases to the disturbance (Bowlby 1958a, 1958b, 1968 1969; Robertson and Bowlby 1952). First the child cries and shows acute distress, the period of '*protest*', he then appears miserable and withdrawn, the phase of '*despair*', and finally there is a time when he seems to lose interest in his parents, the stage of '*detachment*'. When the child returns to his parents he often ignores them at first and then becomes clinging and demanding.

Some investigators have failed to confirm these findings (Davenport and Werry 1970) but on the whole the observations have received support from other studies (Yarrow 1964; Vernon, Foley, Sipowicz and Schulman 1965). Nevertheless a number of important qualifications have had to be introduced. The response described is most marked in children aged six months to four years, but even at this age it occurs in only some children (Illingworth and Holt 1955; Prugh and others 1953; Schaffer and Callender 1959). Moreover it is misleading to regard the separation as only from mother. While children at this age are often most attached to their mother they are also attached to their father and to their brothers and sisters (Ainsworth 1967; Schaffer and Emerson 1964). In the past the strength of these other attachments has often been underestimated. Their importance is shown by the finding that when children are admitted to hospital with their brother or sister they show less distress (Heinicke and Westheimer 1965). Although the separation is probably the principle factor even in hospital admission the care during the separation is also relevant (Faust and others 1964; Prugh and others 1953).

Some of the reasons why children differ in their response to separation can be found in their temperamental characteristics prior to separation (Stacey and others 1970). Similar findings have been found in subhuman primates (Hinde and Spencer-Booth 1970). Finally, with regard to the short-term effects of separation it appears that children used to brief separations of a happy kind are less distressed by *unhappy* separations such as hospital admissions (Stacey and others 1970). This last point suggests that in some circumstances separation experiences may actually be beneficial to the child.

In summary, children are not inevitably distressed by separation from their parents and we are beginning to learn what factors determine whether they are upset, and how we may take steps to diminish the emotional disturbance associated with separation. Even so, despite these qualifications the main point that a child's separation from his family is a potential cause of short-term distress and emotional disturbance, has received substantial support from research findings.

LONG-TERM EFFECTS

The next issue is what *long-term* effects follow separation experiences and this, rather than the immediate response to separation, is what my colleagues and I have been concerned to investigate. In order to discuss our findings it will be necessary to divide separation experiences into several categories. I will start with children whose mothers go out to work.

Working mothers

This is a situation which exemplifies both recurrent very brief separations and also maternal care which is provided by several or even many mother figures. In the past it has been claimed that the children of working mothers are particularly likely to become delinquent or develop some form of psychiatric disorder. Little time need be spent on this topic as there is abundant evidence from numerous studies, including our own, that this is not so (Yudkin and Holme 1963; Douglas and others 1968; Rutter, Tizard and Whitmore 1970). Indeed, in some circumstances, children of working mothers may even be *less* likely to become delinquent (West 1969). There is no evidence that children suffer from having several mother figures so long as stable relationships and good care are provided by each (Moore 1963). This is an important proviso but one which applies equally to mothers who are not working. A situation in which mother figures keep changing so that the child does not have the opportunity of forming a relationship with any of them may well be harmful, but such unstable arrangements usually occur in association with poor quality maternal care, so that up to now it has not been possible to examine the effects of each independently.

Day nurseries and crèches have come in for particularly heavy criticism and, as already noted, the World Health Organization actually asserted that their use inevitably caused permanent psychological damage. There is *no* evidence in support of this view. Of course, day nurseries vary greatly in quality and some are quite poor. Bad child care whether in day nurseries or at home is to be deplored but there is no reason to suppose that day nurseries, as such, have a deleterious influence. Indeed day care need not interfere with normal mother–child attachment (Caldwell and others 1970) and to date there is no reason to suppose that the use of day nurseries has any long-term ill-effects (Yudkin and Holme 1963). Although the evidence is still incomplete, the same conclusions probably apply also to communities such as the Israeli kibbutzim where children are, in effect, raised in residential nurseries although retaining strong links with their parents (Miller 1969; Irvine1966).

Why then have 'experts' asserted that working mothers and day nurseries cause delinquency and psychiatric disorder? The claim was made in good faith but without substantiating evidence and subsequent research has shown the charge to be wrong. It is important that we listen carefully to the advice and testimony of individuals who have studied a problem, but it is equally important that we demand that they present the evidence relevant to their recommendations. Science does not consist of experts' answers, but rather of the process by which questions may be investigated and the means of determining the relative merits and demerits of different explanations and answers.

Transient separations

Transient parent–child separation can lead to acute short-term distress as already discussed. Can it also lead to long-term psychological disturbance? Several independent investigations have shown that children can be separated from their parents for quite long periods in early childhood with surprisingly little in the way of long-term ill-effects (Bowlby and others 1956; Naess 1959;* Andry 1960; Douglas and others 1968). Yet, most studies have shown that children subjected to separation experiences in early childhood do have a slightly increased risk of later psychological disturbance (Ainsworth 1962) and it is necessary to explore the possible explanations for this association. To do this we must examine more closely the nature of the separation experiences.

In our study of patients' families we divided separation experiences into those involving separation from one parent only and those involving separations from both parents at the same time. In each case separations were counted only if they had lasted at least four consecutive weeks.

It was immediately apparent that children separated from both parents came from more disturbed homes than did children who had never experienced separation. Many of the children were separated because they had been taken into care following some family crisis and often this occurs against a background of more long-standing difficulties (Schaffer and Schaffer 1968).

As a measure of family disturbance we used one of our most reliable summary ratings on the quality of the parental marriage. This is based on a wide range of information concerning such items as affectional relationships between the parents, marital

* A further study by Naess (1962) confirmed that prolonged separation experiences were no more frequent in delinquents than in controls, but also suggested that separations might be more frequent in a small group of delinquents. As this study is sometimes quoted in support of Bowlby's 1946 paper, it may be appropriate to give Naess' conclusions in full: 'Our conclusion is that mother–child separation as such is a minor criminogenic factor; it does not stand "foremost among the causes of a delinquent character development", but may be conceived as part of the picture of an unstable family life.'

dissatisfaction, shared leisure activities, communication between husband and wife, mutual enjoyment of each other's company, quarrelling, tension and hostility.

Figure 10.1 (total N=151) shows the association between parent–child separation and anti-social behaviour in boys, after controlling for the quality of the parental marriage. In this and in subsequent figures the measure of children's behaviour used is the

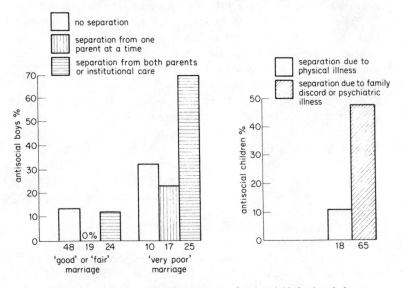

Figure 10.1   Discord or separation as causes of anti-social behaviour in boys
Figure 10.2   Reasons for total parent–child separation and anti-social behaviour in children

On these and all subsequent figures the numbers at the base of the histogram reger to the number of cases for that column.

score on a behavioural questionnaire completed by teachers (Rutter 1967). This has been shown to be a reliable and valid instrument, and it can be scored to differentiate between neurotic and anti-social disturbances (Rutter 1967; Rutter, Tizard and Whitmore 1970). We chose to use this measure because it is the one most independent of our family measures and because it concerns the child's behaviour outside the home. However the comparisons have also been made using more detailed clinical assessments and the findings are closely similar regardless of which behavioural measure is employed.

The largest differences in anti-social behaviour are associated with the marriage rating and not with separation experiences. In each type of separation circumstance the proportion of anti-social boys was higher when there was a 'very poor' marriage than when there was a 'good' or 'fair' marriage.* Furthermore, regardless of the parental marriage relationship, separations from one parent only carried *no* increase in the rate of anti-social disorder. Indeed, although the differences are well short of statistical significance, rather *fewer* of the separated children showed anti-social behaviour.

This comparison took into account neither *which* parent had been separated from the child nor the *age* of the child at the time of separation. Accordingly the comparisons were repeated making these differentiations. Again we found *no* difference. Comparisons were repeated for neurotic disorders and still no differences were found. It may be concluded that in the sample studied there was *no* association between separation from one parent only and any type of psychiatric or behavioural disorder in children.

But there was an association between separation from *both* parents and anti-social disorder in the children. On the face of it this might seem to indicate that this type of separation experience is a factor leading to psychological disturbance in later childhood. But, it can be seen that this difference applied *only* in homes where there was a very poor marriage relationship between the parents ($p < 0.05$). No such difference was found in cases where there was a 'fair' or 'good' marriage. This difference according to the marriage rating suggests that the association may not be due to the fact of separation from both parents but rather to the discord and disturbance which surrounded the separation.

To investigate this possibility we divided separations from both parents into those due to some event *not* associated with discord (namely the child's admission to hospital for some physical illness or his going on a prolonged, usually convalescent, holiday), and those in which the separation was due to some deviance or discord. In the majority of cases this followed family break-up due to quarrels but in some instances separation was due to one parent having a mental disorder and the other parent being unable to keep the family together, the child staying with relatives or going into care.

* The marital rating scale has three main subdivisions, each being split into two parts making a six-point scale in all. There are instructions for raters defining each point.

As shown in figure 10.2 (total $N = 83$), it is the *reason* for the separation that mattered not the separation itself. When the children were separated from both their parents because of physical illness or a holiday, the rate of anti-social disorder was quite low. When the separation was due to some type of family discord or deviance, on the other hand, nearly half the children exhibited anti-social behaviour, a rate over four times as high as in the other children ($p < 0.05$).

It seems that transient parent–child separation as such is unrelated to the development of anti-social behaviour. It only appears to be associated with anti-social disorder because separation often occurs as a result of family discord and disturbance. I should add that this conclusion still holds after taking into account the child's age at the time of separation. As other studies have produced contradictory and statistically insignificant associations with age of separation (Gibson 1969; Douglas 1970), we may conclude that this is not a crucial variable with respect to long-term effects, although it is with respect to short-term effects.

Permanent separations

If we accept that transient separations are of little long-term importance, can we also conclude that prolonged or permanent separations are equally innocuous? To answer that question let us examine what happens when there is an irreversible break-up of the family due to parental death, divorce or separation. In our several family studies we found that children who were in some type of anomalous family situation showed a higher rate of anti-social disorder than did children living with their two natural parents. This finding agrees with the large literature linking 'broken homes' with delinquency (Wootton 1959; Yarrow 1961, 1964; Rutter and Brown 1966; Rutter, Graham and Yule 1970; Rutter, Tizard and Whitmore 1970) and it may be accepted as a fact that, overall, children from a broken home have an increased risk of delinquency. This association does not apply to neurosis but it may apply to some types of depression as well as to delinquency (Wardle 1961; Caplan and Douglas 1969).

But is this association due to parent–child separation, and if not, how is it to be explained? Bowlby (1962) has laid most emphasis on loss of the maternal figure and has suggested that disorder in the child arises from a disruption of the affectional bond with his mother or other parent substitute (Bowlby 1968, 1969). Thus, he suggests that it is the separation or loss which is important and that the disorder in the child has some of the elements of grief and mourning (Bowlby and Parkes 1970). This explanation may well be correct with respect to the short-term effects of mother–child separation (Heinicke and Westheimer 1965), but there are good reasons for doubting the hypothesis with respect to long-term effects and it is these with which we are concerned here.

One important issue concerning the mechanisms involved in the association between 'broken homes' and delinquency is whether the harm comes from disruption of bonds or distortion of relationships. This question may first be examined by comparing homes broken by death (where relationships are likely to have been fairly normal prior to the break), and homes broken by divorce or separation (where the break is likely to have been preceded by

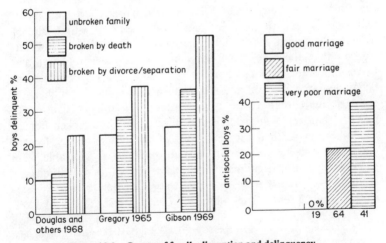

Figure 10.3   Causes of family disruption and delinquency

Figure 10.4   Marital relationship and anti-social behaviour in boys living with both natural parents

discord and quarrelling – or at least by a lack of warmth and affection). Figure 10.3 shows this comparison as made in three independent investigations.

In all three studies the delinquency rates are nearly *double* for boys whose parents had divorced or separated (Gregory 1965;

Douglas and others 1966; 1968; Gibson 1969), but for boys who had lost a parent by death the delinquency rate was only slightly (and non-significantly) raised. In other studies, too, delinquency and conduct disorders have been found to be associated with parental divorce or separation but *not* with parental death (Glueck and Glueck 1950; Brown 1966).

This suggests that it may be the discord and disharmony, rather than the break-up of the family as such, which lead to anti-social behaviour. To test that hypothesis it is first necessary to show directly that parental discord is associated with anti-social disorder in the children even when the home is unbroken. There is good evidence from several studies that this is the case (Craig and Glick 1965; McCord and McCord 1959; Tait and Hodges 1962) and figure 10.4 (total N=124) shows our own findings in this connection from the study of patients' families.*

The rate of disorder in boys rises steadily from 0 per cent in homes where there is a 'good' marriage to 22 per cent when the marriage is 'fair' to 39 per cent when there is a 'very poor' marriage (linear trend significant: $p < 0.001$). Parental discord is associated with anti-social disorder in the children. However, we can take the matter one stage further. If parental discord is more important than break-up of the home as a cause of deviant behaviour, the rate of anti-social disorder should be higher for children living with their two natural, but unhappily married, parents than for children living in harmonious but broken homes. In our study we had too few cases of the latter variety for the comparison to be meaningful, but information is available from several other investigations which have shown that delinquency tends to be commoner in unhappy unbroken homes than in harmonious but broken ones (Jonsson 1967; McCord and McCord

---

* These findings still apply after controlling for social class. In our sample parental occupation was not related to either the marriage rating or to anti-social behaviour. It is frequently assumed that delinquency is commoner in the lower social classes (Wootton 1959) but the evidence is contradictory (Rutter and others 1970b). Furthermore, even in communities where social class is associated with behavioural disorder or delinquency in the children, this association often disappears once the effects of I.Q. are partialled out (Rutter and others 1970b) or family discord and disruption are taken into account (Conger and Miller 1966; Langner and others 1969a, b; Robins and Hill 1966). The association between social class and marital discord or family disorganization is also inconsistent; it applies in some communities but not in others (Barry 1970; Christensen 1964).

1959). For example the McCords (McCord and McCord 1959) in a well-controlled study showed that broken homes resulted in significantly less juvenile delinquency than did unbroken but quarrelsome and neglecting homes.

The conclusions on 'broken homes' are surprisingly straightforward. Although parental death may play a part in the pathogenesis of some disorders (Rutter and Brown 1966; Schlesinger 1969), delinquency is mainly associated with breaks which follow parental discord rather than with the loss of a parent as such. Even within the group of homes broken by divorce or separation, it appears that it is the discord prior to separation rather than the break itself which was the main adverse influence.

The present findings suggest that separation as such is of negligible importance in the causation of delinquency. It is important not to generalise too readily from the results of one study and it could be said that the sample studied was one with a rather high rate of family discord. Perhaps in families with happier relationships, separation experiences could be more influential in the causation of anti-social behaviour. Perhaps, but our evidence suggests not. In this study separation from both parents had some association with anti-social disorders when there was a 'very poor' marriage, but none at all when there was a good marriage. As Gibson's findings (Gibson 1969) were somewhat different it would be unwise to be dogmatic. I cannot state that separation experiences have no adverse effects on a child's psychological development. What we can conclude is that, at most, they can only be a minor factor in the development of delinquent behaviour.

Could it be, though, that we have been looking at the wrong index of psychological development? Maybe separations lead to neurosis rather than delinquency. The evidence is firmly against this proposition. Separation experiences of any kind have never been shown to be associated with child neurosis (Rutter, Graham and Yule 1970; Rutter, Tizard and Whitmore 1970). Indeed, we know surprisingly little about the causes of child neurosis. Disturbed family relationships are associated with anti-social behaviour but not neurosis. Family disruption has been associated also with depression (Caplan and Douglas 1969) and with enuresis (Douglas 1970), but in neither case has it been shown that the disorders are due to separation as such rather than with the family disturbance surrounding separation.

Lastly, in defence of the proposition that separation *per se* is an adverse factor it might be suggested that there is a delayed effect, that the ill-effects are to be found in adult life not in childhood. This remains a possibility. Some studies have suggested that bereavement in childhood is followed by depressive disorders in adult life (Brown 1961; Dennehy 1966; Hill and Price 1967). However other studies have found this association only in severe depression (Munro 1966; Munro and Griffiths 1969; Birtchenall 1970) and yet others have not found it at all (Brill and Liston 1966; Pitts and others 1965; Gregory 1966; Abrahams and Whitlock 1969). It remains uncertain whether or not this is a valid finding. Even if it is, it is probably of little relevance to the present discussion in that most studies indicate that the association is particularly with deaths during *adolescence*, not early childhood. We may still conclude that parent–child separation in early childhood, in itself, is probably of little consequence as a cause of a serious long-term psychological disturbance.

This is not to say that separation experiences in early childhood are without long-term effect. Unhappy separations in a *few* children may lead to clinging behaviour lasting many months or even a year or so. These experiences may also render the child more likely to be distressed by separations when older. However, many children show *no* such long-term effects and even in those that do the effects are generally relatively minor. Serious sequelae are so rare that taken overall they are of very little pathogenic importance.

Parental death and delinquency

Before discussing the effects of parental discord we should pause for just a moment to consider why parental death is followed by *any* increase in disorder. Although in the delinquency studies quoted in an earlier figure the differences were small and statistically not significant, there was an apparent trend for parental death to be associated with a slight increase in delinquency. If it is, and the evidence is only weakly suggestive, does it mean that, after all, parent–child separation is of some importance in its own right, even if it is a minor influence compared with parental discord. Possibly, but there are other equally plausible explanations (Birtchenall 1969). In the first place, death often follows a long illness and it has been shown that chronic physical illness (probably by virtue of the accompanying emotional distress and tension) may be associated with an increased risk of disorder in the children (Rutter 1966). A second factor is the grief of the surviving parent, which often lasts as long as two years (Marris 1958). Children may well be more affected by the distress and emotional disorder of the bereaved parent than they are by the death of the other. Thirdly, families in which a father dies tend to be characterized by other adverse factors and the death is frequently followed by economic and social deterioration (Rowntree 1955; Douglas and others 1968). Again, these may be more important than the death itself. At the moment we do not know which of these influences is the greater. It is clear that when a parent dies the situation is much more complex than just a disruption of parent–child relationship. The association between parental death and delinquency is quite weak and even this weak association may not be attributable to parent–child separation.

Parental discord and disharmony

We should now return to a more detailed consideration of the effects of parental discord and disharmony. If left at this stage we are really saying little more than 'bad homes lead to bad children', which does not take us very far. In order for the association to have much theoretical or practical value we have to go on to ask in more detail about how long disharmony has to last before the child is affected, how permanent are its effects, what sorts of disharmony are particularly associated with anti-social behaviour, what factors in the home may mitigate the effects of discord and tension, and what factors in the child determine why only some children are affected by quarrelsome homes. At the present time we have only partial answers to some of these questions but let us see how far the analysis of findings from our own study can take us.

We have no direct measure of the duration of discord and tension in the home but we do have some indirect measures in the study of patients' families, all of which suggest that the longer the tension lasts the more likely the children are to develop anti-social problems. First, we can look at children going through their second experience of a home with unhappily married parents. When children have experienced parental discord followed by divorce and then after the parents remarry, a second very poor marriage, the rate of disorder is double that for children going through the first experience of parents who cannot get on together $(p < 0.05)$. Secondly, where children were separated from their parents in early childhood because of family discord and were *still* in a quarrelsome home at the time we interviewed the parents, the rate of anti-social disorder was again unusually high (see figure 10.5). Thirdly, within homes with a very poor marriage the children were more likely to be deviant if one or both parents had shown impaired personal relationships throughout the whole of their adult life (see figure 10.11). In each case the differences were large and statistically significant. The evidence is circumstantial but it strongly suggests that the longer the family disharmony lasts the greater the risk to the children. However we have no findings which enable any estimate of how long there must be disharmony before there is any effect on the children.

But we can look at what happens when disharmony *stops*, in order to determine whether the ill-effects of bad family relationships in early childhood are transient or permanent. Figure 10.5 (total $N = 65$) shows the findings on children all of whom were separated from their parents through family discord or deviance. It compares those whose present family situation is still very poor with those whose present situation is fair or good. In most cases the family situation remained rather unsatisfactory and there were only a few children living in happy and harmonious homes. Accordingly, the comparison more accurately concerns children with very poor homes and children with less poor homes. Nevertheless, there is a large and significant difference $(p < 0.05)$; the rate of anti-social disorder was double in children currently in a very poor family situation. The effects are *not* permanent and given a change for the better in the family situation the outlook for the child's psychological development correspondingly improves. How readily, how completely and how often the adverse effects of disturbed relationships in early childhood may be reversed, we cannot answer. That remains one of the many important questions requiring further research.

The next issue is what *type* of family disharmony leads to anti-social disorder in the children. Broadly speaking, unhappy families can be divided into those where there is active disturbance (quarrelling, hostility, fighting and the like) and those which merely lack positive feelings (where relationships are cold and formal and the home is characterized by emotional uninvolvement and lack of concern).

Figure 10.6 (total N=103) compares these two situations. As a measure of active disturbance I have taken 'tension' as a rating which reflects the extent to which discord leads to a persistent

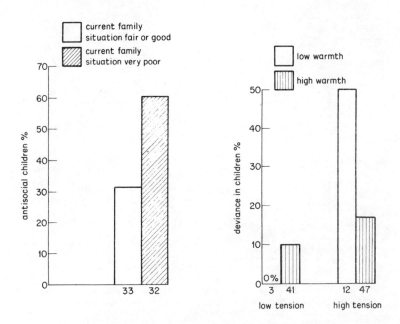

Figure 10.5   Anti-social behaviour in children previously separated through family discord /deviance in relation to current family situation

Figure 10.6   Warmth /tension in the home and anti-social behaviour in the children

atmosphere in the home so that visitors sense the disharmony and feel ill at ease. The warmth rating assesses positive feelings. It is based on feelings expressed by the parents at interview in terms of voice, facial expression and words used. It has been shown to be a reliable measure which accurately predicts emotional expression in other situations. A rating of 'low' warmth means that *both* the parent–child *and* the husband–wife relationship lacked warmth. This is a rather infrequent situation so that the numbers are small. In particular there needs to be a study of more families where there is low warmth but also low tension. However, it seems that there is an interaction effect. There is little disorder in the children when there is low tension but when there is high tension the rate of disorder is significantly higher ($p<0\cdot05$) if there is also low warmth. In short, both a lack of feeling and active discord are associated with deviant behaviour in the children.

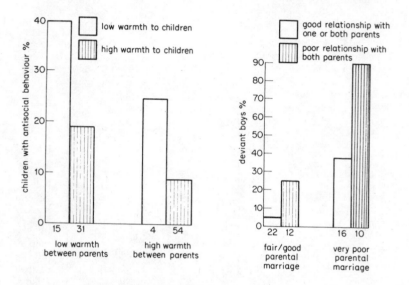

Figure 10.7   Warmth in family relationships and anti-social behaviour in the children
Figure 10.8   Parent/child relationships, parental marriage and deviant behaviour in boys

This last comparison did not differentiate between the marital relationship and the parent–child relationship. So the next figure 10.7 makes this comparison with regard to warmth (total N = 104). On the whole adults who are warm towards their spouse are also warm towards their children so that the number of cases when the two are discrepant is small. Nevertheless (although the differences fall just short of statistical significance), it does seem that the rate of anti-social behaviour in the children is raised if *either* relationship lacks warmth; the rate is particularly high if both relationships are cold.

Quite often in clinical practice one is faced with the problem of a very disturbed home situation with one parent behaving in a very deviant fashion but yet with the child still having a good relationship with the other parent. The question then is: 'to what extent can a good relationship with one parent "make up" for a family life which is grossly disturbed in all other respects?' Figure 10.8 (total N = 60) shows a comparison which provides some answer to this question. Families were first divided according to the quality of the marriage relationship and then within each marriage rating a comparison was made between children who had a good relationship with one parent and children who had a good relationship with neither parent. For this purpose, a good relationship was defined in terms of the parent expressing both positive warmth *and* very little negative feeling. No account was taken of the child's behaviour toward the parent in making the rating.

There was again an interaction effect. Whatever the parent–child relationship the rate of disorder in the sons was significantly higher ($p < 0.05$ for good parent–child relationship and $p < 0.01$ for poor parent–child relationship) if the marital relationship was bad. Conversely, whatever the marital relationship the child was better off if he had a good relationship with at least one parent ($p < 0.05$ for difference within 'very poor' marriage). A good relationship with one parent was *not* sufficient to remove the adverse effect of marital discord but it could go quite a long way in mitigating its effects.

Father–child and mother–child relationships

So far in this talk not much attention has been paid to whether good or bad relationships have been with the father or with the mother. This has been because for the most part in our current studies this has not proved to be a relevant variable. It has not made much difference which parent the child got on well with so long as he got on well with one parent. Yet it would be wrong to assume that it never matters, as other studies have suggested its importance.

For example, in an earlier study of mine (Rutter 1966) examining the effects of parental death and of parental mental illness in children attending a psychiatric clinic there was a sex-linked association. Boys were more likely to show psychiatric disorder if it was the father who had died ($p < 0.05$) or who was ill ($p < 0.05$). Figure 10.9 shows the findings for parental death but the association for parental mental illness was similar.

Or again in a study of delinquent children (figure 10.10), Gregory (1965) found that delinquency rates were higher in boys if the father was absent from the home but in girls the rate was higher if the mother was missing.

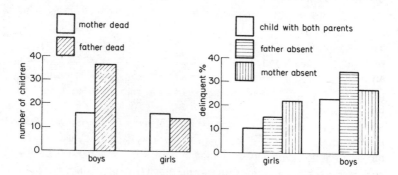

Figure 10.9   **Association between sex of dead parent and sex of child attending psychiatric clinic**
Figure 10.10   **Family composition and delinquency**

We did not find this association in the present study and it has not always been found in other investigations (Gibson 1969) so that the matter must remain open for the moment. It may be that the importance of the same-sexed parent is marked only at certain ages, perhaps in adolescence. The issue requires further study.

I have touched on the subject here, in spite of the inconclusive findings, because, however the problem is finally resolved, it is evident that the father–child relationship is an important one, and in some circumstances it may even be more influential than the mother–child relationship (Peterson and others 1959; Bronfenbrenner 1961; Robins 1966). Of course it is also true that mothers generally have more contact with very young children and their influence on them often predominates (Wolff and Acton 1968). The point, quite simply, is that both parents are important with respect to their children's development and which parent is more important varies with the situation and with the child. It should be added that the influence of each parent cannot be regarded as independent factors. The mental health of one parent may influence that of the other (Kreitman and others 1970) and may also affect the marriage relationship (Barry 1970). It is useful to try to separate the effects of different dyads in the family but it is also important to remember that the family is a social group in its own right (Handel 1967).

THE DIRECTION OF THE RELATIONSHIP

So far the effects of parental discord have been discussed with the implicit assumption that it was the discord that led to the anti-social behaviour, not that the anti-social children caused their parents' marriage to be disturbed. This assumption must be tested for it is important not to forget that children can influence parents just as parents can influence them (Bell 1968). This has been shown, for example, by studies of foster parents (Yarrow 1963), of nursing mothers (Yarrow 1963; Bell 1968) and of parents of children with cogenital handicaps (Bell 1964; Cummings and others 1966).

Accordingly, we must ask whether the anti-social behaviour is a cause or a consequence of family discord (Robins 1969). Our own study provides only circumstantial evidence on this point. However, we found that when children were separated from their parents in the first few years of life because of family discord, anti-social disorders often developed later. In some of these cases the marital difficulties must have preceded the child's birth because older children had already been taken into care following some family crisis.

Other investigations have measured parental behaviour when the children were young and then have followed the development of the children into early adolescence. These studies have shown that it is possible, on the basis of the early family assessment, to predict the development of later delinquency at a considerably better than chance level (Craig and Glick 1965; Tait and Hodges 1962; West 1969).

The effects are not entirely unidirectional and a circular process is probable (Yarrow 1968) but we may conclude that parental discord can start off a maladaptive process which leads to anti-social disorder in the children. This may fairly be regarded as a causal relationship.

PARENTAL PERSONALITY

Genuine and spurious relationships have still to be distinguished (Hirschi and Selvin 1967). Because parental discord leads to later anti-social behaviour it does not necessarily follow that it is the discord itself which is the cause of the anti-social disorder. It could be that the discord is only important because it is associated with some other factor of a more basic kind. One possible factor of this kind is parental personality. In many of the very bad marriages one or both parents had a gross personality disorder. Was this the more basic factor? Were the children anti-social because their parents were abnormal rather than because the home was unhappy? Figure 10.11 (total N = 70) shows findings relevant to that question.

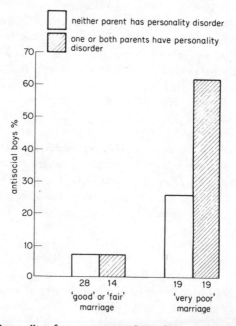

Figure 10.11 **Personality of parents, parental marriage and anti-social behaviour in boys**

Families have been sub-divided both according to the quality of the marriage, as before, and also on the basis of whether either parent showed a handicapping personality disorder. Much the most important factor in relation to anti-social disorder in the sons was the parental marriage rating. Regardless of whether one parent had a personality disorder, anti-social behaviour was many times more common when the marriage was 'very poor' than when it was 'good' or 'fair'. Furthermore, within the group of families with a satisfactory marriage there was *no* effect attributable to parental personality disorder. These findings make it most unlikely that the association between parental discord and anti-social disorder is due to the presence of abnormalities of personality in the parent.

Even so, the difference associated with parental personality within the families with a 'very poor' marriage requires explanation although the difference falls just short of statistical significance at the 5 per cent level ($x^2 = 3.832$). By definition, the parents with a personality disorder had shown disordered behaviour or relationships throughout their adult life and in most cases this was associated with prolonged marital discord (in some cases this having occurred throughout two marriages). We do not have a measure of the duration of marital discord but it is highly probable that discord was of much longer duration when one parent had a personality disorder. Whether this is so, and if so, whether it accounts for the difference is not known. All that can be said is that regardless of whether or not a parental personality disorder acts as a contributory factor in the causation of anti-social disorder its influence is not such as to account for the effects of parental discord.

GENETIC INFLUENCES

This result makes it less likely that the association between parental discord and anti-social disorder in the children could be explicable in genetic terms, but this possibility must be examined. The whole association could be accounted for in terms of heredity if a gene led both to delinquent behaviour and to personality difficulties giving rise to marital disharmony. Again this could not be tested directly but other studies allow an indirect test of the hypothesis. A recent Swedish study by Bohman (1970) examined deviant behaviour in *adopted* children in relation to characteristics of the children's biological parents. Information was available on criminality and alcohol abuse in the true fathers who, of course, had no contact with the children. Bohman (1970) found *no* association between these characteristics of the true fathers and deviant behaviour in the adopted children. This negative result stands in sharp contrast to the findings of many studies that criminality and alcoholism *are* associated with deviant behaviour in the children when the children are brought up by their criminal or alcoholic parents (Nylander 1960; Robins 1966; Jonsson 1967). This finding and similar findings from studies of foster children (Roe and Burks 1945) strongly suggest that the passing on of delinquent behaviour from parent to child largely involves environmental rather than genetic influences.

Twin studies also suggest that genetic factors play but a small part in the pathogenesis of delinquency (Rosanoff and others 1941; Shields 1954, 1968). The concordance of monozygotic pairs with regard to anti-social disorders is only slightly greater than that of dizygotic pairs, showing that genetic factors have only a minor influence. That concordance rates are high in both types of twins suggests the importance of familial influences of an environmental type.

In short, the evidence shows that delinquent behaviour is not inherited as such and that personality disorders in the parents probably lead to anti-social difficulties in the children through their association with family discord and disturbance rather than through any direct genetic influence. Of course, that is not to say that genetic factors play no part. They probably are of importance with respect to the temperamental features which render children more susceptible to psychological stress (see below). Also, it may well be that genetic factors are more influential in cases of delinquent behaviour which is associated with a personality disorder persisting through adult life (Rutter and Madge 1976).

FACTORS IN THE CHILD

In concentrating, as I have for the purpose of this paper, on the effects associated with family discord, it should not be thought that I am suggesting that this is the only factor involved in the causation of anti-social behaviour. Obviously it is not. Other studies have shown that a variety of social, cultural, psychological and biological factors all play a part in the genesis of delinquency (West 1967). The Tower Hamlets studies of Power and his colleagues (Power and others 1967) suggest that factors in the school as well as in the home may be important. In addition, there are a number of factors in the child himself which may make him more likely to develop some type of behavioural disorder. For example, our own studies on the Isle of Wight showed that children with organic brain disorders were more likely to develop deviant behaviour (Rutter, Graham and Yule 1970) and that children with severe reading difficulties were especially prone to exhibit anti-social tendencies (Rutter Tizard and Whitmore 1970).

However, at the moment we can only be concerned with the factors which aggravate or ameliorate the adverse influence of family discord. In this connection there are two factors in the child which have to be discussed.

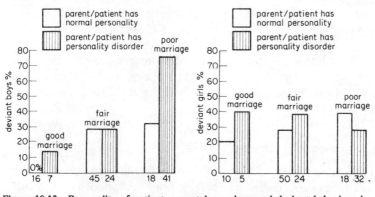

Figure 10.12   Personality of patient, parental marriage and deviant behaviour in boys

Figure 10.13   Personality of patient, parental marriage and deviant behaviour in girls

Unlike figure 10.11, figures 10.12 and 10.13 refer to personality disorder in the patient alone (not both parents). This information was available on a larger sample.

Sex

The first of these is the child's sex. Nearly all the findings mentioned so far have referred to boys. This is not accidental. In our studies the effects of parental discord have been found to be much more marked in boys than in girls. The size of this difference is illustrated in figures 10.12 and 13. Figure 10.12 (total $N = 151$) shows the association between marital disharmony and deviant behaviour in boys. As noted previously, the rate of deviant behaviour rises steeply the worse the parental marriage, and there is an association with parental personality disorder.

In girls this association was not found (figure 10.13; total

N = 139). The rate of deviant behaviour was much the same in girls regardless of whether a parent had an abnormal personality and regardless of the state of the parental marriage. This implies that boys may be more susceptible to the effects of family discord than are girls. The evidence from other studies is incomplete and rather unsatisfactory but there does seem to be a tendency for the male to succumb more readily to psychological stresses (Rutter 1970b), in parallel perhaps with the very well-documented finding that the male is much more susceptible to biological stresses (Rutter 1970b; Tanner 1962). The evidence on children's responses to acute separation is somewhat contradictory but both in humans and in subhuman primates there is some suggestion that the young male may be more vulnerable (Vernon and others 1965; Stacey and others 1970; Sackett 1969; Spencer-Booth and Hinde 1971). The matter is far from settled at the moment and further research is required, but on the whole the evidence tends to point to the male being more likely to suffer from the ill-effects of parent–child separation and family discord.

Temperamental make-up

The other factor in the child which we have to consider is his temperamental make-up. There is now substantial evidence that, even in the infancy period, children differ sharply one from another (Berger and Passingham 1973). The young child responds selectively to stimuli in terms of his idiosyncratic and developmental characteristics; to a considerable extent he *elicits* responses from other people (Yarrow 1968). Thomas and his colleagues in New York have shown that it is possible to measure the temperamental attributes of young children (Thomas and others 1963). In the course of a longitudinal study, they have followed a group of children from soon after birth up to middle childhood. A proportion of the children have developed emotional and behavioural difficulties and it has been found that the children's temperamental attributes as measured at the age of one to three years were associated with the development of behavioural difficulties a few years later (Rutter and others 1964). Children who were irregular in their eating and sleeping habits, who were very intense in their emotional responses, who adapted slowly to new situations and who showed much negative mood were those most likely to develop behavioural problems.

This study showed that a child's own characteristics influenced the development of emotional and behavioural disorders and it seemed that it did so through effects on parent—child interaction (Thomas and others 1968).

In our study of patients' families (Graham and others 1973) we investigated children's temperamental attributes in a somewhat similar way. These were assessed when the children were four to eight years-old and the influence of temperament was measured against behavioural deviance in the school (i.e. in a different situation) one year later. Figure 10.14 shows the findings.

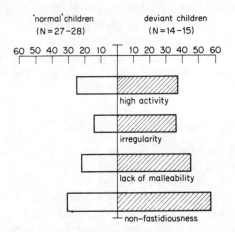

Figure 10.14 **Temperamental characteristics and deviant behaviour (one year later) in children of mentally ill parents**

Children who lacked fastidiousness (that is, they did not mind messiness and disorder) were significantly more likely ($p < 0.05$) to show deviant behaviour one year later. The same was true of children who lacked malleability ($p < 0.05$), whose behaviour was difficult to change (a measure quite similar to the New York group's category of non-adaptability). As in the New York study, children who were markedly irregular in their eating and sleeping patterns were also more likely to develop behavioural problems ($p < 0.01$). There was a similar, but statistically insignificant ($p < 0.2$), tendency for highly active children to be at greater risk.

The findings demonstrated that children differed in their susceptibility to family stress and they showed which temperamental attributes were important in this respect. The attributes were not ones concerned with deviance but rather were features which determined *how* a child interacted with his environment. That we were measuring more than just aspects of deviant behaviour is suggested by the finding that the attributes tended to have a stronger association with deviance one year later than with deviance at the time. Furthermore, the association was as strong with respect to the child's deviance at school as at home in spite of the fact that temperament was assessed only in relation to the child's mode of behaviour when with his family.

It is no new observation that children differ in their responses to stress situations but until recent years surprisingly little attention has been paid to this side of parent–child interaction. It warrants further study and the dividends of such study should be great.

THEORETICAL EXPLANATIONS

It has been found that a child's separation from his family constitutes a potential cause of short-term distress, but that separation is of little direct importance as a cause of long-term disorder. Moreover, even the short-term effects cannot be regarded solely as a response to maternal separation. Other family members are also very important in this context. Although separation experiences have an association with the later development of anti-social behaviour, this is due, not to the fact of separation itself, but rather to the family discord which accompanies the separation. The same applies to the more permanent separations due to family disruption consequent upon parental death or divorce. For the most part, the child is adversely affected by the tension and disharmony; the break-up of the family is only a minor influence. Studies of unbroken families show that boys in homes where there is an unhappy marriage between the parents are much more likely to become deviant than are boys in harmonious homes. Both active discord and lack of affection are associated with the development of anti-social disorders. A good relationship with one parent can go some way towards mitigating the harmful effect of a quarrelsome, unhappy home. The longer the family discord lasts the greater the effect on the child but the effects are not necessarily permanent. If the child later lives in a harmonious home the risk of anti-social problems drops. The association between family discord and anti-social disorders seems to be largely due to environmental influences with hereditary factors of lesser importance. Nevertheless the family discord cannot be regarded as an independent influence; it acts through the medium of parent–child interaction. This is a dyad in which the child also plays an active role and both the child's sex and his temperament attributes have been shown to affect the interaction.

While these findings have added to our understanding of the long-term consequences of family disruption, this is far from the end of the problem, although it is where we will have to leave it today. I should just remind you that we have still to determine the psychological mechanisms involved. *Why* and *how* does family discord interact with a child's temperamental characteristics to produce anti-social behaviour?

Let me conclude with three suggestions on possible mechanisms. First, there is evidence from both retrospective and prospective studies that the parents of delinquent boys differ from other parents in their approach to the discipline and supervision of their children (Glueck and Glueck 1962; West 1969; Sprott and others 1955; Craig and Glick 1965). Could it be that it is the child-rearing practices which are the main factor in the causation of delinquency and that the discord is important only in so far as it is associated with erratic and deviant methods of bringing up children? Secondly, experimental studies have shown how readily children imitate other people's behaviour and how a model of aggressive or deviant behaviour may influence the children to behave similarly (Bandura 1969). Perhaps the family discord is important only because it provides the child with a model of aggression, inconsistency, hostility and anti-social behaviour which he copies. The third alternative is that the child learns social behaviour through having a warm stable relationship with his parents, that this relationship provides a means of learning how to get on with other people and that difficulties in interpersonal relationships constitute the basis of anti-social conduct.

It is not difficult to think of situations in which these three hypotheses lead to different predictions, but that is another story. We have come a long way from the simple question with which we started: 'Is separation from their parents bad for children?' The conclusions from research suggest a more complex interaction than that implied in the original question, but one which is still susceptible to critical analysis. There is some distance yet to go before we understand the mechanisms and processes by which family life helps shape children's psychological development. However, the problems are soluble and the solutions should be of practical importance in knowing how best to help children and families who are going through a period of psychological difficulties.

The studies were financed in part by a grant from the Association for the Aid of Crippled Children.

ADDENDUM: DECEMBER 1975

A recent paper by Douglas (1975) has reopened the issue of whether separation experiences in early life can predispose children to disorders in adolescence. The findings from his longitudinal study of the 1946 National Survey cohort confirmed the earlier observations that a single hospital admission of one week or less was *not* associated with an increased risk of any kind of disorder. But the findings did indicate an association between *prolonged* or *repeated* hospital admission in early childhood and an increased risk of behaviour disturbance or delinquency in adolescence. Douglas argued that the evidence was highly suggestive of a causal relationship.

His findings refer to hospital admission which involves many stresses other than separation but on the face of it the results do suggest that quite brief acute stresses can have long-term effects – a conclusion which runs counter to the arguments in the present paper. However there are reasons for caution before accepting Douglas's conclusions in view of certain limitations in the data (Quinton and Rutter 1976). First data were missing on a very substantial proportion of the population. Second, even on the data given, the increase in troublesome behaviour associated with hospital admission contributed little to the total number of disturbed children in the population. Third, it appears possible that the association applied equally when admissions occurred after the onset of delinquent acts. Fourth, the findings refer to children admitted to hospitals in the very different conditions existing a generation ago. Fifth, the findings could be an artefact resulting from an association between hospital admission and family discord (on which Douglas did not have data). On the other hand our negative findings with respect to separations in early childhood did not take into account *repeated* separations and the data applied to a sample with a high rate of family pathology.

The matter required further study and fresh data. Both were available from two recent epidemiological studies of the general population of ten-year-old children living on the Isle of Wight and in an inner London borough (Rutter, Cox and others 1975). The combined studies provided a sample of four hundred children with systematic data on hospital admission *and* on a variety of detailed aspects of family functioning and social circumstances. On the basis of these findings a psychosocial disadvantage index was constructed which showed a strong association with child psychiatric disorder.

The findings confirmed Douglas's finding that single hospital admissions lasting a week or less were *not* associated with any form of later emotional or behavioural disturbance. This was so both for individual psychiatric ratings based on detailed sensitive interviewing and for teacher questionnaire scores. The study also confirmed that *repeated* hospital admissions were significantly associated with later disturbance (provided the first admissions occurred before age five years). However the children with multiple admissions were much more likely to come from disadvantaged homes, and it was necessary to take this into account. After standardising the groups on the psychosocial disadvantage index the association between repeated admission and psychiatric disorder remained but was more marked in the case of children from disadvantaged homes. It may be concluded that single hospital admissions rarely have long-term sequelae, that *repeated* admissions may sometimes constitute a cumulative stress resulting in disorder but that this is most likely to occur when the multiple acute stresses are also associated with chronic psychosocial disadvantage.

The data did not confirm Douglas's claim that single prolonged admissions also led to disorder. We, too, found an association between admissions of four weeks or more and later disorder. However, children with prolonged admissions were twice as likely to have also experienced multiple admissions and twice as likely to come from disadvantaged homes. When attention was confined to single admissions of four weeks or more in children from non-disadvantaged homes only three out of four hundred children remained. To determine whether these few children had an increased risk of psychiatric disorder would require a very much larger sample, but even if there was a risk it must apply to a tiny proportion of children.

The original conclusion, therefore, remains. Single brief acute stresses rarely have long-term sequelae. However *recurrent* stresses may have a cumulative effect and they are particularly likely to do so in the presence of chronic disadvantage.

Editorial note: see also pages 81–8.

CHAPTER ELEVEN

Adopting Older Children: Summary and Implications

Alfred Kadushin

This chapter summarizes the study, introduces selective statistical data resulting from analyzing the relationship between background factors and outcome measures, makes explicit some general conclusions which derive from the study, and briefly discusses these conclusions.

This is a follow-up study of the experience of parents who adopted white, healthy, older children through one agency, The Division of Children and Youth, Wisconsin State Department of Public Welfare, over a ten-year period (1952–62). The agency placed a hundred and fifty such children who, at the time of adoptive placement, were older than five years of age but younger than twelve. Of the total number of such placements twelve failed some time during the first year, and the child was removed from the home. In 138 cases legal adoption was completed. The 138 children included some multiple placements so that 112 families met all of the delimitations of the study. Failure to locate, movement out of the area, and refusal by one county judge of permission to contact the family reduced the number of the study sample to ninety-five families. Four families refused an interview, a rate lower than in most adoptive follow-up studies. The final study group, then, consisted of ninety-one families who met the delimitation of the study, were located, contacted, and who consented to participate.*

* Editorial note: Where, within a given family, multiple adoptive placements had occurred, only one of the children was selected for study, generally the older of two or three children, except where the older violated some delimitation of the study (i.e. was not of average intelligence, or twelve years of age or older when placed; on the former grounds very few were so excluded [Kadushin, personal communication]).

Reprinted from Kadushin, A. (1970) *Adopting Older Children* (New York: Columbia Univ. Press)

Data for the study were obtained from the agency records, joint interviews with the adoptive parents, and response forms completed by the parents at the end of the interview. The two- to three-hour interviews were tape recorded, only four families refusing permission for this. Typescripts of the interviews, averaging some fifty pages, were used as a basis for analysis of outcome by three typescript readers, all of whom were graduate social workers with experience in adoption.

Two criteria for outcome were developed. One was a composite score of overall parental satisfaction in the adoptive experience. This was derived by averaging independent judgments of the parents, the interviewer and each of the three typescript readers, all of whom used the same five-level scale to assess the extent of parent satisfaction. The second criterion was the ratio of discrete satisfactions to dissatisfactions expressed by the parents in the interviews and identified by at least two of the three readers. The two measures of outcome were related to each other at a level beyond 0·001, and each gave slightly different overall percentages of successful outcome, but with neither method was successful outcome less than 82 per cent of the cases nor more than 87 per cent. The percentage of successful cases in this study was compared with other follow-up studies of adoptions. Despite the fact that the subjects of all these studies were infant adoptions the level of success achieved was no different, in terms of statistical significance, from the level of success achieved with these older children.

The two outcome measures were consistently supported, in the results they offered, by additional, supplementary data – parents' free response to sentence stubs requiring completion, as well as their replies to unstructured probes about advice they would give to friends regarding adoption of older children, and so on.

The children in this study group became available for adoption, in all instances, as a result of court action to terminate parental rights because of neglect and/or abuse.* The families from which

* Editorial note: Of the 91 children studied, in the case of 26, one or both parents were dead, had deserted, or could not provide care; for 14, one or both parents were hospitalized, imprisoned or deserted; in 24 cases, the marriage was breaking up, or had broken up, or divorce was contemplated or completed, neither parent wanting the child; 12 children suffered gross neglect and/or abuse; in 13, the mother was unmarried and arrangements for the continuation of care broke down; and for two children 'other reasons' dictated action for terminating parental rights.

they came were atypically large, 52 per cent having five or more children. During their infancy they had lived in socially deprived circumstances, in substandard housing with families whose incomes were, most often, below poverty level. Natural parents had limited education, only 2 per cent of the fathers having completed high school. When employed they worked in unskilled or semi-skilled occupational categories. The marital situation in the natural home was, in almost all instances, conflicted. In addition, the natural parents presented a picture of a considerable personal pathology compounded of promiscuity, mental deficiency, alcoholism, imprisonment, and psychosis. The mean number of specific social and personal pathologies exhibited by each of the natural families from which these children came was 5·7. Neither socioeconomic background of natural parents nor number of pathologies evidenced in the natural home was related to outcome.

The relationship between the natural parents and these children was most frequently characterized by physical neglect, although 31 per cent of the group were described as having experienced an emotional relationship which was 'normally warm and accepting'. Physical abuse was encountered in only 4 per cent of the mothers and 10 per cent of the fathers. The natural mother's relationship to the child when 'normally warm and accepting' was highly related to outcome. However, a negative relationship to the child was not related to outcome. In only about 15 per cent of the cases was termination of parental rights actively opposed by the parents, and their attitude towards such termination was not related to outcome.

The group of children included forty-nine boys and forty-two girls. Sex was not related to outcome. They were of average intelligence,* had been removed from their own home at a mean age of 3·5 years, placed for adoption at the mean age of 7·2 years, and were at the mean age of 13·9 years at follow-up. They had experienced, on an average, 2·3 changes of homes prior to adoptive placement and throughout the period in placement had exhibited an average of 2·9 behavioral problems. The group as a whole, however, showed a greater degree of psychic health and stability

---

* Editorial note: 'based on psychological scores available in the child's record', 85 per cent lay between I.Q. 90 and 115; one child lay between 80 and 84; three between 84 and 89, and five above 115. Very few were excluded for being below I.Q. 80 (Kadushin, personal communication).

than might have been anticipated given the nature of their backgrounds and developmental experiences. The child's capacity to develop interpersonal relationships, as assessed by the record readers based on the material included in the record by the social worker, was rated as 'good' or 'fair' in 79 per cent of the cases. 'Capacity to develop interpersonal relationships' was highly related to outcome. The older the child was at time of placement (seen in the context of the fact that all these children were 'older' by adoption standards) the greater the likelihood of less favorable outcome.

Outcome was related to the number of placements experienced, although it might be of interest to note that replacements were more frequently for administrative and/or situational reasons than because of a child's unacceptable behavior in the foster home. The latter set of reasons accounted for only 19 per cent of the total replacements experienced by this group of children. The number of pathologies manifested by the child was, as expected, related to outcome. The more behavioral disturbances exhibited the less likely was outcome to be favorable. The child was 'weaned', or 'weaned' himself, gradually during placement from emotional attachments to his natural home and parents. The change in strength of such attachment was related to outcome, and when the child had not resolved such earlier ties, outcome was less likely to be favorable.

Since the older child, unlike the illegitimate infant placed for adoption, is likely to have developed a relationship with siblings, it is not unexpected to find that in 43 per cent of the cases these children were placed for adoption with siblings; this fact was not related to outcome.

The mean age of the adoptive mother at placement was 40 and of the fathers, 41·5. They are consequently older than most adoptive parents. However, the age difference between these adoptive parents is similar to the age difference between the more typical younger parents and their adoptive infants. Age of adoptive parents was not related to outcome, nor was religion of the adoptive parents.

The adoptive parents were socioeconomically at a higher level than the natural parents, and almost all of these children were displaced upward in moving from their own to the adoptive home. Neither the degree of displacement nor the socioeconomic level of the adoptive parents was related to outcome.

In contrast to most adoptive parents a high percentage of the group (37 per cent) either had their own or an adopted child already in the home at time of placement. Previous experience as a parent was not related to outcome; nor was composition of the family at time of placement. Thirty per cent had previously been rejected as adoptive applicants, primarily because of age. As a group, these adoptive parents had experienced few developmental difficulties, but where such difficulties had been noted in the record it was not related to outcome.

Reason for sterility was related to outcome. Where a woman had experienced miscarriages or where reason for infertility was not clearly established the likelihood was that outcome would be less favorable. While few parents preferred the older child at the point of placement, most were reconciled to the realities of the adoptive situation so as to be accepting of this. Reaction to the idea of adopting an older child was not related to outcome. While most of the parents reacted positively to the presentation of the child, reaction to presentation was not related to outcome. The largest percentage of the adoptive children and parents adjusted readily and without great difficulty to the placement, and in 75 per cent of the cases legal adoption was completed within the minimum period of time. In only two of the ninety-one families contacted did the adoption end in the child's subsequent removal from the home. In all other instances the child was still in the home at the time of the follow-up interview which took place on an average of six years after placement.

Outcome was positively related to parents' acceptance of the child, in their perception of him as a member of the family, and negatively related to self-consciousness by parents regarding adoptive status. However, very few of these parents were perceived as being self-conscious about their adoptive status. Almost all openly accepted their status as adoptive parents but at the same time felt there was little essential difference between biological and adoptive parenthood as this related to implementing parental roles in relation to the older child. Their perception of the community's attitude toward adoptive parents was essentially positive. There was no relationship between perception of community attitude as positive or negative and outcome.

Parents derived satisfaction from many areas: the child himself – his personality, temperament, mannerisms and disposition;

his achievements – artistic, athletic, social, educational – at school, in the community, with peers and in the home; the parent–child relationship, companionship with the child, affectional responses from him, his obedience to, respect for, and sympathetic understanding of the parent, as well as in the child's pride in them, identification with and sharing of confidences. In addition there was the occupation of parenthood itself as a lifelong interest, in the pleasure it affords in helping a child grow and develop, in successfully handling the problems of child rearing, and the appreciation it stimulates of the simple pleasures of life, as well as the opportunity to act as an exemplar to a dependent child. Additional sources of satisfaction were the positive relationship between the child and siblings and the child and the extended family, and the ability to resolve the problems of adoption. All were potential dissatisfactions as well. In aggregate, some 1,740 discrete satisfactions and dissatisfactions were identified by at least two of the three typescript readers as having been expressed by this group of parents. The overall ratio of satisfaction to dissatisfaction was 3·9 to 1.

Parents discussed some particular advantages of adopting the older child. The fact that the parent-age spread is more appropriate for the older adoptive parent was mentioned most frequently (66 per cent). In descending order of frequency of mention were the following advantages: the child is old enough to do things with, there is none of the drudgery of training a totally dependent infant, the child is old enough to reason with, and because he consciously experienced adoption the parent is not faced with the problem of sharing this with him.

The parents talked about special problems in adopting the older child. The following were related to outcome measures: the fact that the child, having lived under stress, is apt to come to the adoptive home somewhat disturbed; he is difficult to understand because the parent has not shared a significant segment of his life; and he has been molded by others and in some measure 'belongs' emotionally to others. Other special problems were mentioned but were not related to outcome: the disadvantage of missing the joy of having the child during his dependent infancy, the problems occasioned by lack of specific details regarding the child's health and developmental history. Despite the supposed separation between the child's adoptive family and his previous life, in 28 per cent of the cases these children had contact with 'significant others' whom they had known in the past: foster parents, siblings in other homes, grandparents, etc.

THE REVERSIBILITY OF TRAUMA

The most significant general overall conclusion of the study is that older children can be placed for adoption with expectation that the placement will work out to the satisfaction of the adoptive parents. The level of expectation of satisfying outcome is only slightly lower than that which might be anticipated in adoptive placement of infants.

The general conclusion is unexpected and raises a question of considerable interest. The data on the background factors and developmental history of these children, which were reviewed in chapters 3 and 4 [of *Adopting Older Children*] on the natural parents and the children, indicate that almost all lived, during early childhood, under conditions of social and emotional deprivation. The families into which they were born and from which they were removed by court action, after the community had recognized the dangers of such an environment for healthy child development, were characterized by considerable social and interpersonal pathology. The early lives of these children, who spent their most impressionable years under conditions of poverty, inadequately housed, with alcoholic, promiscuous parents who frequently neglected them, sometimes abused them, and only rarely offered them the loving care prerequisite to wholesome emotional development, make it difficult to explain the generally favorable outcome of these placements.

We echo the surprise expressed by some of the workers whose records we read in doing this study. One worker in her adoption summary statement said:

I think that this child will continue to make good adjustment and to develop into a secure, happy child in an environment which can continue the permissive, understanding, and warmly accepting attitudes he has found in the receiving home. It is difficult, in view of the home environment from which the child came, and the type of separation which he has experienced, to account for the apparent lack of traumatizing and destructive influences in this picture. I cannot adequately explain where he might have developed his inherent ego strength and ability to accept normal and satisfying relationships, but I do feel that there is a remarkable amount of resiliency and ability in the child.

Before attempting an explanation, however, it might be well to point out that other studies have come to the same unexpected conclusion with similar expressions of surprise; in each instance the children studied turned out to be more 'normal', less 'malad-justed' than they had any right to be, given the trauma and insults to psyche experienced during early childhood.

Van Theis, in summarizing her impression derived from one of the first large-scale follow-up studies of foster children, expresses some surprise at the adjustment of the group, 80 per cent of whom came from 'bad backgrounds'.

Our study of the group as a whole, insofar as the subjects have demonstrated their ability to develop and to adjust themselves to good standards of living, and perhaps even more strikingly, our study of individual members of it, leave us with a distinct impression that there exists in individuals an immense power of growth and adaptation. Our studies of these individuals and of the groups of individuals have shown that there were potentialities within these people which revealed themselves only under certain conditions. We would certainly not say that anything could be made of any child – that a favorable environment could produce any kind of development desired, but rather that our study leads us to believe that there are tremendous latent powers within an individual awaiting development, and that under favorable conditions these powers may be developed and directed toward accomplishment. (1924, p. 163)

Roe and Burks, both psychologists, did a follow-up study of thirty-six young adults who had, as children, been removed from their home and placed in foster care because their own parents were chronic alcoholics. Other types of deviant behaviour were associated with alcoholism; 81 per cent of the fathers of these children 'were guilty of mistreatment or neglect of their children'; 44 per cent of the mothers 'mistreated or neglected their children' (1945 p. 38). Since most of the children 'became dependent as a result of court action – this means that the first few years of life of these children were spent in a home situation which left much to be desired – and that they were probably subjected to traumatic experiences during the early years of their lives' (Roe 1972, pp. 382—3). The mean age at placement for the group was 5·6 years.

As adults, at the time of the follow-up interview, 'most of these subjects have established reasonably satisfactory lives, including adequate personal and community relationships and most of them are married' (Roe 1972, p. 388). When this group was contrasted with a group of adult former foster children who had come from 'normal' homes broken by death and illness, it was noted that 'there is no difference between the two groups in the percentage who feel reasonably secure and it does not appear that the proportion is much lower, if at all, than would be found in an unselected population' (Roe 1972, p. 338).

Here, too, the authors are prompted to ask:

How did it happen that these children turned out as well as they did? How did it happen that in spite of these |adverse| factors many of them have become not only useful citizens but reasonably contented persons working adequately, with pleasant family lives and sufficient friends? No one who has read the records of some of these lives and pondered on them can escape a profound sense of awe at the biological toughness of the human species. (Roe 1972, p. 391)

Maas conducted a follow-up study of twenty children who had been removed from home during infancy and early childhood and placed for at least a year in a residential nursery. He reviewed agency records, interviewed parents and saw the children themselves, who at the time of the follow-up study some twenty years later were young adults. Maas reports:

... although these 20 young adults may have been seriously damaged by their early childhood separation and residential nursery experiences, most of them gave no evidence in young adulthood of extreme aberrant reductions ... To this extent the data supports assumptions about the resiliency, plasticity and modifiability of the human organism rather than those about the irreversibility of the effects of early experience. (Maas 1963, pp. 66–7)

In the follow-up study of independent adoptions conducted by Witmer and others, a group of fifty-six children were identified as having lived under 'possibly traumatizing conditions' prior to adoption. These children had lived under adverse physical conditions and the psychological situation 'was even more pathetic'. At follow-up, there was little difference in the adjustment ratings achieved by this group of children as contrasted with other adoptees placed at a similar age and in similar adoptive homes but who had not experienced such 'possibly traumatizing conditions' (Witmer 1963, p. 286—7).

Meier completed a follow-up study of sixty-one young adults who had grown up in foster care. All of the group had experienced five years or more in foster care and none had returned to their own families. About half of the group had been removed from their own home before the age of five. Between their first foster placement and their discharge from foster care at eighteen, these children had experienced an average of 5·6 living arrangements. Most of them had been removed by the courts from their own homes 'in which they had experienced inadequate care' (Meier 1962, p. 197).

Based on lengthy interviews with the group, now young adults, Meier concludes:

The vast majority of the subjects have found places for themselves in the community. They are indistinguishable from their neighbors as self-supporting individuals, living in attractive homes; taking care of their children adequately, worrying about them, and making some mistakes in parenting, sharing the activities of the neighborhood and finding pleasure in their association with others. (p. 206)

Meier says:

Child welfare workers are continuously baffled, as well as heartened, by the fact that over and over again they see children removed from impossibly depriving circumstances who, by all the rules 'ought' to be irreparably harmed, who, nevertheless, thrive and grow and learn to accept love and affection and respond to it. (p. 12)

Rathbun reported on a follow-up of thirty-three foreign children who, after having suffered considerable deprivation in their own country, were placed for adoption in the United States. Interviews by case workers with the adoptive parents six years after placement, supplemented by contact with the schools, showed that 'the adjustment of the majority was judged adequate and in some cases notably superior' (Rathbun 1964, p. 6). The report concludes by noting that 'the consistence of the ratings for all categories in which assets outweigh liabilities, points in the direction of a considerable degree of reversibility of the effects of early psychic damage' (1964, p. 131).* Another research group studied twenty-two Greek children

* Editorial note: for a more detailed description of the Rathbun and others reports, see pages 76–80.

institutionalized during the first two years and subsequently placed for adoption in the United States. Testing and interviews, five years after adoption, rated only two of the children as 'poorly adjusted . . . We can conclude, therefore, that despite early deprivation the children have done remarkably well' (Research Institute for the Study of Man 1964, p. 19).

Welter studied seventy-two children placed for adoption in America when older than five years of age. Thirty-six of the group were born outside America and transferred to that country for adoption. Some 85 per cent of the children were judged to be showing 'good' to 'excellent' adaptation on follow-up (1965, p. 126).

Welter notes, in summarizing her report that

. . . perhaps the single most important implication may be drawn from the fact that according to the social workers [responsible for working with the children] both of these groups of older adoptive children . . ., despite extended exposure to massive deprivation, have indicated a degree of responsiveness to a restitutive environment and a reversibility of early psychic damage which seems to exceed even the most optimistic assessments of the studies on maternal deprivation and separation we have seen thus far. (1965, p. 164)

A follow-up study by Tinker (1952) of 112 emotionally disturbed children in foster care indicated that 'when basic needs are met many of these disturbed children do outgrow some, or all of their behavior and personality problems.' Evaluation at follow-up was made in terms of the child's adjustment at home and school and in the community as reported by caseworkers, foster parents, and others familiar with the child's behavior. Most of the children in the study 'had spent their early formative years in homes disorganized by desertion, alcoholism, immorality or other forms of social breakdown'.

Heston studied the effects of institutional care on adult adjustment. Hospital, school, police and armed forces service records were used in addition to personal interviews and Minnesota Multiphasic Personality Inventory. Three psychiatrists independently gave each subject a mental-health rating in terms of a mental-health sickness rating scale formulated by the Menninger Clinic. The general conclusion was that the 'long term effects of childhood institutional care are much less drastic than had been feared.'

In explanation of the findings the researchers point out that 'the factor most clearly related to the effects of institutional care as seen in the subjects of this report is the corrective experience of family living – it appears that the human organism has the happy capacity of reversing the effects of childhood emotional trauma of the type connoted by institutionalization' (Heston and others 1966, p. 1109).

If the studies reviewed by Bowlby (1951) in his widely disseminated and influential report point to the dramatic negative effects of early trauma, it might be significant to call attention, in this context, to the fact that, as Yarrow reminds us (1962, p. 20), a sizable proportion of the children in each of the studies listed did not show the predicted negative reactions to separation and deprivation.

While the studies cited above vary in precision of methodological approach one might note, as did Bowlby, that 'What each individual piece of work lacks in thoroughness, scientific reliability or precision is largely made good by the concordance of the whole' (1951, p. 15).

The idea of irreversibility of trauma is related to the continuity hypothesis. This presupposes that the disturbed child will become the disturbed adolescent, who then becomes the disturbed adult. Studies by Robins (1966), Morris and others (1954, pp. 743–54, 1956, pp. 991–7), and Livson and Peskin (1967, pp. 509–18) tend to suggest that the hypothesis needs further refinement and specification. Children manifesting neurotic symptoms very frequently become well-adjusted adults. Childhood anti-social behavior, while outgrown in some cases, is more likely to lead to maladjustment in adulthood. As Kohlberg and others (1970) note, however, there is no linear relationship between childhood diagnosis and adult prognosis.

FACTORS RELATING TO REVERSIBILITY

Does the above then imply a contradiction of the most important tenets of child rearing: that continuous contact with one set of loving, accepting, understanding parents providing the proper emotional as well as physical support is the best basis for healthy biopsychosocial development? We are not suggesting that neglect, abuse, and physical deprivation are not harmful. Each of the studies cited above shows that a more detailed contrast within the follow-up group invariably favors subsets of children with a more benign environment prior to separation. For instance, while most of the children in the Maas study and most of those in the study by Roe turned out reasonably well adjusted, those who came from less pathological backgrounds did better than those who had been subjected to more trauma (Maas 1963, pp. 67, 72, 381–2). In the present study, outcome is related to natural mother's acceptance. Nor do the results contradict the objection that while these children may have achieved normal levels of functioning they may not, because of early deprivation, have realized their full psychosocial potential. There is no way of knowing what levels of functioning these children might have achieved if they had had a continuous positive experience from birth.

The data do not argue for a rejection of the generally accepted tenets but rather refinement of such principles and a qualification of them. They argue, it seems to me, for a recognition that children have varying capacities to deal with potentially traumatic conditions and that these strengths enable them, when provided with a healthier environment, to surmount the damaging influences of earlier developmental insults.

Social and emotional childhood deprivations may be the necessary preconditions for later maladjustment; for some they are not sufficient conditions. Certain children possess greater capacity for recovery from hurt. Others may be less vulnerable, so that situations which are damaging to most children affect them less adversely. What is generally regarded as traumatic may be merely annoying, irritating and inconvenient to them. The core of self remains relatively undamaged.

In the balance between what the child brings and what the environment has to offer, we have developed the conviction that what the environment offers, or fails to offer, is by far the major determinant of developmental outcome, and that early environment is of crucial importance. Yet the outcome for the very deprived children in this study and the outcome for similar groups of children who were the subject population of studies cited above suggest giving greater consideration to what the child brings to the environment and greater weight to the influence for change of a later, healthier environment.

Empirical evidence supports such an explanation of the unexpected outcome of this and similar studies. Studies of differences between children immediately after birth, before one can say differences are due to the effects of variations in their surroundings, indicate that children differ in many ways which have significance for the resultant of interaction between themselves and their environment. Thus, Thomas and others studied a hundred and thirty children from the first months of life onward. From the moment of birth, children differed in terms of activity, adaptability, distractability, persistence, mood, intensity of reaction to sensory stimuli, threshold of responsiveness, and so on. He notes:

... all infants will not respond in the same fashion to a given environmental influence. Rather, given constancy of environmental factors the reaction will vary with the characteristic of the child upon whom the relatively constant stimulus is brought to bear ... This holds true for all aspects of the child's functioning ... including reactions to situations of special stress, such as illness, radical change in living conditions or abrupt shifts in geographic environment ... This view of the child stands in contrast to the assumption that environmental influences, as such, have determinative effects ... Underlying the environmental approach is the assumption that all children will tend to react similarly to the same developmental influences ... Our findings suggest that exclusive emphasis on the role of environment in child development tells only part of the story and that responses to any regimen will vary in accordance with primary patterns of reactivity. (1963, pp. 84–5)

Similarly Dr Wagner Bridger, director of a longitudinal team study of three hundred children from birth at the Albert Einstein Medical College, concludes – as a result of the research thus far – that 'the role of environmental variables in growth and development has to be evaluated in the context of the biological endowment of the individual' (Levin 1965, p. 134). These conclusions are supported by additional research which points to the same fact: that children are different at birth in ways which are crucial for personality development (Escalona 1968; Fries and Woolf 1953; Witkin and others 1962).

If biological determination of individuality, as contrasted with environmental or experiential determination of individuality, is given greater consideration, the resiliency of the children in this study group may be more explicable. One child's trauma, which makes future positive adjustment very improbable, may be another child's inconvenience, the effects of which, given reasonable opportunity, can be reversed.

Such research concerned with biological differences in vulnerability to trauma, capacity to adapt to trauma, and levels of resiliency and 'recoverability' in the face of trauma is perhaps one general approach to explaining the contradiction between anticipated outcome, given the pathology in the background of these children, and the outcome in response to placement in an adoptive home which met the child's essential needs.

However, there may be another, more sociological explanation. These children made two important shifts in moving from their own home to the adoptive home. They made the change, referred to above, from a home which offered little in the way of meeting their needs in terms of affection, acceptance, support, understanding and /or encouragement to the adoptive home, which offered some measure of these essential psychic supplies.

They also made a change from a lower-class, multiproblem family in a slum to a middle-class reputable home in an area of the community which had some status. A child's self-concept is developed as a result of his experience in the intense relationship with significant others within the intimacy of the family group, particularly in relation to the most significant of all others, the parents. A child who perceives himself as acceptable to the parents perceives himself as acceptable to himself.

But however important this factor is in building the child's self-concept, it ignores the impact of the wider world which soon begins to transmit messages to the child which affect his conception of self. The Negro child has to have a much stronger positive self-image, initially, to withstand the corrosion on this image of the thousands of overt and covert cues which come from the predominantly white environment, all of which say black is bad, white is better.

The white child with an initially shaky self-concept, supported, reinforced, and strengthened by an environment which affirms his acceptability, is likely to end up with a more positive conception of self than is a Negro child born into a loving, accepting family which gives him, initially, a strong self-concept subsequently denied by a society which manifests its open rejection of him.

This problem operates along class lines as well as along color lines. The same kind of messages are received by subsets within the white community. The standard bearers of the white community behave toward the lower-class, multiproblem, disreputable white family so as to transmit the message that they are unacceptable. The child in such a family, carrying its name and associating with its members, inevitably begins to be affected by this pervasive, negative labeling.

We then remove the child from this family and place him in an apparently decent, middle-class home in an attractive neighborhood, and identify him with a well-organized family of father and mother who act in a responsible, respectable manner. He now receives messages which proclaim his acceptability, and support, reinforce, and strengthen whatever components, however limited, of self-acceptance he has been able to develop as a result of whatever small amount of affection he received in his former home. The effect of positive parent-child relationships within the home are now buttressed by social relationships outside the home rather than vitiated by the contradiction between the acceptance of the lower-class child in the lower-class home and his rejection by the community.

Burks and Roe, in attempting to explain the better-than-anticipated outcome in foster care of children removed at an average age of five from homes in which the parents were alcoholic and/or psychotic, point to this as a factor which needs consideration.

Had these children remained with their own families, they too, would have been, in a sense, outcasts. The children of respectable families would, in all likelihood, not have been permitted to play with them. They would not have been invited to their parties; and nasty remarks about their fathers and mothers would have been shouted after them on the street. They could react only by identifying with their families and rejecting the community and all its customs, or by rejecting their families and striving ceaselessly somehow to achieve membership in the group which had despised them.

The children were removed from such homes and placed in acceptable ones, and the authors note that:

It seems very probable that residence in a home which is a respected part of the community, and the child's acceptance as a member of that community, make possible the formation of an organized ideal derived from the attitudes and forms of behavior of the community which can function as an integrating force . . . (Roe and Burks 1945, p. 16)

Srole, in his report of a large-scale effort to assess the level of 'mental health' of people in midtown Manhattan, reports that the mental impairment was related to socioeconomic level. More of the 'poor' were apt to be 'mentally impaired'. In attempting to explain this, the report points to the factor of community rejection of the lower-class child which intensifies tendencies toward maladjustment. 'In many areas of his experience the lower-class child encounters the contempt, implicit but palpable, in the non-verbal behavior of others who think of him in the symbolism of such words as rubbish, scum, dregs, riffraff and trash. These devastating judgments inevitably force their way into his own self-evaluating processes' (Srole and others 1962, p. 198).

In moving the child from a lower-class home and social environment to a middle-class adoptive home and social environment the agency has 'rescued' him from a situation which intensifies the problem of adjustment to one which assists the making of a positive adjustment. A recognition of these factors – the factor of biological potential providing a resiliency which permits the child, despite past deprivation, to make a healthy response when provided with a healthy environment, and the implication of a changed social context which reinforces, rather than opposes, change in the child toward a more positive adjustment – has implications for adoptive practice in addition to providing some reasons for unanticipated results.

Social workers, together with mental hygienists, have tended to overemphasize the importance, significance and power of the past. Although we say that the past is structured in the present and is *one* of the determinants of present behavior, we tend to see the past as more powerful than the present and the most significant determinant of present behavior. History, despite the historian's interest in the past, favors a situational psychology. Hitler transformed a nation in a decade so that there were few to support a democratic ethos; southerners who only yesterday swore not to ride in desegregated buses and eat in desegregated restaurants are doing that today. The situation, the living context in which one lives and with which one is forced to come to terms, demands a mobilization of those latent aspects of ego which are congruent with situational demands; contrariwise, it forces a defense against those aspects of ego which make adjustment to the situation difficult, hazardous, and precarious.

We may need a reorientation in emphasis with a greater respect being accorded the present and the more recent, proximate experiences. The past does, of course, intrude to shape perception, and in the case of the psychotic and seriously neurotic it may even be decisive. But for those less ill, which includes the children in the present study as well as most children available for adoption, the present is a countervailing force which exerts a constant pressure, demanding that we live in response to it.

The whole rationale of therapy presupposes that experience in the present can free us from the past. The provision of a different environment, social class, neighborhood and family is perhaps the most therapeutic of all therapies for a child. The new living situation offers the opportunity for making manifest the potential for changed feeling and behavior.

This point of view is supported by the results of other recent follow-up adoption studies. Analysis of the data of one study, obtained through tape-recorded interviews with two hundred adoptive families, showed that only one of the many background factors regarding the adoptive child and his early developmental experience was related to the level of success of the adoption (Lawder and others 1966, p. 163). Detailed agency records made available developmental information such as age at adoption, preadoptive placement history, psychological evaluation and rating of emotional deprivation. These background factors showed remarkably little relationship to later functioning. Whatever experiences the child may have encountered earlier seem to be compensated for by the experience of living in a good adoptive home. The study notes that 'it appears very much as though background variables take on less and less impact as prognostic factors through the passage of time . . . With time, in a relatively normal family setting, the children are free to gain, and realize, their basic potential' (Josslyn 1948, pp. 149–50).

A recent follow-up study of a hundred and sixty Negro and white children showed no significant relationship between background factors, such as child's age at adoptive placement, number of preadoptive placements, early behavior of the child and adjustment at follow-up (Ripple 1968, p. 485). The researchers conclude that 'in general, factors pertaining to the child and particularly those used to assess potential risks to development, did not prove discriminating' (p. 496).

For the children whose lives were carefully reviewed in both these studies, the pre-adoptive past seems to have been of less importance and significance for determining adjustment than the experiences in the adoptive present. Adoption is not psychotherapy. But its psychotherapeutic potential is like that of a good marriage, a true friendship, a new satisfying job, or an enjoyable vacation. It can help to repair old hurts.

The child could not make of himself what he was not. However, personality is multifaceted, and we are capable of a much greater repertoire of behavior than we are generally called upon to manifest. The altered situation, requiring a 'change' in personality for the child, means an emphasis on the kinds of feelings and behavior which helped him fit in to the adoptive home and a de-emphasis of those kinds of feeling and behavior unacceptable in the present environment.

What is involved here are different approaches to an explanation of what is psychotherapeutic. The rationale basic to the traditional social-work approach to therapy (specific remedial measures) suggests that the behavior itself is not of primary importance since it is merely a manifestation of some underlying intrapsychic conflict. Since behavior is merely symptomatic of underlying disturbances the inner causes, rather than the behavior itself, should be the focus of attention. The behavior itself is purposive and beyond rational control, simple re-education, exhortation or persuasion since the individual is motivated to act in this way in response to a conflict which he cannot resolve because its nature is not fully available to conscious awareness. Changes in behavior may be achieved, but unless the basic conflict is resolved, other, equally disabling, symptoms may be substituted for the symptom which is no longer manifested.

It would be futile to seek to change behavior and/or relieve symptoms without attempting to trace and resolve the conflict, the 'real' problem, from which the symptoms originate. It follows then that effective therapy is directed not toward changing behavior but toward achieving understanding, toward an 'expansion of consciousness' so that it includes the hidden sense of conflict. 'If the client can be helped to understand why he behaves as he does or to recognize and understand the origin of his neurotic tactics that continually defeat him, he will gradually abandon the inappropriate behavior and substitute therefor more rational tactics in the management of his life' (Hobbs 1964, p. 474). The promotion of self-understanding and insight is the most effective approach toward helping people with their problems, and all strategies – reassurance, universalization, desensitization, catharsis, clarification, and interpretation – are valued because they free emotional energy or change the balance of intrapsychic force so as to maximize the possibility for self-understanding. Even environmental manipulation, reducing, modifying, and mitigating external stress infringing on the client, is regarded as a desirable tactic primarily because this, too, frees ego energy (previously devoted to struggling with the environment) for dealing more effectively with the basic intrapsychic conflict. These postulates are fundamental to one view of what is psychotherapeutic deriving primarily from psychoanalytic psychology.

Another view of therapy follows from the learning and conditioning psychologies. Here, the primary concern is with the behavior itself without concern for underlying 'causes'. The behavior is viewed as the result of some unfortunate learning and conditioning experiences which have taught undesirable, unadaptive approaches to interpersonal relationships. 'The concept of symptoms', as a response to an underlying conflict, in this view is unnecessary and superfluous (Thomas and Goodman 1965, p. 8).

Here therapy focuses primarily on the behavior itself; it is concerned with providing an opportunity for 'unlearning' the unadaptive behavior and learning new, more adaptive modes of behavior. The therapy seeks to identify 'unsuitable stimulus-response connections', to dissolve them and to teach more desirable 'stimulus-response connections'. It seeks to identify the specific environmental conditions through which the undesirable behavior is controlled and sustained and to change these. The stress is on immediate experience and specific behavior.

Our view of what is therapeutic about adoptions is closer to the second rationale for therapy outlined, the learning–conditioning rationale, than it is to the first – the psychoanalytic psychology rationale.

The child's previous living experiences may have 'taught' a view of parents and parental surrogates which resulted in neurotic, unadaptive behavior. Defenses were developed and behavior manifested which was in response to the nature of the situation to which the child was subjected. Moving into the adoptive home meant moving into an environment which was set up to condition the child to a change in behavior. Previously learned, now inappropriate, behaviors went unrewarded or were actively discouraged; new, more appropriate, more adaptive behaviors were rewarded and actively encouraged. Without any explicit effort to resolve whatever underlying intrapsychic conflict may or may not have been present, without any explicit effort to have the child develop insight or self-understanding into his distorted perception of himself in the parent–child relationship and/or his distorted expectations with reference to the parents' behavior toward him, the living experience provides the corrective in day-to-day learning. The living experience teaches new ways of relating to people and new ways of perceiving oneself. In this sense, life is therapeutic. It acts as a large scale conditioning matrix which stimulates and supports changes in the child's feeling and behavior. As Franz Alexander says: 'No insight, no emotional discharge, no recollection, can be as reassuring as accomplishment in an actual life situation in which the individual has failed' (Alexander and French 1946, p. 40).

Psychotherapy is, in effect, a condensed, systematic attempt to imitate curative, real-life situations and assure the availability of such a curative configuration to the patient. Environmental therapy – therapy which actually affords the child the opportunity to live in a healthier family situation and experience the possibility of successful interaction with parents – is, as Josslyn notes, 'the least artificial form of therapy' (1948, p. 120).

The curative resource, the adoptive home, is made available as the result of the institutionalization of an area of concern such as the field of child welfare in the profession of social work. The resource itself is the regenerative force, and while the effectiveness of the resource in application in each individual instance may be increased or diminished somewhat by the work of the individual practitioner, it is the availability of the resource itself which is of prime importance.

By far the most important thing the social agency does for the child is to provide him with an adoptive home. All else is commentary. All the casework preparation, all the casework efforts in easing transition, all the casework in follow-up during the postplacement year is frosting on the cake of the potential for change provided by a different environment. The agency achieves its supreme importance in making available a responsible, formally organized channel for bringing together the adoptive home and the child needing such a home. In the case of the group of children studied here, providing this change in environment for the child was social work's greatest contribution. The agency arranged the living situation of these children so that they were offered a therapeutic environment – a healthy restitutive living experience. The social agency, the institutionalized apparatus sanctioned and supported by the community, made it possible for the community to identify the children needing help, to act to remove the children from a clearly damaging situation, and then to find adequate substitute homes for these children. It made available a formally organized channel through which people interested in adoptive children could apply and be received with understanding. If it had not been for the social workers engaged in this work, some percentage of the children might never have found a home, and some percentage of the parents would never have found these children. This is the true and ultimate contribution of the social agency; that it was instrumental in making available to the child a second chance at growing up, this time in a reasonably healthy environment.

If the therapeutic potential of such a situation is so rich, if the therapeutically beneficient present reacting with the child's capacity for a healthy response offers fertile possibility for positive change, then the agency should take greater risks in moving more expeditiously to place children. Discharging the community .nandate with a sense of professional responsibility would still require that the agency make a careful selection of children for placement and of parents to receive them; it would still require that the agency prepare both parents and children carefully to mitigate the inevitable problems which arise in the difficult transition as strangers meet to become a new family. But it might temper caution with the recognition that children are perhaps capable of more positives than they have ever been able to actualize, and that these may never become manifest unless the child is given the opportunity of living in an adoptive home. It might temper caution by the recognition that the only way the child can be made ready for adoption is to be given the opportunity of living as an adopted child. No amount of preparation for marriage can achieve what is achieved by the experience of being married. Similarly, the child in living adopted becomes adopted. A sense of responsibility might be tempered by an optimistic orientation toward the positive potentials of the adoptive situation, as such, for evoking what both parents and children can offer, if given the chance, to make the adoption a success.

We have come to realize that expectations are a powerful force in determining outcome. The self-fulfilling prophecy, the placebo effect, and the Rosenthal effect (1966) all point to this same phenomenon. Every adoptive placement is an experiment. If the social worker communicates an expectation of success this, in itself, is a factor which increases the likelihood of success of the placement. The study suggests that we can justifiably communicate expectation of success.

In a symposium on the adoption of oriental children in American homes, one of the participants said:

I think we need a gambling attitude or a probability attitude towards our work. We need to think in terms of probability chances. We might try thinking of probability chances, with a big role given to the unknown factors. But I think part of the fault lies in our own evaluation standards. We're always looking for 100 per cent success. I would prefer to set up as a criterion of success in an agency the fact that there is a percentage of failures of a given size. We want a certain per cent of failures (if we have a selection of cases) before the agency is considered to be doing its job. It means that the agency has accepted risky cases and extended itself for maximum service in the selection, and not eliminated those cases which are unsure. A small loan company area manager said that he rates his area office not on the fact that they may have zero or a very small percentage of failure of repayment of loans. He claimed that there had to be certain percentage of failures to repay, because otherwise the district manager was playing too conservative a game, and was not developing the proper range of business. He was turning down fair risks as well as poor risks! The same point of view might probably hold for the evaluation of a social agency. (Child Welfare League of America 1960, pp. 56–7)

Perhaps this is the most important result of the study. Agencies can take the risk in placing of older children with a high probability of success. Some failures are inevitable. But unless it takes the risks, a sizable number of children, however pessimistic a prognostication one might make from background data, will be denied the opportunity for a therapeutic experience to which they can respond. The agency – and the parents – accepting the risk will have rescued these children for life.

But the results have implications beyond the adoptive agency and the adoptive family. The adoptive child is first a child and secondly an adoptive child; the adoptive family is first a family and secondly an adoptive family. All children in all families face the possibility of injury, illness, and death of parents. Many children must adjust to family conflict which often leads to divorce, separation, or desertion. Life gives no guarantees to any child, anywhere, that life will be without trauma, without limited or prolonged periods of separation from parents, without hurts. The results speak, then, to all children, in all families, who at all times face the possibility of some measure of deprivation. And the results suggest that a child's resiliency and capacity for adaptation very often enable him to struggle effectively and successfully with the tragic circumstances of life. Despite the inevitability of tragic circumstances, many children have emerged from such struggles reasonably healthy, reasonably happy, reasonably well-adjusted people.

Section IV

Changing the Course of Human Development II

CHAPTER TWELVE

Some Contrived Experiments

Ann M. Clarke and A.D.B. Clarke

INTRODUCTION

The recognition that the course of human development might to varying extents be modified for good or ill was, as noted in the previous section, recognised in the 1930s and 1940s. It arose first from the tracking of the correlates of 'natural' events such as institutionalisation, being reared on canal boats, adoption or rescue from isolation. Once established it virtually demanded that planned prospective studies should take place in which the whole environment, or at least significant parts of it, might be altered in such a way as to produce desirable changes to order. Perhaps this sounds like naive, Watsonian environmentalism and, indeed, it may have been so in the earlier work of the Iowa school. Later, however, it is clear that evidence for the importance of constitutional and genetic factors was not overlooked by these investigators.

The obvious advantage of the prospective experimental study is the possibility of identifying selective factors at source, of following representative samples over sometimes lengthy periods, and of systematically testing hypotheses by means of environmental changes. Once again, however, it is important to point out that the belief in the crucial long-term role of early experience provides the context and inspiration for such work. Very few attempts to alter experimentally the course of development have been initiated except in the first few years of life.

To understand the ways in which potentialities for change have been regarded, our review must begin in the 1930s with some of the most important work of the Iowa Group, work which for its methodological weakness called forth a vitriolic attack by McNemar (1940). As noted earlier in this book, however, later independent findings largely support the conclusions of these workers, although nowadays more detached observers would wish to give an equally great emphasis to individual differences in response to change, which no doubt largely reflect constitutional factors.

One of the most carefully documented studies of environmental change and its effect upon retarded children has been provided by Skeels and Dye (1939), Skeels (1966) and Skodak (1968). The initial observation was accidental. Two children under eighteen months old, in residence at a state orphanage, gave unmistakable evidence of marked mental retardation. Kuhlmann-Binet Intelligence Tests were given to both, the results on one (at thirteen months) being I.Q. 46, and on the second (aged sixteen months) I.Q. 35. Qualitative and behavioural assessments supported these results. There was no indication of organic defects.

These two children were recommended for transfer to a state school for the mentally deficient but prognosis was at the time regarded as poor. After transfer they were placed in a ward of older girls whose ages ranged from eighteen to fifty years and in mental age from five to nine years. Six months later the psychologist visiting the wards of this institution was surprised to notice the apparently remarkable development of these children. They were accordingly re-examined on the same test as before, this time gaining I.Q.s of 77 and 87 respectively. A year later their I.Q.s had risen to 100 and 88. At the age of about three and a half the two children's scores were 95 and 93.

The hypothesis to explain these results was that the ward attendants had taken a particular fancy to these two babies who were the only pre-school children in their care. They were given outings and special play materials. Similarly, the older and brighter inmates of the ward particularly attached to the children and would play with them during most of their waking hours; for these two it was clearly a stimulating environment. It was considered that a further change would be desirable if the intellectual alteration was to be maintained, and accordingly they were placed in rather average adoptive homes at the age of three and a half. After about fifteen months in these homes re-examination, this time with the Stanford-Binet, resulted in I.Q.s of 94 and 93 respectively. These unexpected findings raised a number of important questions. Observation suggested that similar children left in an orphanage nursery made no such gains in the rate of mental growth. Adult contacts were

at a minimum and limited largely to physical care. Adoptive placement was clearly inappropriate, owing to the lack of certainty
that progress would occur. The most reasonable solution would
seem to lie in a repetition of the 'accidental experiment' but this
time in a planned and controlled manner. Thus research was started
involving an experimental group of thirteen children whose ages
ranged from seven to thirty months, and Kuhlmann-Binet I.Q.s
of 35 to 89. Mean age at the time of transfer to the state school
was nineteen months and mean I.Q. was 64. Once again clinical
observation supported the I.Q. classification; for example, a seven-
month-old child in the group could scarcely hold his head up
without support, while another at thirty months could not stand
alone and required support while sitting in a chair. After the close
of the experimental period it was decided to study a contrast group
of children remaining in the orphanage. This group consisted of
twelve children, whose ages ranged from eleven to twenty-one
months, and I.Q.s from 50 to 103. Mean age at the time of the
first test was sixteen months, with a mean I.Q. of 86. No marked
differences in the birth histories of the two groups were observed,
nor in their medical histories. Family histories indicated that the
majority came from homes of low socioeconomic levels with parents
of low intellect, and there were no important differences between
them.

The members of the experimental group in general repeated
the experiences of the first two children and also attended the
school kindergarten just as soon as they could walk. In the case
of almost every child, some adult, either older girl or attendant,
would become particularly attached to him or her and would
figuratively 'adopt' him. This probably constituted an important
aspect of the change. Members of the contrast group, however,
had environments rather typical of the average orphanage. The
outstanding feature was the profound lack of mental stimulation
or experiences usually associated with the life of the young child
in an ordinary home. Up to the age of two years, the children
were in the nursery of the hospital. They had good physical care
but little beyond this; few play materials were available and they
were seldom out of the nursery room except for short walks or
periods of exercise. At the age of two they graduated to cottages
where overcrowding was characteristic. Thirty to thirty-six children
of the same sex under six years of age were under the care of

one matron and three or four untrained and reluctant teenage girls. The matron's duties were so arduous that a necessary regimentation of the children resulted. No child had any personal property. The contrast between these two environments is obvious.

During the course of the experiment the average increase in I.Q. of the experimental group was 27·5 points, the final I.Q.s at the conclusion having a mean of 91·8. Gains ranged from 7 to 58 points; three made increments of 45 points or more, and all but two increased by more than 15 points. The length of the experimental period depended in an individual case upon the child's progress, varying from 5·7 months to 52·1, with a mean of 18·9 months.

The development of the children in the contrast group was almost precisely the opposite from those in the experimental group. The average I.Q. at the beginning was 86·7 and at the end was 60·5, an average loss of 26·2 points. Apart from one child who gained 2 points, all showed losses varying from 8 to 45 points. Ten of the twelve children lost 15 or more points. The average length of the experimental period was 30·7 months.

In commenting upon these data, one notes (1) the initial superiority of the contrast group; (2) the reversal of the status of the two groups; and (3) the differing lengths of the evaluation periods for the groups.

As soon as the experimental group showed intellectual functioning approaching the normal range, with two exceptions they were placed in adoptive homes. The adoptive parents were, with one exception, lower-middle class. The selection of relatively modest levels of adoptive homes was made because of the poor social background of the children and the fact that, at one time, they had all been mentally retarded. It was therefore felt advisable to select homes where aspirations for achievement might not be too high.

Contrast children, on the other hand, either remained in unstimulating and in some cases actively adverse orphanages or state schools for the mentally retarded (with one exception: see below).

The transfer to adoptive homes of the eleven children from the experimental group took place round an average age of three and a half years, well beyond the critical period for achieving normality suggested by Dennis (1973). The major I.Q. changes had taken place within the mental-retardation institution and were followed by average increments of only 4 points (mean I.Q. 96) over the two and a half years of first follow-up. Contrast children averaged a 5-point increment over three years follow-up, with a terminal mean I.Q. of 66. However, as is well known, infant intelligence tests have little predictive value, and these results are useful only in indicating that there is no clear reason to believe that the Contrast Group was constitutionally inferior to the members of the Experimental Group.

Later, Skeels, with the assistance of Marie Skodak, carried out an impressive second follow-up of both groups after being completely out of touch with their members for over twenty years (Skeels 1966; Skodak 1968). The aims of the follow-up were simple. What happened to the children as adults, how have the early childhood differences been reflected in adult achievement and adjustment, and have the divergent paths been maintained? A major problem was of course to locate the subjects, and the Skeels monograph describes in vivid detail the problems and frustrations in so doing.

Very marked differences between the two groups were found in educational and occupational status and general life style. The experimental group had completed an average of 11·68 grades of school (median 12); their spouses had virtually identical educational attainments. The contrast group, on the other hand, had completed an average of 3·95 grades of school (median 2·75).

In considering occupational levels it should be noted that the experimental group contained only three males, while the contrast group contained eight.

There were marked differences in the occupational levels of the two groups. The three males in the experimental group were: a vocational counsellor, a sales manager for an estate agent and a staff sergeant in the Air Force. Eight of the ten girls were married and of those who were employed, one taught elementary school grades, another was a registered nurse, another a licensed practical nurse, another had passed State Board examinations and practised as a beautician. Another girl was a clerk, another after graduating from high school passed the examinations and was accepted as a stewardess in an airline. Two were domestics in private homes.

In the contrast group four were still residents in institutions and unable to engage in employment. Seven were employed, one washing dishes in a nursing home, two were dishwashers in small restaurants, another worked in a cafeteria. One of the men had been in and out of institutions for years, and when out lived with his grandmother, doing odd jobs. Another man was a 'floater' travelling from coast to coast, engaging in casual and unskilled labour. Yet another was an employee in the state institution where he was originally a patient. Finally, the deviant of this group, to be referred to later, was a typesetter for a newspaper in a large city. It will be apparent that, of those who were employed, with the exception above (Case 19), all were in unskilled manual occupations. It might also be added that, unlike the experimental group which had shown considerable geographical mobility, and whose members were very difficult to trace, there were only minor problems in locating by means of institutional records the members of the contrast group.

Space precludes a detailed consideration of all the evidence presented in the 1966 monograph. Although inevitably in a study of this kind there are some gaps in information available, sufficient data are presented on the status of the children as infants, the socioeconomic and educational backgrounds of at least one parent, the status of the adoptive parents and the final outcome for the twenty-five children as adults, for certain conclusions to be drawn with considerable confidence.

Although the majority of the experimental group were adopted, two were not, for reasons which are not stated. The majority of the contrast group remained in poor institutions during their childhood, but there was one exception. What is clear is that the eventual outcome for all these children was closely related to the long-term environmental circumstances surrounding the major part of their later development. It is our belief, based on this and other evidence, that the relatively brief pre-school stimulation programme, which was initially a major focus of interest for Skeels and his colleague Skodak, is probably of little long-term relevance, except as initiating a differentiation between experimental and contrast groups, and thus providing the belief that the experimental children would not grow up to be mentally retarded.

This thesis will be illustrated with reference to the bare outlines of some specific case histories.

Case 10 (experimental group) at 23 months, before transfer to the 'stimulating conditions', had an I.Q. of 72. On retest at 45 months, his I.Q. was 79. His natural mother was educated to eighth grade and had six months of high school education. His natural father was a theatre manager in a small town, and was presumably at least of reasonable intelligence. His adoptive father, educated to ninth grade, was a milkman and his adoptive mother had been educated to eighth grade. The subject himself graduated from high school, and attended college for two and a half years. At the time of follow-up he was sales manager in a real-estate firm.

Case 11 (experimental group) at 26 months, before transfer, had an I.Q. of 75. On retest at 51 months, after the special programme, he had an I.Q. of 82. His natural mother had an I.Q. of 66 and was diagnosed as a psychotic mental defective. Nothing is known of his natural father. His adoptive father was a college graduate, the only one of the adoptive sample who occupied a professional post. The adoptive mother was a high-school graduate, drawn from a somewhat affluent family. The subject himself was a university graduate, with a B.A. degree and some postgraduate work at the time of follow-up. His occupation was that of vocational counsellor in a state-welfare programme.

By contrast Case 2 (experimental group) had an I.Q. of 57 at 13 months. On retest, after the programme, at 37 months her I.Q. had risen to 77. Her natural mother had completed eighth grade at school and was said to be 'slow mentally'. The natural father, a farm labourer, was said to be mentally slow; he, too, had completed eighth grade. The subject was never adopted and completed only five grades at school. On follow-up, about 1942, she was in residence at the institution for the mentally retarded and 'in all probability will continue to show marked mental retardation to a degree necessitating continued institutionalisation'. At final follow-up, she was a housewife married to a labourer and had been in domestic service.

Case 24 (contrast group) had an I.Q. of 50 at 22 months. On retest, at 52 months his I.Q. was 42. His natural mother went as far as eighth grade at school and then took a short evening-class course in business studies. She worked as a telephone operator and did general office work. His natural father graduated from high school but was unemployed at the time of his birth. The subject was brought up in the institution for the mentally retarded where he did rather well. At the age of twenty his Wechsler I.Q. scores were: Verbal 76; Performance 106; Full Scale 84. An attempt was made to place him in open employment but this proved to be unsatisfactory and he asked for return to the institution where, at the time of follow-up, he was assistant to the Head Gardener. He was reported to be an exceedingly good gardener but institutionalised.

Case 19 (contrast group) had an I.Q. of 87 at 15 months. On retest at 45 months this had decreased to 67. His natural mother graduated from high school and had an I.Q. of 84; his father was a farmer. Although he was never adopted, he was the only member of the contrast group not brought up in the institution for the mentally retarded. By chance he was included in an intensive stimulation programme as part of a doctoral research which emphasised language training and cognitive development. When he entered regular school he was discovered to have a moderate hearing loss following bilateral mastoidectomy in infancy. At about the time of retest, at the relatively late age of six, he was accordingly transferred to a residential school for the deaf where the matron of his cottage took a special fancy to him as one of the youngest children, and one who had no family. He was a frequent guest in her home and in that of her daughter and son-in-law. He graduated from high school, had one semester of college and at the time of follow-up was employed as a compositor and typesetter. His marriage was stable, he had four intelligent children, owned his house in a comfortable middle-class district, and was earning as much as the rest of the contrast group put together.

In summary, the diverging early histories of both groups have been maintained in adult life. Skeels writes (1966):

It seems obvious that under present day conditions there are still countless numbers of infants born with sound biological constitutions and with potentialities for development well within the normal range, who will become mentally retarded and a burden to society unless appropriate intervention occurs . . . we have sufficient knowledge to design programs of intervention which can counteract the devastating effects of poverty, sociocultural deprivation and maternal deprivation.

Apart from its important implications for the influence of environment on adult status and adjustment, this study contains evidence on the relative influence of the early years and later periods of development. The experimental group started life in a bad orphanage: they were then transferred to an institution for the mentally retarded, and finally (rather late) placed with adopting families. All these changes took place during a period regarded as critical in terms of developing a close, permanent relationship with a mother or permanent mother substitute. In fact these children were in Bowlby's words 'passed like parcels from one mother to another'. Moreover, Case 19 (contrast group) was left in the orphanage for several years before his hearing loss was discovered and he was transferred to a residential school where he was in a sense 'adopted' by someone who presumably gave him sufficient affection and attention to ensure a normal development.

The work of Kirk (1958) was important for two reasons. First, it was clearly inspired by the findings of Skeels, and was the first perfectly controlled group study of children exposed to significant environmental change in the form of pre-school programmes. Second, its results predicted in some detail the outcome of Project Head Start. One of the eminent sponsors of the latter once remarked that it would of course have been appropriate to run pilot Head Start schemes, but time was short and the political pressures great. Kirk's results, published some six years before Head Start was planned, nullify part of this explanation, for his study constituted *the* pilot experiment which was needed. Had the Head Start planners paid heed to it, a great opportunity might not have been so conspicuously wasted. It will therefore be appropriate to offer an account of this research which was designed to provide factual data for or against the general contention that special educational provision early in life could alter the children's rate of development.

Eighty-one retarded children, aged between three and six, were identified and studied for between three and five years. Twenty-eight formed the Community Experimental Group, attending a pre-school in the community and being followed up for between one and four years after leaving. Fifteen children were members of the Institution Experimental Group, attending an institution pre-school, and being followed up in the same way as in the first group. Twenty-six children constituted the Community Contrast Group and a further twelve, in a different institution from the second experimental group, constituted the Institution Contrast Group.

The I.Q.s of the subjects ranged from 45 to 80. They were examined at the beginning of the experiment, during the pre-school period and again on follow-up after leaving the pre-school. The results were analysed both by case studies of the children in the experimental groups, and by the more conventional type of statistical comparisons. For the former, each child was placed in one of seven developmental levels, ranging from 'uneducable' to 'average'. It was found that thirty of the forty-three children who had received pre-school stimulation showed an acceleration in growth rates during the experimental period and retained that level subsequently. They had raised their developmental classification from between one and three levels.

Analysis of test scores showed differential increase on the Binet, Kuhlmann and Vineland scales, all significant beyond the 0·05 level. On the Binet, for example, the range of I.Q. changes from the beginning to the end of the study for the Institution Experimental Group varied between a loss of 17 points and a gain of 33. The average increment was 10 points. For the Institution Contrast Group, however, there was an average decrement of $6\frac{1}{2}$ points, with a range of from -19 to $+10$. The Community Experimental Group showed a total average Binet increment of nearly 12 points, while the Community Contrast Group showed a 7-point increment. The difference between the two Contrast Groups is interesting, and obviously has a bearing upon interpretation of the effects of some kinds of institutional upbringing. In brief, it was clear that pre-school education whether in the community or the institution had positive and (within the time limits of the study) lasting effects on intellectual and social development. Nevertheless, as Kirk indicates, group comparisons may well mask intra-group differences. It became apparent that it was much more difficult to displace the growth rates of those children with definite organic aetiologies. This finding is in accord with the Clarkes' work on I.Q. changes (see pages 71–4). The results also suggested two further conclusions: first, that 'within limits the greater the changes that are made in the environment, the greater are the changes in the rate of growth'; and second, that holding the home factor constant by studying siblings from the same family one of whom did, and the other who did not, attend pre-school, it was clear that the pre-school had provided compensation for inadequate home environment, during the programme.

An unexpected finding by Kirk was that the Community Contrast Group after a year in school showed an upward trend in I.Q.s and S.Q.s, thus narrowing the gap between its members and those who had had the advantage of pre-school stimulation. Kirk notes that 'this could mean that pre-schools for mentally handicapped children are not necessary, since the children will accelerate their rate of development after entering school at the usual age of six.' A further study of the Community Contrast Group, however, suggested that children from adequate homes tended to accelerate their growth rates during later school experience, while those from inadequate homes did not. This difference was, however, not significant statistically, no doubt partly because of the small number (eight out of twenty-six) in this group who came from inadequate homes.

The general inference from this study was that differences between those who had received an adequate and quite lengthy pre-school programme, and matched children who had not, tended to reduce or 'wash out' during the primary school, either because of the accelerating development of the contrast children or, as we shall see later, the deceleration of growth rates for those who had pre-school experience earlier.

PRE-SCHOOL INTERVENTION

With the publication of books by Hunt (1961) and Bloom (1964), among others, who in effect both argued for the power of early experience, the stage was set for more widespread attempts to combat the effects of social disadvantage by means of pre-school intervention. Ignoring the implications of Kirk's work (1958), and making unjustified inferences from the results of Skeels's study (1966), both politicians and behavioural scientists combined, under President Johnson's Anti-Poverty Bill, to set up Project Head Start nationwide in the mid-1960s, after only a few months' planning. It was seriously expected that a few weeks or months of pre-school experience would be sufficient to counteract previous disadvantage, so that the child would enter regular schooling fully equipped to profit from normal education.

Project Head Start was founded upon at least four erroneous principles: (1) the use of mainly very short programmes; (2) the common use of a play-school approach, offering the child little education and little cognitive activity; (3) treating the child out of his home context which remained inimical to normal development; and (4) failing to reinforce any gains by repeating the 'enriched' experiences after the child had moved into regular school. The whole project was the clearest expression of a blind and unthinking belief in the pre-school years as truly formative in the long term.

It did not take long for a more austere attitude to gain currency. In an excellent review Bereiter and Engelmann (1966) predicted what was to become increasingly apparent, that 'enrichment' (in the sense of play-school activities) would be ineffective. 'Normally the young child has a lot of time; but the disadvantaged child who enters pre-school at the age of four-and-a-half has already used most of his up.' Hence a highly structured programme concentrating upon key cognitive activities was the only appropriate approach. In a paper delivered in 1967 a warning was given that 'the Head Start Programme will, however, stand or fall not on what it achieves in the pre-school years, but on whether or not these diversions of development are subsequently reinforced' (Clarke 1968). Taking as his starting point the report of the United States Commission on Civil Rights (1967), Jensen (1969) published his well-known review indicating large-scale failure of Head Start, attributing this to intractable genetic factors, and postulating a 'threshold' model for environmental action. The environment will operate significantly only when very adverse, as in the studies of formerly isolated children (see section II). The ordinary slum environment is far less damaging and is therefore not a significant factor in cognitive development. We do not propose here to consider Jensen's review in any detail, for we have recently analysed it elsewhere (Clarke and Clarke 1974) and Bronfenbrenner's contribution has summarised admirably the few properly conceived and properly executed pre-school studies of the last decade (see pages 247–56). Suffice it to say that, apart from the influence of genetic factors to which Jensen drew attention, it is very possible that the failure of the Head Start programmes was in environmental terms due to the short duration of the programmes at too early an age to be effective. Apparently the idea of, for example, a long-term, intensive compensatory programme in the middle-school period (about age eight to thirteen) seemed not to have entered anyone's mind.

Heber and Garber (1971, 1975) have outlined a study of considerable relevance to our theme. In its planning, methodology and execution it far surpasses the work of Skeels. Intervention with the retarded mothers and their children from their earliest months of life in a Milwaukee slum produced much greater changes in the latter than anticipated, and highly significant differences in many measures occurred as between experimental and control children. On the most familiar I.Q. measures, (and many other assessments were undertaken) at age five the averages for the former were in the low 120s and for the latter in the 90s. Both groups experienced repeated retesting. Unfortunately the very unusual intervention ceased at age six, when the children entered regular school. And, as we predicted before the subsequent results were available to us, there followed a decline, but in both groups this was such that the discrepancy remained. The children in the experimental group decremented first to an average of 112, then 110 and (Garber, personal communication 1975) to 106. More importantly, differences in reading abilities between the groups had disappeared. The study, summarised in Bronfenbrenner's reprinted contribution, is of interest in this book largely because of the decrements since intervention ceased, decrements which we would expect to continue slowly and surely, year by year.

What is now required is both longer intervention and also attempts to reveal its crucial ingredients for success. Moreover programmes for similar children, but commencing and ceasing at different ages, is also an obvious next step. Since some natural experiments make it apparent that improvements in response to environmental change can occur throughout development, it would seem clear that initial intervention might commence at say, five or ten years, and have prospects of success (even though early intervention is to be recommended since prevention is better than cure, on humane grounds).

In the meanwhile one or other of two alternative hypotheses might logically account for the findings of the Milwaukee Experiment: (1) that the intervention was insufficiently lengthy to enable the children, in their still rather adverse home and school contexts, to maintain their degree of gain; or (2) that the early acceleration of development has merely enabled them to reach their genetic limits earlier, and that these will progressively exercise constraints upon development, reflected in decelerating growth. This study, terminated too soon as we believe, will never answer these questions. We would guess, however (and guess is the right word), that the first hypothesis is the more likely to be correct. Future research will settle the question.

COMMENTS ON REPRINTED CONTRIBUTIONS

The Early Training Project of Gray and Klaus (1965, 1970) was no doubt inspired both by the Skeels and Kirk programmes. It is not to be considered as one of the Head Start Studies, since it both ante-dated this programme in its origin, and because of its great sense of realism and its excellent research design. The second paper (1970) is reprinted later in this section and can speak for itself. As the authors point out, their programme, which involved both structured pre-school activity over either three or two summers (i.e. from age three or from age four) for disadvantaged children, and which also included home visits weekly during the rest of each year, might be seen as a massive intervention. Yet these children spent less than 2 per cent of their waking time with Project staff between birth and school entry. 'Such programs, however, cannot be expected to carry the whole burden of providing adequate schooling for children from deprived circumstances; they can provide only a basis for future progress in schools and homes that can build upon that early intervention.' This statement is a clear expression of the view stated as part of our general hypothesis in section I. While it is not very difficult to alter the course of development early in life, such alterations must be followed by long-term repetition of the type of experience which induced such change, if there is to be any real hope of permanency.

Bronfenbrenner's (1974) book offers a masterly review of early intervention studies and their effects. The summary, which is re-printed, is so succinct and clear that our comments can be very brief. Attention is mainly directed to some twenty-six of the most satisfactory investigations. The immediate responsiveness of children to intervention is underlined, particularly in structured rather than free-play programmes, a point independently noted by both Tizard (1974) and Clarke (1974). A relative decline sets in, however, on termination of the intervention, particularly during the first year of school. The vital role of the home in maintaining, or more usually undoing, the effects of intervention is noted; hence the involvement of both parents and child is more often effective. The most severely deprived families, however, 'have neither the energy nor the psychological resources necessary to participate . . .' Elsewhere we have indicated the usual problem that those most in need of help are least likely to seek or accept it, or if accepted, to profit by it.

Bronfenbrenner is, in our view, rightly pessimistic in implying that, for the most deprived, only an 'ecological intervention' is likely to be effective. This means either a massive and long-lasting attack upon home and child problems (e.g. Heber and Garber 1975) or removal of the child from pathological conditions (e.g. Skeels 1966) by a complete environmental change followed by adoption.

It is clear that the author recognises fully that brief early experiences have effects which are not perpetuated unless the conditions giving rise to these changes are continued. His book illustrates, and is completely consistent with, our general theme.

CONCLUSIONS

The conclusions to this chapter are very closely similar to those in chapter 6, which outlined the results of some natural experiments. The main message is absolutely unequivocal. Brief intervention, offering even a radical change of environment, while inducing immediate effects, has no chance of long-term influences upon development unless the changed circumstances are perpetuated over a very long period. Pre-school education by itself has absolutely no possibility of breaking the cycle of disadvantage, nor has brief intervention with parents. For the child who is severely deprived, only a massive and lengthy attack upon his problems and those of his family is likely to be rewarding. Even so for the child in such desperate conditions, removal therefrom offers the best hope, for as Bronfenbrenner has indicated, the most deprived are highly unresponsive to intervention. Of course there are important ethical problems here, problems which society needs to face more unflinchingly and less emotively. Half-hearted attempts to 'prop up' families which may be essentially irredeemable are by definition useless. Society does, in fact, deal with such problems daily; the prime question here is where the line should be drawn. At the moment it appears to be too close to sentimentalism, and insufficiently in children's best interests.

The result of life-long intervention following highly disturbing early life experiences is best illustrated in the Skeels study. The Heber and Garber investigation is also extremely impressive, but its premature (as we would think) termination allows alternative interpretations. Nevertheless the bulk of the evidence cited in this chapter clearly illustrates and illuminates our main theme: early experience by itself, if unrepeated, has effects which fade.

Areas of ignorance include uncertainty on the number of years necessary for repetition of early experiences in order that effects may become self-perpetuating. We do not know either how far different processes can show different degrees of change, and we cannot delineate the essential environmental ingredients for change. While it is clear that in certain circumstances a relatively late change of circumstances can be followed by personal changes, we do not know how late this can be to remain effective. Moreover, we believe it probable that there is a 'wedge' effect for environmental influence, that is, the nearer the child to long-term optimal conditions of rearing, the less likely will positive change affect his level of functioning. The more adverse his conditions, the greater the potential for change, a potential more often than not unrealised because society fails to take appropriate action.

CHAPTER THIRTEEN

The Early Training Project: A Seventh-Year Report

Susan W. Gray and Rupert A. Klaus

The Early Training Project has been a field-research study concerned with the development and testing over time of procedures for improving the educability of young children from low-income homes. The rationale, the general design and methodology, and findings through the second year of schooling have been reported in some detail by Klaus and Gray (1968). A briefer report, up to school entrance, is given in Gray and Klaus (1965). The purpose of this report is to present the findings at the end of the fourth grade, three years after all experimental intervention had ceased.

The major concern of the Early Training Project was to study whether it was possible to offset the progressive retardation observed in the public school careers of children living in deprived circumstances. In addition, the writers undertook to study the spillover effect upon other children in the community and upon other family members.

The general research strategy was one of attempting to design a research 'package' consisting of variables which – on the basis of research upon social class, cognitive development, and motivation – might be assumed to be relevant to the school retardation which is observed in deprived groups and which at the same time might be subject to the effects of manipulation. Because this was a problem with major social implications, we also tried to design a general treatment approach which would be feasible to repeat on a large scale in the event that the procedure proved successful.

Subjects were eighty-eight children born in 1958. Sixty-one of these lived in a city of 25,000 in the upper South. The remaining twenty-seven, who served as a distal control group, resided in

Reprinted from *Child Development* 41 (1970), 909–24

a similar city 65 miles (100 kilometres) away. The children were all Negro. When we initiated the study the schools of the city were still segregated; we chose to work with Negro children because, in this particular setting, we had reason to believe that our chances of success were greater with this group.

The children were selected on the basis of parent's occupation, education, income, and housing conditions. At the beginning of the study, incomes were considerably below the approximate $ 3,000 used as the poverty line for a family of four. Occupations were either unskilled or semi-skilled; the educational level was eighth grade or below; housing conditions were poor. The median number of children per family at the beginning of the study was five; in about one-third of the homes there was no father present.

From the sixty-one children in the first city three groups were constituted by random assignment. The first group (T1) attended, over a period of three summers, a ten-week pre-school designed to offset the deficits usually observed in the performance of children from disadvantaged homes. In addition, this group had three years of weekly meetings with a specially trained home visitor during those months in which the pre-school was not in session. The second group (T2) had a similar treatment, except that it began a year later; the children received two summers of the special pre-school and two years of home visits. The third group (T3) became the local control group, which received all tests but no intervention treatment. The fourth group (T4), the distal-control group, was added to the design because of the somewhat ghetto-type concentration of Negroes in the first city. The local and distal-control groups also made possible the study of spillover effects upon children and parents living in proximity to the experimental children. The general layout of the experimental design is given in table 13.1. By reading down the columns, one may see the particular treatment and testing sequence followed for each of the four groups. Periodic testing is continuing for the children through elementary school.

THE INTERVENTION PROGRAM

The overall rationale for the intervention program grew out of the literature on child-rearing patterns in different social classes, plus the writers' own observations in low-income homes. On the

treatment time	three summer schools (T1)	two summer schools (T2)	local controls (T3)	distal controls (T4)
first winter (1961–2)	criterion development, curriculum planning, general tooling up			
first summer (1962)	pre-test, summer school, post-test	pre-test, post-test	pre-test, post-test	pre-test, post-test
second winter (1962–3)	home visitor contacts	—	—	—
second summer (1963)	pre-test, summer school, post-test	pre-test, summer school, post-test	pre-test, post-test	pre-test, post-test
third winter (1963–4)	home visitor contacts	home visitor contacts	—	—
third summer (1964)	pre-test, summer school, post-test	pre-test, summer school, post-test	pre-test, post-test	pre-test, post-test
fourth winter (1964–5)	home visitor contacts	home visitor contacts	—	—
fourth summer (1965)	follow-up tests	follow-up tests	follow-up tests	follow-up tests
fifth summer (1966)	follow-up tests	follow-up tests	follow-up tests	follow-up tests
seventh summer (1968)	follow-up tests	follow-up tests	follow-up tests	follow-up tests

Table 13.1 Layout of general research design

basis of this study, the intervention program for children was organized around two broad classes of variables: attitudes relating to achievement, and aptitudes relating to achievement. Under attitudes we were particularly interested in achievement motivation, especially as it concerns schooltype activities, in persistence, in ability to delay gratification; generally interested in typical school materials, such as books, crayons, puzzles, and the like. We were also concerned with the parents' attitude toward achievement, particularly in their aspirations for their children, especially as they related to schooling.

In the broad class of aptitude variables relating to achievement, we were particularly interested in perceptual and cognitive development and in language. Children from low-income homes have been shown to have deficits in these areas, all of which appear closely related to school success in the primary grades.

In the summer months, for ten weeks the children met in assembled groups. Each of the two experimental groups had a head teacher, who was an experienced Negro first-grade teacher. There were, in addition, three or four teaching assistants. These assistants were divided about equally as to race and sex.

The work with the parents in the project was carried on largely through a home-visitor program in which a specially trained preschool teacher made weekly visits to each mother and child. Both the home program and the school program are described in considerable detail in Gray, Klaus, Miller, and Forrester (1966) and in Klaus and Gray (1968).

Prior to and after each summer session, children in all four groups were tested on several instruments. From the first summer certain standardized tests of intelligence and language were used, along with a number of less formal instruments. At the end of the first grade, achievement tests were added. This testing schedule is shown in table 13.1. In general the 0·05 level of significance was used.

RESULTS

The detailed results of the testing program through May 1966, the end of the second grade for the children, are given in Klaus and Gray (1968). This paper gives the results as they relate to the spring and summer testings of 1968 with some additional information on performance of younger siblings. The same kinds of analyses were used for the 1968 data as were used in the earlier paper.

In 1968 the following tests were administered to all children still residing in middle Tennessee: the Stanford-Binet, the Peabody Picture Vocabulary Test, and the Metropolitan Achievement Test. The analyses here reported are based only upon those children available for testing with the exception of one child in the distal control group.

The Stanford-Binet scores are given in table 13.2, and are portrayed graphically in figure 13.1. A Lindquist (1953) Type 1 analysis of the results of 1962–8, in terms of I.Q. gave a significant F of 4·45 for the four groups, F of 16·81 for repeated measures, and F for interaction of groups over time of 3·51. All of these were significant at the 0·01 level or beyond. Next an analysis was made by the use of orthogonal comparisons. These are given in table 13.3. Here it may be seen that the two experimental groups remained significantly superior to the two control groups. The comparison of the first and the second experimental groups for 1968 showed an F of less than 1·00. The comparison

date of admini- stration	T1(N = 19) M.A. (Mo)	I.Q.	T2(N = 19) M.A. (Mo)	I.Q.	T3(N = 18) M.A. (Mo)	I.Q.	T4(N = 23) M.A. (Mo)	I.Q.
May 1962	40·7	87·6	43·8	92·5	40·3	85·4	40·3	86·7
August 1962	50·7	102·0	46·9	92·3	44·3	88·2	43·4	87·4
May 1963	55·6	96·4	56·0	94·8	53·2	89·6	50·4	86·7
August 1963	59·3	97·1	60·6	97·5	55·0	87·6	52·3	84·7
August 1964	68·0	95·8	71·6	96·6	62·3	82·9	59·4	80·2
August 1965	83·8	98·1	86·3	99·7	79·4	91·4	77·0	89·0
June 1966	88·7	91·2	93·4	96·0	86·8	87·9	82·9	84·6
July 1968	106·0	86·7	111·4	90·2	104·7	84·9	96·2	77·7

Table 13.2   Mean Stanford-Binet M.A. and I.Q. scores for the four treatment groups
at each administration

of the two control groups, however, yielded an F that, although not conventionally significant, was still large enough (3·52 where $F_{·95} = 3·96$) to be suggestive of a sharper decline in the distal than in the local control group. As was true of earlier analyses, the larger part of the variance appeared to be carried by the second experimental group and the distal control group.

The scores across the ten administrations of the Peabody Picture Vocabulary Test are given in table 13.4. in M.A. and I.Q. form. A Lindquist (1953) Type 1 analysis of variance was performed for

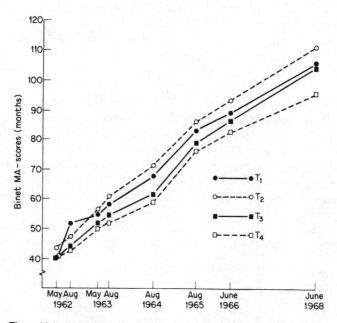

Figure 13.1   Mental ages for the four groups on the Stanford-Binet Test

the M.A. scores. For groups F was 5·16, indicating a significant effect of the experimental treatment upon the children's performance. For repeated testings F was 376·73, an effect that would be clearly expected when M.A. scores were used. These were selected in preference to I.Q. scores on this particular test since the I.Q. scores appear to lack discrimination at certain levels. The interaction between groups and time was nonsignificant. Orthogonals were next used. Here it was found that T1 + T2 was significantly greater than T3 + T4 up until 1968, in which year differences were not significant. As may be seen from table 13.4, differences in

date of administration	hypothesis T1 = T2 + T3 + T4		hypothesis T2 = T3 + T4		hypothesis T3 = T4	
	F-ratio	conclusion	F-ratio	conclusion	F-ratio	conclusion
August 1962	12·67*	T1 > T2 + T3 + T4	1·44	T2 = T3 + T4	<1·00	T3 = T4
May 1963	2·91	T1 = T2 + T3 + T4	3·36	T2 = T3 + T4	<1·00	T3 = T4

date of administration	hypothesis T1 + T2 = T3 + T4		hypothesis T1 = T2		hypothesis T3 = T4	
	F-ratio	conclusion	F-ratio	conclusion	F-ratio	conclusion
May 1962	2·07	T1 + T2 = T3 + T4	1·53	T1 = T2	<1·00	T3 = T4
August 1963	18·53*	T1 + T2 > T3 + T4	<1·00	T1 = T2	<1·00	T3 = T4
August 1964	29·94*	T1 + T2 > T3 + T4	<1·00	T1 = T2	<1·00	T3 = T4
August 1965	11·12*	T1 + T2 > T3 + T4	<1·00	T1 = T2	<1·00	T3 = T4
June 1966	5·99*	T1 + T2 > T3 + T4	1·18	T1 = T2	<1·00	T3 = T4
July 1968	7·50*	T1 + T2 > T3 + T4	<1·00	T1 = T2	3·53	T3 = T4

$* \; p < ·05; \; F ·95 = 3·97$

Table 13.3 Orthogonal comparisons of treatment-group sums for Stanford-Binet I.Q. scores for the eight administrations

date of administration	test form	T1(N = 19)		T2(N = 19)		T3(N = 18)		T4(N = 23)	
		M.A. (Mo)	I.Q.	M.A. (Mo)	I.Q.	M.A. (Mo)	I.Q.	M.A. (Mo)	I.Q.
May 1962	A	30·0	69·5	30·6	70·1	29·4	66·4	32·2	74·0
August 1962	B	36·8	75·3	33·1	63·9	32·7	65·8	30·7	62·8
May 1963	A	44·8	79·0	40·7	69·6	39·1	69·3	39·5	69·8
August 1963	B	45·0	78·4	50·7	83·6	38·4	64·0	37·6	63·8
May 1964	B	55·6	81·2	60·1	85·5	45·8	65·4	48·7	70·9
August 1964	A	59·1	83·0	62·0	87·0	50·6	72·4	48·7	69·6
June 1965	B	74·2	89·0	76·2	90·3	67·6	83·0	67·3	84·0
August 1965	A	70·6	86·2	76·5	91·8	65·4	80·2	66·3	83·4
June 1966	A	78·1	86·7	81·9	89·3	75·4	83·9	71·2	80·7
July 1968	A	96·4	84·5	100·3	86·7	91·7	81·8	89·3	78·7

Table 13.4 Mean P.P.V.T. mental-age scores and I.Q. equivalents for the four treatment groups for the ten administrations

mean scores were still apparent. Heterogeneity had increased over time, however, so that differences were no longer significant. In no analysis at any point of time was either experimental group significantly superior to the other. Nor did either control group show itself to be significantly superior to the other one.

The results for the Metropolitan Achievement Test are given in table 13.5. A Lindquist (1953) Type 1 analysis was performed on each subtest, and orthogonal comparisons made. In the interest of brevity a table of orthogonal comparisons is not given. In 1965, at the end of first grade, the experimental children were significantly superior on three of the four tests used at that time: word knowledge, word discrimination, and reading. For arithmetic computation

subtest and year	T1	T2	T3	T4
word knowledge				
1965	1·69	1·73	1·79	1·37
1966	2·32	2·47	2·29	1·98
1968	3·58	3·90	3·54	3·27
word discrimination				
1965	1·68	1·81	1·82	1·37
1966	2·64	2·73	2·65	2·20
1968	3·73	3·95	3·76	3·47
reading				
1965	1·72	1·82	1·84	1·46
1966	2·52	2·75	2·56	2·11
1968	3·52	3·89	3·72	3·10
arithmetic computation				
1965	1·52	1·62	1·54	1·43
1966	2·41	2·55	2·49	2·05
1968	3·92	4·07	4·06	3·79
spelling				
1966	2·42	2·85	2·60	1·99
1968	4·26	4·69	4·24	3·67
language				
1968	3·52	4·00	3·63	3·17
arithmetic problem solving and concepts				
1968	3·31	3·54	3·75	3·26

Table 13.5   Metropolitan Achievement Test grade equivalent mean scores for the various subtests for the three administrations

score, F was less than 1.00. The local controls were also somewhat superior to the distal controls on these tests, an indication possibly of horizontal diffusion or, either in interaction or independently, a somewhat better instructional program. In 1966 five subtests were given. This time only two were significant, word knowledge and reading On the other three tests, however, the F's ranged from 2.69 to 2.84, suggesting probabilities at about the 0.10 level. In neither year was T1 significantly superior to T2. The highest F was 1.16, where $F_{.95}$ is 3.97. In the comparisons of T3 and T4, T3 was superior to T4 on reading and arithmetic computation. On word knowledge, word discrimination, and spelling the F's ranged from 3.19 to 3.85, suggesting probabilities beyond the 0.10 level ($F_{.90} = 2.77$). At the end of the fourth year no significant effects were found with the single exception of reading, on which T3 was superior to T4. There is some suggestion of residual effect since, in six of the seven possible comparisons of experimentals and controls, the experimentals were superior. Also, on all seven possible comparisons the local control group was superior to the distal control group.

The Stanford-Binet was administered in all four groups to those younger siblings who were of testable age. This was first done in 1964 and again in 1966. Since the 1966 findings have not been previously reported, they are presented here in table 13.6. In 1964, fifty-seven children were tested. Fifty of these same children were tested again in 1966, along with forty-three additional siblings who were too young to test in 1964.

An analysis of covariance was performed on these scores, with the I.Q.s at first testing of the target-age children used as the covariable. Also, where there were two younger siblings in the same family, one was dropped, so that the analysis was based on eighty-seven children. Separate analyses were also performed for the 1964 and the 1966 results of all children who were retested. In addition, an analysis was performed on the 1966 results for those children who were being tested for the first time.

On all younger siblings tested in 1966 F between groups was not significant at the 0.05 level ($F = 3.97$). It was significant beyond the 0.10 level, and therefore we made further analyses. Orthogonal comparisons were used, with the hypotheses shown in table 13.7. This is the same general approach as used with the target children. All orthogonal comparisons showed significant differences for the testing of all younger siblings in 1966: the combined experimental group siblings were superior to the combined control group siblings; the T1 siblings were superior to the T2 siblings; and the T3 siblings were superior to the T4 siblings. When the children who were tested for the first time are separated out, it is clear, both

testing and groups	mean scores (first testing, 1962) for treatment-group children with younger siblings			mean scores for younger siblings		
	N	C.A.	I.Q.	N	C.A.	I.Q.
1964 testing of younger siblings born in 1959 and 1960						
T1	12	47	82	13	54	82
T2	16	46	89	21	53	83
T3	7	50	84	9	54	71
T4	12	48	88	14	62	74
1966 retesting of younger siblings initially tested in 1964						
T1	12	47	82	13	78	85
T2	14	46	92	19	76	85
T3	5	46	82	7	76	78
T4	11	48	86	13	77	75
1966 testing of younger siblings born in 1961 and 1962						
T1	10	44	87	11	58	84
T2	9	47	91	10	52	87
T3	7	48	83	9	56	76
T4	12	47	88	15	55	84
1966 testing of all younger siblings						
T1	15	50	84	24	69	84
T2	17	46	91	29	68	86
T3	8	47	84	16	65	77
T4	15	47	86	28	63	80

Table 13.6   Initial Stanford-Binet scores of treatment-group children and younger siblings in two testings

in the 1966 and the 1964 data, that most of the variance was being carried by younger siblings closer in age to the target-age children. There are some interesting implications of these general results on younger siblings which will be examined in more detail in the Discussion.

DISCUSSION

The results on the one test of intelligence which was used consistently, from the initiation of the program in 1962 until the testing at the end of the fourth grade in 1968, are very much in line with what might be expected. For this was an intervention program that used a broad-gauge approach and which was relatively successful in terms of improving the educability of young children from low-income homes. Intervention caused a rise in intelligence which was fairly sharp at first, then leveled off, and finally began to show decline once intervention ceased. The control groups on the other hand tended to show a slight but consistent decline with the single exception of a jump between entrance into public school and the end of first grade. Differences between experimentals and controls on Stanford-Binet I.Q. were still significant at the end of the third year after intervention ceased. All four groups have shown a decline in I.Q. after the first grade, but the decline, as shown in figure 13.1, tended to be relatively parallel. Perhaps the remarkable thing is that with the relatively small amount of impact over time, differences should still be significant. After all, the child experienced only five mornings of school a week for ten weeks for two or three summers, plus weekly home visits during the other nine months for two or three years. This suggests that the impact was not lost. It was not sufficient, however, to offset the massive effects of a low-income home in which the child had lived since birth onward.

The results on the P.P.V.T. showed a pattern that is not dissimilar. There was a rise during intervention, including the first grade, then a leveling off and a slight decline. Here, however, difference between groups, although consistent, was no longer significant.

The importance of the school situation for the maintenance or loss of a gain should be weighed. The children for the most part remained in schools in which the entire population was Negro.

	HO*: T1 + T2 = T3 + T4		HO: T1 = T2		HO: T3 = T4	
	F-ratio	conclusion	F-ratio	conclusion	F-ratio	conclusion
all younger siblings 1966	3·48	T1 + T2 = T3 + T4	0·75	T1 = T2	0·00	T3 = T4
younger siblings first tested in 1966	0·77	T1 + T2 = T3 + T4	0·04	T1 = T2	0·80	T3 = T4
younger siblings retested in 1966						
1964 results	8·13+	T1 + T2 > T3 + T4	0·74	T1 = T2	0·01	T3 = T4
1966 results	4·72+	T1 + T2 > T3 + T4	5·11+	T1 > T2	2·07	T3 = T4

Table 13.7   Orthogonal comparisons of Stanford-Binet scores of younger siblings

* HO = hypothesis
+ $p < ·05$; F·95 = 3·97

Eight of the local children at the end of first grade did enroll in schools that had previously been all white. Four more changed during the next two years. None of the distal children attended schools with white children. Since in this area, as in many places, race tends to be confounded with social class, the children in the study did not in general have the advantage of classmates with relatively high expectancies. There is some evidence that in both of the all-Negro schools the general teaching-learning situation, although fair, was less adequate than in the schools that had formerly been all white. This, plus the continuing effect of the home situation and the immediate community, took its toll. There are some data on achievement-test scores to be presented later which suggest the impact of the two all-Negro schools which most of the children attended.

On the one achievement battery administered from first to fourth grade, the Metropolitan Achievement Test (table 13.5), significant differences did not appear in 1968 on any of the subtests with sole exception of the reading score, in which the local control group was superior to the distal control group. The experimentals had been superior to the controls on three tests in 1965 and on two tests in 1966. One might interpret this as showing that the intervention program did have measurable effects upon test performance at the end of first grade, but that by the end of fourth grade, the school program had failed to sustain at any substantial level the initial superiority. Although disappointing, this is perhaps not surprising in a test battery so dependent upon specific school instruction.

An interesting sidelight is thrown on this matter by looking at the performance on the Metropolitan Achievement Test of the eight children from the local school who enrolled in previously all-white schools at the end of first grade. An attempt was made, on the basis of first-grade achievement tests and home ratings of educational aspirations, to match these eight children with eight who remained in the Negro school. Admittedly, this is a chancy business, and one which should not be taken too seriously. Table 13.8 presents the gains in grade equivalents on the Metropolitan Achievement Tests from the end of first grade to the end of fourth grade. On the four subtests common to both grade levels, the picture is a clear one of more gain in the children who changed schools, varying from 0·8 to 1·4 year's greater gain. These data did not seem appropriate for subjection to statistical analysis. They do suggest, however, the fairly obvious: that performance on achievement tests is directly related to school experience. The children who changed schools have made approximately 'normal' gain for their three years; the children who did not change have gained two years or less during the three years from first through fourth grade.

The results on the younger siblings are to the writers among the most interesting findings of the study. We have termed the process by which such results are achieved and the product of that process 'vertical diffusion', to suggest that this is a spread of effect down the family from the mother and possibly the target-age child to a younger child.

| | mean gains 1965–8 | | | |
	word knowledge	word discrimination	reading	arithmetic
E.T.P. Ss in integrated schools beginning Fall 1965	3·1	2·8	2·7	2·9
E.T.P. Ss in Negro schools matched to the first group on Spring 1965 M.A.T. and on verbal rating by home visitor	1·7	2·0	1·6	1·7
difference	1·4	0·8	1·1	1·2

Table 13.8   Mean gains on the M.A.T. over a three-year period for eight E.T.P. children in integrated schools and matches in Negro schools

In this study the effects of the older sibling and the mother upon the younger child were confounded. Some research currently being carried on under the direction of one of the writers has made possible the separation of the influence of mother and older siblings. Results so far indicate that most of the effect is coming from the mother. It is plausible to assume that the role of the mother was the more influential since considerable effort was expended by the home visitor over a period of three years with the first experimental group and over two years with the second experimental group. The emphasis of the home intervention was on making the mother a more effective teacher, or more generally, an effective educational change agent for her target-age child. Also worthy of note is the finding that vertical diffusion appeared more clearly in the younger siblings born in 1959 and 1960, who were within one to two and a half years in age of the older siblings. The siblings born in 1961 and 1962, when pulled out for separate analysis, did not show an effect which approached statistical significance. Vertical diffusion also appeared more operative in the first than in the second experimental group. A plausible explanation is that intervention lasted a year longer with the first group and began a year earlier. There is also in the data some suggestion of a process we have examined in more detail elsewhere (Klaus and Gray 1968), one that may be termed horizontal diffusion, the spread of effect from one family to another. This we have in general analyzed by comparing the local and distal control groups. Here we find that the younger siblings in the local control group showed themselves to be superior to the distal control group.

To the extent that the findings on vertical diffusion have generality, they seem to point to the efficacy of a powerful process in the homes, presumably mediated by the parent, which may serve to improve the educability of young children. Before a second conclusion is reached by the reader, however, to the effect that 'parent education' is the answer, we would like to point out that our procedure was clearly parent education with a difference. It was conducted in the homes; it was done by skilled pre-school teachers with some experience in working in the homes; it was highly concrete and specific to a given mother's life situation; it was continuous over a long period of time. Indeed, parent education probably is the answer, but in low-income homes a very different kind of parent education from that usually provided may be needed.

Seven years after the Early Training Project began, in 1969, intervention programs for young children from low-income homes were nationwide. These programs differ tremendously in the length and timing of the intervention, in the objectives and consistency with which they are followed, in the degree of specificity of the program, and in the length and extent of follow-up study of the sample.

It is hardly surprising, with the wild heterogeneity of such programs, that nationwide assessment of programs, such as the

Westinghouse Survey of Project Head Start (1969), would find relatively small evidence of positive effects upon the child's achievement and personal adequacy. Leaving aside all the problems of measuring personal adequacy and even achievement in young children, such lack of results is only to be expected in situations where the bad or inappropriate so cancels out the good that little positive effect can be found, especially if the evaluation is somewhat premature.

At this point in time it seems appropriate to look more closely at those programs which have clearly followed an adequate research design, specified and carefully monitored their treatments, and conducted adequate follow-up study of the sample. Such programs are relatively few in number, for their history is short.

In the Early Training Project we have been more fortunate than most. The study was initiated nearly four years before the tidal wave of interests in such early intervention that came about through such nationwide programs as Project Head Start and Titles 1 and 111 of the Elementary and Secondary Education Act. We have worked in a setting in which we have been free from administrative pressures either to change our procedures or to make premature conclusions from our data. The two communities in which families live have had little outward mobility; even at the end of seven years attrition is only a minor problem. For these reasons we believe the data collected over seven years with our four groups of children do shed some light upon the problem of progressive retardation and the possibility that it can be offset.

Our answer as to whether such retardation can be offset is one of cautious optimism. The effects of our intervention program are clearly evidenced through the second year of public schooling, one year after intervention ceased. There is still an effect, most apparent in the Stanford-Binet, after two more years of non-intervention. Our data on horizontal and vertical diffusion, especially the latter, give us some hope that intervention programs can have a lasting effect that goes beyond the children that were the target of that intervention program.

Still, it is clear from our data, with a parallel decline across the four groups in the second through fourth grades, that an intervention program before school entrance, such as ours, cannot carry the entire burden of offsetting progressive retardation. By some standards the Early Training Project might be seen as one of relatively massive intervention. And yet a colleague of ours (Miller 1970) has estimated that in the years prior to school entrance the maximum amount of time that the children in the project could have spent with the Early Training Project staff was approximately 600 hours, less than 2 per cent of their waking hours from birth to six years. Perhaps the remarkable thing is that the effect lasted as well and as long as it did. In a similar vein, we have estimated the amount of these contacts in the home as a maximum of 110 hours, or about 0·3 per cent of the waking hours of the child from birth to six years. Surely it would be foolish not to realize that, without massive changes in the life situation of the child, home circumstances will continue to have their adverse effect upon the child's performance.

In 1968 we wrote:

The most effective intervention programs for pre-school children that could possibly be conceived cannot be considered a form of inoculation whereby the child forever after is immune to the effects of a low-income home and of a school inappropriate to his needs. Certainly, the evidence on human performance is overwhelming in indicating that such performance results from the continual interaction of the organism with its environment. Intervention programs, well conceived and executed, may be expected to make some relatively lasting changes. Such programs, however, cannot be expected to carry the whole burden of providing adequate schooling for children from deprived circumstances; they can provide only a basis for future progress in schools and homes that can build upon that early intervention.

In 1969 we saw no reason to alter this statement. Our seventh-year results serve only to underscore its truth.

Major financial support for this study was received from the National Institute of Mental Health, under Mental Health Project grant 5-R11-MH-765. Additional support for research staff during the later phases of the study was made possible through grant HD-00973 from the National Institute of Child Health and Human Development, from the Office of Education, contract OEC 3-7-070706-3118, and grant 9174 from the Office of Economic Opportunity.

CHAPTER FOURTEEN

Is Early Intervention Effective? Facts and Principles of Early Intervention: a Summary

Urie Bronfenbrenner

The conclusions of this analysis are presented in the form of a summary of the research findings and a set of generalizations to which they give rise.

SUMMARY OF RESEARCH RESULTS

PRE-SCHOOL INTERVENTION IN GROUP SETTINGS

The results are based on twelve studies involving children ranging in age from one to six. Eight of these researches included comparisons between randomly constituted experimental and control groups. Conclusions regarding program effectiveness are cited only if supported by results from such comparisons.

1 Almost without exception, children showed substantial gains in I.Q. and other cognitive measures during the first year of the program, attaining or even exceeding the average for their age.

2 Cognitively structured curricula produced greater gains than play-oriented nursery programs.

3 Neither earlier entry into the program (from age one) nor a longer period of enrollment (up to five years) resulted in greater or more enduring cognitive gains.

4 By the first or second year after completion of the program, sometimes while it was still in operation, the children began to show a progressive decline, and by the third or fourth year of

Reprinted from *A Report on Longitudinal Evaluations of Pre-school programs*, vol. 2 *Is Early Intervention Effective?* (Washington D.C., 1974: D.H.E.W. Publication no [OHD] 74–25).

follow-up had fallen back into the problem range of the lower 90s and below. Apparent exceptions to this general trend turned out to be faulted by methodological artifacts (e.g. self-selection of families in the experimental group).

5 The period of sharpest decline occurred after the child's entry into regular school. Preliminary data from the Follow-Through program suggest that this decline may be offset by the continuation of intervention programs, including strong parent involvement, into the early grades.

6 The children who profited least from the program, and who showed the earliest and most rapid decline, were those who came from the most deprived social and economic backgrounds. Especially relevant in this regard were such variables as the number of children in the family, the employment status of the head of the household, the level of parents' education, and the presence of only one parent in the family.

7 Results from a number of studies pointed to factors in and round the home as critical to the child's capacity to profit from group programs both in pre-school and in the elementary grades. For example, several researches revealed that the greatest loss in cognitive performance of disadvantaged children took place not while they were in school, but over the summer months. During this same period, disadvantaged children living in favorable economic circumstances not only maintained their status but showed significant gains.

HOME-BASED TUTORING PROGRAMS

The results of the two studies in this area were similar to those for pre-school programs in group settings. Children showed dramatic gains in I.Q. while the project was in operation but began to decline once the home visits were discontinued.

PARENT–CHILD INTERVENTION

A total of nine studies, involving children from the first year of life through elementary school, focused simultaneously on parent and child (almost exclusively the mother) as the targets of intervention. In seven of these researches, the principle of random assignment (either of individuals or groups) was employed in the designation of experimental and control subjects. Again conclusions regarding program effectiveness are cited only when supported by results from comparisons of randomly constituted experimental and control groups.

1 Parent–child intervention resulted in substantial gains in I.Q. which were still evident three to four years after termination of the program (Gordon 1972, 1973; Levenstein 1972a). In none of the follow-up studies, however, had the children yet gone beyond the first grade.

2 The effects were cumulative from year to year, both during intervention (Levenstein 1972a) and, in some instances, after the program had ended (Gordon 1973, Levenstein 1972a).

3 The magnitude of I.Q. gain was inversely related to the age at which the child entered the program, the greatest gains being made by children enrolled as one and two year olds (Gilmer and others 1970; Karnes and others 1968, 1969a, 1969b, 1970; Levenstein 1972a; Radin 1969, 1972; Stanford Research Institute 1971a, 1971b).

4 Parent intervention was of benefit not only for the target child but also for his younger siblings (Gilmer and others, 1970; Klaus and Gray 1968; Gray and Klaus 1970).

5 Gains from parent intervention during the pre-school years were reduced to the extent that primary responsibility for the child's development was assumed by the staff member rather than left with the parent, particularly when the child was simultaneously enrolled in a group intervention program (Gilmer and others 1970; Karnes and others 1969c).

6 By the time the child was five years old, parent intervention appeared to have little effect so far as gains in intellectual development are concerned. *But children who were involved in an intensive program of parent intervention during, and, especially, prior to their enrollment in pre-school or school, achieved greater and more enduring gains in the group program* (Gilmer and others 1970; Gordon 1972, 1973; Radin 1969, 1972; Standford Research Institute 1971a, 1971b; Smith 1968). This effect on group programs did not appear until children were at least three years of age, but was still strongly in evidence in the one project in which parent intervention was continued through the sixth grade (Smith 1968). Thus, from the third year onward, parent intervention seemed to serve as a catalyst for sustaining and enhancing the effects of group intervention.

7 Parent intervention influenced the attitudes and behavior of

the mother not only toward the child but in relation to herself as a competent person capable of improving her own situation (Gilmer and others 1970; Gordon 1973; Karnes and others 1970).

8 Families willing to become involved in parent intervention programs tended to come from the upper levels of the disadvantaged population. Research findings indicate that, at the most deprived levels, families are so overburdened with the task of survival that they have neither the energy nor the psychological resources necessary to participate in an intervention program involving the regular visit of a stranger to the home (Klaus and Gray 1968; Radin and Wikart 1967).

9 The complexity of findings on the effects of parent intervention prompted a more detailed analysis of the role of parent–child interaction in fostering the child's psychological development. An examination of the research literature (Bronfenbrenner 1968a, 1968b, 1972a) indicated that, in the early years of life, the key element was the involvement of parent and child in verbal interaction round a cognitively challenging task. A second critical feature was the fact that the mother not only trained the child but the child also trained the mother. A third factor was the existence of a mutual and enduring emotional attachment between the child and adult. It is by capitalizing on all these elements, by taking as its focus neither the child nor the parent but the parent–child system, that parent intervention apparently achieves its effectiveness and staying power. It is as if the child himself had no way of internalizing the processes which foster his growth, whereas the parent–child system does possess this capability.

10 Along with advantages, parent intervention appears to have serious limitations in terms of its applicability and effectiveness with families at the lowest extreme of the socioeconomic distribution.

ECOLOGICAL INTERVENTION

The research results indicate that for the children from the most deprived groups no strategy of intervention is likely to be effective that focuses attention solely on the child or on the parent–child relationship. The critical forces of destruction lie neither within the child nor within his family but in the desperate circumstances in which the family is forced to live. What is called for is intervention at the *ecological level*, measures that will effect radical changes in the immediate environment of the family and the child.

Only three studies of this kind were found in the research literature (Heber and others 1972; Skeels 1966; Skodak and Skeels 1949). The major findings were as follows:

1 *Severely disadvantaged children of mothers with I.Q.s well below average (i.e. below 70 or 80) are not doomed to inferiority by unalterable constraints either genetic or environmental.*

2 Substantial changes in the environment of the child and his principal caretakers can produce positive developmental changes considerably greater (gains of 25 to 28 I.Q. points) and more enduring than those achieved by the most effective intervention techniques when the home environment is left essentially unaltered.

3 The processes and effects produced through ecological intervention substantiate the critical role in early development played by an enduring one-to-one relationship involving the child in verbal interaction with an adult around cognitively stimulating activities.

SOME PRINCIPLES OF EARLY INTERVENTION

The principles are stated in the form of propositions specifying the elements that appear essential for early intervention programs to be effective. Although derived from results of a substantial number of studies by different researchers, these generalizations should still be regarded as tentative. Even where the supportive findings have been replicated, they are susceptible to alternative interpretations, and the crucial experiments are yet to be done.

To indicate the extent to which each of the following generalizations are supported by research results, we shall label each one by a symbol. The superscript 'i' denotes that the conclusion is *inferred* from the evidence; the superscript 'r' means that the generalization is supported by *replicated results* obtained in two or more well-designed studies described in the main body of this analysis, but that there is need for further research designed specifically to test and refine the proposition in question.

General Principles*

FAMILY CENTERED INTERVENTION

The evidence indicates that the family is the most effective and

* The propositions are stated in terms of parent rather than mother alone in the belief that subsequent research will indicate that they apply as well to the father, or any other older member of the household who is prepared to assume a major and continuing responsibility for the care of the child.

economical system for fostering and sustaining the development of the child.[r] The evidence indicates further that the involvement of the child's family as an active participant is critical to the success of any intervention program.[r] Without such family involvement, any effects of intervention, at least in the cognitive sphere, appear to erode fairly rapidly once the program ends.[r] In contrast, the involvement of the parents as partners in the enterprise provides an on-going system which can reinforce the effects of the program while it is in operation, and help to sustain them after the program ends.[r]

ECOLOGICAL INTERVENTION

The first and most essential requirement is to provide those conditions which are necessary for life and for the family to function as a child-rearing system.[r] These include adequate health care, nutrition, housing, employment, and opportunity and status for parenthood.[i] These are also precisely the conditions that are absent for millions of disadvantaged families in our country.[r]

To provide the conditions necessary for a family to function will require major changes in the institutions of the society and the invention of new institutional forms.[i] The results of this analysis offer no guidance on the development of new systems for providing adequate health care, nutrition, housing or income, but they do suggest strategies for increasing opportunity and social reward for the functions of parenthood. These include extending the number and status of part-time jobs available to disadvantaged parents of young children,[i] establishing more flexible work schedules,[i] introducing parent apprentice programs in the schools to engage older children in supervised care of the young, involving parents in the work of the school,[i] creating patterns of mutual assistance among disadvantaged families living in the same neighborhood,[i] meeting the basic needs of young families (including supervised experience in child care) before they begin to raise children,[i] providing homemaker services,[i] making available insurance to meet family emergencies,[i] and using television as an adjunct to parent–child intervention.[i] *

---

* A more extended discussion of the rationale and nature of the foregoing proposals appears in Bronfenbrenner 1972b.

A SEQUENTIAL STRATEGY OF INTERVENTION

A long-range intervention program may be viewed in terms of five stages. Although the program may be begun with benefit to the child at any age,[r] initiating appropriate intervention at earlier stages can be expected to yield cumulative gains.[r] Ideally intervention should not be interrupted (for then the gains achieved are gradually eroded,[r] and there should be continuity from one phase to the next.[i] During every stage the first requirement is to meet the family's basic needs as outlined above.[i] Thereafter intervention is differentiated to accommodate the developmental level of both family and child as indicated below.

STAGES OF INTERVENTION

STAGE 1   PREPARATION FOR PARENTHOOD

Ideally intervention begins before the family is formed when the future parents are still in school. This initial phase involves providing school children of both sexes practicum experiences in the care of the young.[i] In addition, attention is given to the health requirements of the future mother in terms of nutrition and preventive medical care.[i]

STAGE 2   BEFORE CHILDREN COME

The next critical point for intervention is after the family is formed but before any children are born. Here the initial emphasis is to insure adequate housing, health care, nutrition, and economic security before, during, and after pregnancy.[i] This is also the optimal period for introducing a parent intervention program with some experience with young children provided before the family's own offspring arrive on the scene.[i]

STAGE 3   THE FIRST THREE YEARS OF LIFE

During this period the primary objective is the establishment of an enduring emotional relationship between parent and infant involving frequent reciprocal interaction[r] around activities which are challenging to the child.[r] The effect of such interaction is to strengthen the bond between parent and child,[r] enhance motivation,[r] increase the frequency and power of contingent responses,[r] produce mutual adaptation in behavior,[r] and thereby improve the parent's effectiveness as a teacher for the child,[i] further the latter's learning,[r] and, in due course, establish a stable interpersonal system capable of fostering and sustaining the child's development in the future.[r] The development of such an enduring pattern of attachment and interaction can be facilitated through a parent intervention program involving the following elements.

1 The program includes frequent home visits in which parent and child are encouraged, by example and with the aid of appropriate materials, to engage in sustained patterns of verbal interaction around tasks which gradually increase in cognitive complexity as a function of the child's development.[r]

2 The parent devotes considerable periods of time to activities with the child similar to those introduced during the home visit.[r]

3 The role of the parent as the primary agent of intervention is given priority, status and support from the surrounding environment.[r] Intervention programs which cast the parent in a subordinate role or have the effect of discouraging or decreasing his participation in activities with the child are likely to be counter-productive.[r]

4 The effectiveness and efficiency of parent intervention can be increased by extending activities so as to involve all the members of the family.[i] In this way the effects of vertical diffusion to younger siblings can be maximized[r] while older family members, including father, relatives and older brothers and sisters, can participate as agents of intervention.[i] Such expansion, however, should not be allowed to impair the formation and uninterrupted activity of enduring one-to-one relationships so essential to the development of the young child.[i]

5 The effectiveness and efficiency of parent intervention can be enhanced through group meetings designed to provide information, to demonstrate materials and procedures, and to create situations in which the confidence and motivation of parents (and other family members) is reinforced through mutual support and a sense of common purpose.[r] Such meetings, however, must not be allowed to take precedence over home visits or the periods which the parent devotes to playing and working with the child.[r]

STAGE 4   AGES FOUR THROUGH SIX
During this period, exposure to a cognitively oriented pre-school curriculum becomes a potent force for accelerating the child's cognitive development,[r] but a strong parent-intervention program

is necessary to enhance and sustain the effects of the group experience.[r] This combined strategy involves the following features.

1 The effectiveness of pre-school experience in a group setting is enhanced if it is *preceded* by a strong parent-intervention program involving regular home visits.[r]

2 After pre-school begins, the parent program must not be relegated to secondary status if it is to realize its potential in conserving and facilitating the effects of group intervention.[r] Both phases of the combined strategy should reinforce the parents' status as central in fostering the development of the child.[i] A program which places the parent in a subordinate role dependent on the expert is not likely to be effective in the long run.[r]

STAGE 5   AGES SIX THROUGH TWELVE

Of especial importance for sustaining the child's learning in school is the involvement of parents in supporting at home the activities engaged in by the child at school and their participation in activities at school directly affecting their child.[i] The parent, however, need no longer be the child's principal teacher as at earlier stages. Rather he acts as a supporter of the child's learning both in and out of school, but continues to function, and to be identified by school personnel, as the primary figure responsible for the child's development as a person.[i]

Taken as a whole, the foregoing principles imply a major reorientation in the design of intervention programs and in the training of personnel to work in this area. In the past, such programs were primarily child-centered, age-segregated, time-bound, self-centered and focused on the trained professional as the powerful and direct agent of intervention with the child. The results of this analysis point to approaches that are family centered rather than child-centered, that cut across contexts rather than being confined to a single setting, that have continuity through time, and that utilize as the primary agents of socialization the child's own parents, other family members, adults and other children from the neighborhood in which he lives, school personnel, and other persons who are part of the child's enduring environment. It is beyond the scope of this paper to attempt to spell out the implication of this reorientation for the organization of services, delivery systems and training. Many developments in the desired direction are already taking place. It is hoped that this analysis may accelerate the process of social change in the major institutions of our nation directly affecting the lives of young children and families.

In completing this analysis, we reemphasize the tentative nature of the conclusions and the narrowness of I.Q. and related measures as aspects of the total development of the child. We also wish to reaffirm a deep indebtedness to those who conducted the programs and researches on which this work is based, and a profound faith in the capacity of parents, of whatever background, to enable their children to develop into effective and happy human beings, *once our society is willing to make conditions of life viable and humane for all its families.*

Section V

Conclusions

CHAPTER FIFTEEN

Overview and Implications

Ann M. Clarke and A.D.B. Clarke

Before discussing the evidence and attempting to reach some conclusions, it is important to emphasise what this book is *not* about.
We are not primarily concerned with the major problem of whether
and to what extent the physical and social environment influences
the development of personal attributes such as intelligence and
social adjustment. Had this been our aim, a large number of,
often excellently documented, empirical studies would have been
included, some of which also emphasise the importance of genetic
and constitutional variables. We are concerned *solely* with the
problem of the implications of *early* environmental events for later
development. Without exception, the authors whose work is cited
are aware of the importance of genetic variables; they are sensitive
to the possibility of environmental effects; a majority have, sometimes to their own surprise, produced evidence suggesting that
events occurring in the first few years of a child's life are not
necessarily of any great significance for later development.

In chapter 1 we outlined in some detail what appeared to be
the origins of the modern view that the first few years of life
are of vital long-term importance. These views have entered into
received wisdom, and are rarely challenged. Indeed, they appear
to be reinforced both by selective perception and clinical experience.
For example, the social worker or psychiatrist assessing the problem
of a deviant or abnormal individual has traditionally directed his
initial attention to early development. As Vernon (1964) pointed
out, this may for the individual be a welcome escape from discussing current problems. Equally one might add that both clinician
and patient may unwittingly act as mutual reinforcers in discovering
anomalies in early life, anomalies which in such cases are usually
to be found both then and later.

It has been widely argued that various forms of often loosely defined deprivation in early childhood may find expression in a variety of deviant behaviours in later life. These range from maternal separation with hospitalisation leading to delinquency in adolescence, to severe lack of cognitive and emotional stimulation leading to subnormal intellectual functioning in adoptive homes in childhood. In evaluating the evidence our first difficulty is that, with one exception (Koluchová), there is a total lack of detailed description of the social transactions between the child and his caretakers and peers following the early depriving experience.

Furthermore it is absolutely clear that, among other things, the research findings reported in this book are to some degree attributable to the type of sample studied, the life histories of its members, the measures used, both of the individual and his environment, the crudity or sensitivity of such measures, the duration of study, to name but a few. The different estimates (68-72 per cent versus 22 per cent) in the Prugh and others, Schaffer and Douglas studies (see pages 81–7) of immediate disturbances in behaviour following early hospitalisation are a case in point. It could well be that each estimate is correct for the sample concerned and the particular type of measure of disturbed behaviour used. Yet these estimates at face value are wildly discrepant. Thus there is great difficulty in comparing the results of one study with another.

In order to summarise and evaluate the evidence, a skeletal sketch of the more important studies follows:

1 **Davis** (1947: chapter 3 above) Six-year-old girl rescued from life-long isolation with deaf-mute mother. Specialist speech treatment. Very rapid normalisation from rickets, lack of speech, severely subnormal ability. Limited follow-up to age fourteen. Regarded then as normal.

2 **Koluchová** (1972 and chapter 5 above) Twin boys, developed normally first in an institution, and later with an aunt until aged eighteen months. Then isolated and cruelly treated until rescued at age seven. Rickets, I.Q.s in 40s, little speech, fears of normal objects, unable to understand meaning of pictures. Rapid I.Q. increments, then slower and smaller to normality. Educational retardation decreasing to normality. Severe emotional maladjustment decreasing under unusual adoptive care; now rare traces of the past. Essentially normal outcome. I.Q.s 100 and 101 at age fourteen.

3 **Goldfarb** (1943) Two groups, 'matched for heredity' from very bad orphanage. One adopted in early months, other adopted about

age three. Age ten to fourteen on follow-up. Average Wechsler I.Q.s for early versus late adopted, 95 and 72, respectively. All-round inferiority of latter on other measures. But what selective factors were associated with early versus late adoption? Would a longer follow-up have reduced the gap? (see Clarke and Clarke 1954, 1958, whose follow-up of deprived children *started* later than the age at which Goldfarb's ceased).

4 **skeels and Dye** (1939); **Skeels** (1966) Early life of twenty-five children in exceedingly bad orphanage; thirteen moved to a mental-retardation institution at average of nineteen months, then moved aged three and a half to adoptive homes of rather average status. Diverging I.Q.s, and above all, diverging life experiences of thirteen experimental and one contrast case, compared with other contrast cases. Poor matching of groups, but contrast group initially superior. Wide range of rather average outcomes for experimental subjects, rather homogeneous poor outcomes for contrast cases (except one with fortunate life experiences). In spite of uniform early experience in orphanage, and in the case of the experimental group relatively late adoption after two different residential experiences, outcome related to life-long changes or non-changes in environment.

5 **Dennis** (1973: chapter 8 above) Foundlings from very bad institution either adopted at different ages by Lebanese or American adopters, or, if female, transferred about six years to another very bad institution, if male to a very good one. Outcome related to direction of environmental shift or non-shift. Only about half of those adopted were available for study. Evidence of selective adoption policies relating to age at adoption. Average I.Q. outcome for those adopted before age two, subaverage outcome for those adopted later. Very poor status of older institutionalised girls, sub-average for boys. Did differing 'age of adoption' policies or adoption preferences impinge on constitutionally different children? Were children adopted at very different ages taken on by different types of home? Why are results somewhat discrepant with those of Skeels, when the experimental children were all adopted after age two?

6 **Tizard and Rees** (1974 and chapter 9 above) Sixty-five children reared from infancy in three residential nurseries. High staff–child ratio, material provision good; multiple caretaking, constant staff changes, official disapproval of close personal relationships. Between ages two and four and a half, twenty-four were adopted and fifteen restored to their mothers. At age four and a half

I.Q.s were at least average, the adopted children had higher I.Q.s and appeared more stable than those restored or remaining in institution. At eight and a half there was inevitable sample attrition. Children still average or above; earlier adopted higher than a small group adopted after four and a half, or children restored to parents. Children remaining in institution had declined slightly in I.Q. ($n = 7$). Reading ages reported; little difference among the groups.

7 **Kadushin** (1970: chapter 11 above) Large sample of eighty-plus I.Q., healthy children, typically coming from large families in substandard circumstances, often below poverty level, and suffering physical neglect. Natural parents showed a picture of considerable personal pathology compounded of promiscuity, mental deficiency, alcholism, imprisonment and psychosis. At average age three and a half, the children had been removed from their homes by court order, and after an average of 2·3 changes of foster home, were placed for adoption just over average age seven, and followed up at an average of almost fourteen years. Adoptive parents older than natural parents and of a considerably higher socioeconomic level. Data obtained from agency records and detailed statements by adoptive parents. The children in general were a source of satisfaction to the adoptive parents and showed a greater degree of psychic health and stability than might have been expected from their background. It is not precisely known how many were excluded from adoption by virtue of low I.Q.s. Population background very similar to those in the Clarke and Clarke, and Hilda Lewis studies. Outcome also similar in so far as it is better than would have been predicted (1) from social history; (2) after several foster changes; and (3) following very late adoption.

8 **Rathbun and others** (1958, 1965) Refugee children (thirty-eight), age range five months to ten years, brought to United States from Korea and Greece, hence change of language and culture. Considerable personal disturbance on arrival; adopted by thirty-three families, five children unavailable for six-year follow-up. On average these had above average health, I.Q. and general competence; twenty-one had adequate or superior adjustment, ten problematic and two were clinically disturbed. Authors believe problematic adjustment arose in response to present rather than past problems. The picture is one of 'almost incredible resiliency'. No background details exist, almost certainly a group selected by overseas welfare workers in refugee camps.

9 **Lewis** (1954) Five hundred children with poor backgrounds, the worst in Kent, majority aged over five years, admitted to reception centre. Wide range of presenting disorders (delinquency 32 per cent; severely neurotic 18 per cent; psychopathic 3 per cent; normal behaviour but with slight neurotic symptoms 21 per cent; normal behaviour 25 per cent). One sample of a hundred followed up two years later by means of personal interviews with staff, foster parents, teachers and systematic recording of school data. Another sample of a hundred and twenty followed up by post. Wide variety of placements; no one type of placement had a monopoly of success. Essentially similar results from both follow-ups. Whereas on admission only 15 per cent of the samples had been in 'good' condition, two years later this had increased to 39 per cent. The 25 per cent in 'fair' condition increased to 36 per cent. Thus 75 per cent of the most deprived were in 'good' or 'fair' condition after only two years of better experiences.

10 **Clarke and Clarke** (1954, 1959); **Reiman** (1958) Two total samples of certified 'feeble-minded' adolescents and young adults drawn from bad or very bad homes (independently assessed from case histories) followed by, on average, several moves through residential schools or institutions, followed by certification. All exhibited mild subnormality, poor scholastic attainments, poor social competence and work capacity. I.Q.s and measures of work and social adjustment taken $2\frac{1}{4}$, $4\frac{1}{2}$ and 6 years after initial assessment. Greater (and substantial) I.Q. and social improvement in those from the worst homes. All groups had average ages in the mid-twenties at follow-up, but such changes could occur at any time between age fifteen and about thirty, and perhaps slowly and steadily throughout the period. Estimates for change were very conservative owing to selective sample wastage from the loss of the more successful individuals. All data collected independently before being brought together.

11 **Bronfenbrenner**'s (1974: chapter 14 above) review of the twelve most adequate studies of pre-school intervention in group settings outlines a number of very clear findings. Almost without exception children showed substantial I.Q. and other cognitive gains during the programmes, by comparison with control groups, attaining or exceeding average norms for their age. By the first or second year after completion, the children showed a progressive deceleration in I.Q., and by the third or fourth year this had fallen back

towards the lower 90s and below, with sharpest decline after entry into the regular school.

Similar findings emerged in home-based tutoring programmes. Reviewing a further nine studies on intervention with both parents and their children, from the first year of life until the children had reached elementary school, it emerged that such programmes were associated with substantial I.Q. increments, still evident three to four years after their termination, presumably because of alterations in parent–child interaction, reflected also in gains for younger siblings. Children involved in an intensive programme of parent intervention, achieved greater and more enduring gains than in group programmes. There has as yet been no adequate follow-up of parent-intervention programmes, so it is not possible to state to what extent such a procedure may be effective. Furthermore Bronfenbrenner makes clear that those mothers who agree to participate in controlled studies of this kind are a self-selected sample from the 'upper crust' of poor families.

12 **Kagan** (chapter 7 above) studied Guatemalan, rural and city children of different ages. From a position of considerable retardation during early life, related to environmental conditions and modes of child care, the rural children advanced in several cognitive areas by pre-adolescence, attaining Guatemala City and American norms. The report emphasises plasticity of development and its potential discontinuity in relation to changing environmental demands, and that early retardation has no important implication for ultimate normality.

13 **Douglas** (1975) Subsamples of large national sample, those who had experienced early or repeated admission to hospital. Relations found between these admissions and ratings in adolescence. Surprisingly 68 per cent, according to mothers' reports, showed no disturbance on discharge, but suggestion of a 'sleeper effect' apparent in adolescence. Such later ratings for 'troublesomeness', 'poor reading', 'delinquency', 'unstable job pattern' clearly associated with early hospitalisation. Even stronger associations with longer periods of admission after five years. Douglas indicates that the 'evidence . . . though highly suggestive, does not establish the existence of a causal relationship between early hospital admissions and later behaviour. For that an experimental study would be required.' Yet he also shows that children hospitalised in the early years are more likely to return to hospital, to have persisting

physical disability, to be boys, from large families, with manual-worker parents who take little interest in their schooling. We believe data are inconclusive allowing either Douglas's interpretation or our own that early hospitalisation (and particularly repeated admissions) represent significant actuarial signs of present and future disadvantage.

14 **Bowlby and others** (1956) Sixty children who before age four had spent a period (range less than six months – more than two years) in a T.B. sanatorium, matched with three controls per child, adjacent in age in same school class in follow-up. Latter took place within age range six years ten months to thirteen years seven months. Average I.Q. 107, S.D. 22·8, controls 110, S.D. 16·8. Capacity for friendship normal. Maladjustment 63 per cent compared with 42 per cent regarded as usual expectancy. This excess 21 per cent might have arisen from social class and family contexts rather than separation and hospitalisation. Indeed, authors carefully point out that such children tend to 'come from families where other members . . . have tuberculosis, so that illness and death are common with their attendant disturbed family relations and depressed economy' (1956 p. 213). Thus 10 per cent of the mothers were dead at the time of follow-up. The authors indicate that 'part of the emotional disturbance . . . is to be attributed to factors other than separation' (see Rutter).

15 **Rutter** (1971) Part of a total sample of nine- to twelve-year-old children on the Isle of Wight, plus a representative group of London families in which one or both parents had been in psychiatric care. Anti-social behaviour in boys was associated with ratings of parents' marriage, not separation experiences. Where separation had occurred, the cause was relevant: holiday or illness, no effect; family discord or deviance, larger effect. On the whole separation due to parental death had little effect. It is also suggested that the longer the family disharmony lasts, the greater the risk to the children.

As yet there is no clearly developed comprehensive model of how the physical and social environment affects children during the course of growth. We do, however, have evidence which calls into question certain assumptions which appear to have guided the thinking of a large number of professional workers. These are stated in the form of hypotheses. In each case, of the studies assembled in this book, the most pertinent are cited.

The generic hypothesis, to which the others are related, states that environmental events in the first few years of life influence the developing organism in a way which is critical for later development.

HYPOTHESIS 1

What is believed to be essential for mental health is that an infant and young child should experience a warm, intimate and continuous relationship with his mother (or permanent mother-substitute) in which both find satisfaction and enjoyment' (Bowlby 1951).

This hypothesis has already been extensively examined by Rutter (1972) in a book entitled *Maternal Deprivation Reassessed*, and by Morgan (1975); further contrary evidence is provided in connection with other more specific hypotheses.

HYPOTHESIS 2

That temporary separation of a very young child from its mother may result in later behaviour problems.

This widely held hypothesis must be subdivided into at least two research areas: hospitalisation, involving much more than mother–child separation; and other brief separations.

1 Douglas (pages 81–7 and summary 13) shows an association between early hospitalisation and adolescent problems, but indicates himself that the problem is complex (see discussion).

2 Rutter (pages 153–86 and summary 15) presents contrary evidence, emphasising that the nature of the separation experience is important.

HYPOTHESIS 3

That young children cannot develop normally in an institution.
Contrary evidence: Skeels (pages 214–21 and summary 4); Bowlby and others (page 80 and summary 14); Tizard and Rees (pages 135–52 and summary 6); Klackenberg (page 9). The evidence suggests that the quality of the institution is important.

HYPOTHESIS 4

That where children have suffered from adversity, late adoption cannot be successful in bringing them to normal intellectual functioning or emotional adjustment.

Goldfarb (pages 9–10 and summary 3) offers evidence in support; and Wayne Dennis's (pages 122–34 and summary 5) data appear to confirm this hypothesis for average intellectual status. Certainly among those adopted after age two there were many children who were subnormal. Unfortunately nothing is known of the natural parents, but there may well have been an unusual combination of biologically determined vulnerability and severe social deprivation, a possible point of difference between these children and Koluchová's twins. So far as social-emotional adjustment is concerned, the evidence of Lewis (pages 74–5 and summary 9), Rathbun and others (pages 76–9 and summary 8) and Kadushin (pages 187–210 and summary 7) strongly suggests that late removal of children from adverse circumstances should lead in most cases to a satisfactory outcome.

HYPOTHESIS 5
That there is a critical period about the age of two for normal (average) cognitive development (Dennis pages 122–34 and summary 5).
Contrary evidence: Davis (pages 35–43 and summary 1); Koluchová (pages 45–66 and summary 2); Sutton and Francis (pages 31–4) and Kagan (pages 97–101 and summary 12). Clarke and Clarke (pages 71–4 and summary 10) found that some of their population of formerly deprived certified mental retardates reached average status during late adolescence and early adult years.

HYPOTHESIS 6
That early compensatory educational programmes of demonstrable efficacy should have permanent effects regardless of later cognitive and social deprivation or stimulation.
Contrary evidence: Kirk (pages 221–3); Gray and Klaus (pages 229–46) and Bronfenbrenner (pages 247–56 and summary 11).

In short, if there is a critical period, it is difficult to know how to define it; clearly chronological age is not a good contender; mental age fares worse; perhaps one should consider social age? Moreover, it does not seem any more promising to think in terms of critical events: apart from those which make it impossible to sustain life, *it appears that there is virtually no psychosocial adversity to which some children have not been subjected, yet later recovered*, granted a radical change of circumstances.

Attention should perhaps be drawn to the fact that Goldfarb (summary 3), Kadushin (summary 7), Dennis (summary 5) and Tizard and Rees (summary 6) all agree independently that those adopted later had a poorer outcome than those adopted early. But, in this context, 'later' describes a number of widely different chronological ages. The samples which they studied differed from one another; on the one hand, Goldfarb and Dennis were recounting the sequelae of early and very austere or impoverished institutional upbringing. On the other hand, Tizard's children came from good children's homes. Kadushin's, however, had been taken from inadequate or adverse parental homes, then fostered and finally adopted. If sample differences between these four studies were irrelevant to the general principle that late adoption is less satisfactory than early, this might seem strongly supportive for the power of early experience. One must, however, in light of other evidence, raise the alternative possibilities that there may be selective differences between late and early adoptees, such that one is dealing with different populations or different types of adoptive homes. Finally, it has been clear that one mechanism by which the effects of adversity may be perpetuated is reflected in the Transactional Model (see page 14). The child's problems may selectively alter the new environment, making it less satisfactory, and this in turn reinforces problem behaviour. Such effects may well become attenuated in good circumstances, and are rapidly overcome in the ideal situation (e.g. Koluchová). Hence while these findings are important 'natural history' descriptions, they do not unequivocally either support or deny the importance of early experience. Other findings (e.g. Davis summary 1; Koluchova summary 2 and Sutton and Francis pages 31–4) may legitimately sway the interpretation.

It is perhaps no coincidence that evidence of personal change from advantage to disadvantage is on the whole lacking. Fortunate young children appear rarely to suffer great and prolonged deprivation in later childhood; it is difficult to be sure of the theoretical implications of the data summarised here in the absence of its converse.

As indicated in chapter 1, the view that the early years of infant development are of crucial importance has become so widely accepted as to be implicit in the writings and decision-taking of research workers and practitioners alike. We have assembled a body of evidence which suggests a reformulation; this should not be interpreted literally as a counter-balance, which might be an equal and opposite extreme, but rather as an attempt to achieve a balanced view.

H.R. Schaffer (personal communication) unaware of our 1968 formulation, independently reached a rather similar conclusion to our own in an unpublished paper delivered at the annual meeting of the British Association for the Advancement of Science in 1971. He then indicated that there was little firm evidence on the alleged potency of early experience. Subsequently he has developed these ideas, arguing that 'early experiences, however drastic at the time, do not necessarily set into motion patterns of behaviour that cannot subsequently be modified.' Single delineated occurrences rarely produce permanent effects, although one misfortune may initiate 'a whole sequence of further misfortunes, each confirming the child's expectation of what life has to offer him . . .' These then involve situations which continue to sustain and encourage original responses. Schaffer also draws attention to changes in parental behaviour and their interactional and reciprocal relations with their children. He points out that even such factors as the effects of minimal brain damage in the child may in one family be modified and normalised; in another they may be exaggerated and become the starting point of considerable behaviour problems. An interactional model of development is thus much more valid than a critical period model (Schaffer 1976). Schaffer's independently initiated reappraisal of the alleged importance of early experience thus offers substantial support to our own.

Although, as we have indicated, there is at the present time no clearly formulated model of child development, nor, as we see it, has empirical research advanced sufficiently to build one, there is a growing consensus that ultimately such a model must take account of discontinuities as well as continuities, the child as an active agent in social transactions, and the potentiality for modification of behaviour patterns within the limits set by constitutional factors (Kagan and Klein 1973; Clarke and Clarke 1976; Schaffer

1976; Sameroff and Chandler 1975). We have already drawn attention to the contribution of the latter writers who indicate that the outcome of pregnancy and perinatal disorders cannot be accommodated either by Main Effect or Interactional Models for constitutional and environmental influences; rather a Transactional Model is more appropriate.

As a general rule, only when information regarding the nature of the subsequent caretaking environment has also been taken into account have such long-range predictions about the later consequences of pregnancy and birth complications been successful. These results argue strongly against any 'simple and sovereign' approach to the definition of risk and emphasize the necessity of assuming a much more transactional attitude toward the study of childhood vulnerability. Unfortunately those investigators who have directed their attention to the study of the caretaking environment have, in turn, largely ignored the contributions of the child and his or her cumulative prenatal and perinatal complications, to his or her own social environment. As a consequence this literature has tended to be as one-sided and unilateral as the research on prenatal complications already reviewed and rarely reflects the transactional emphasis which seems to be required . . . In the light of the great variety and range of influences on development, there are a surprisingly small number of developmental outcomes. The human organism appears to have been programmed by the course of evolution to produce normal developmental outcomes under all but the most adverse of circumstances (Waddington, 1966). Any understanding of deviancies in outcome must be seen in the light of this self-righting and self-organizing tendency which appears to move children towards normality in the face of pressure towards deviation. (Sameroff and Chandler 1975)

This is what elsewhere we have termed resilience, presumably an internal factor, but one should not ignore the effects of the increasingly wider experiences such a child undergoes, outside the context of adverse family or other influences, which may assist this self-righting tendency.

The evidence we have outlined supports such a view. All the studies are concerned with children who have suffered some social disadvantage and, in so far as one can ascertain the facts, the majority had parents of average-to-low personal status in terms of intelligence, achievement, adjustment and socioeconomic status. Unless one were incautious enough to overlook constitutional factors, one would hardly expect the average ultimate outcome to be very superior to the general population. And this is, of course, the case. However, one may legitimately argue that the outcome might have been a great deal worse.

A review of the literature on child development, including the material summarised here, suggests certain implications for future research. There has been a disproportionate amount of time and effort devoted to the earliest years of development. We suspect that one reason for this is the belief in the long-term implications of bio-social factors operating in the pre-school stage. Far too little is as yet known, in a detailed way, about cognitive and social behaviours at later stages, or their biological and environmental correlates. Developmental research requires effort over a broad spectrum of time if it is to be of any significance. In this connection a methodological point requires emphasis: unless it can be positively shown that there was a significant discontinuity between early and late environmental circumstances, no conclusions can legitimately be drawn concerning the effect of the former.

What emerges very strongly from our evidence is the need for a greater recognition of the possibility of personal change following misfortune. For example, as Kadushin (personal communication) makes clear, in children offered late for adoption, having very poor backgrounds, an I.Q. score below 80 probably prevented an unknown number from even being considered for such placement, in a situation already perceived as highly risky. Thus the perception of risk, based upon conceptual models which may be wholly or partially incorrect, leads to administrative decisions and their possible self-fulfilling prophecies. Perhaps the single most important finding is thus that for an unknown number of children the options for personal change following environmental change are open during the whole of development, even up to young adulthood.

It must, however, equally be stressed that constitutional factors appear to be responsible both for individual differences and for upper limits to improvement.

It is unclear whether the limits to personal change are the same throughout the period of development, or whether, as we rather suspect, they get progressively smaller as age increases and as personal characteristics in adolescence and young adult life begin to achieve an autonomy and self-perpetuation. This is our so-called 'wedge' hypothesis, suggesting a greater potential responsiveness during early life and childhood at the 'thick' end, tailing off to little responsiveness in adulthood, the 'thin' end of the wedge. This hypothesis is difficult to test because children needing help either do or do not get it rather early in life; and the extreme cases of social isolation can scarcely remain undetected beyond the age of school entry. Hence data on comparable environmental changes at very different ages hardly exist (Clarke and Clarke 1976).

Early in this chapter we thought it right to indicate what this book is *not* about; it may be equally useful to outline what are *not* the implications. The swing of the pendulum which resulted from Bowlby's (1951) monograph had many humane effects, sensitising the public to the needs of children. It would be more than unfortunate if this book played any part in a reaction against the new humanism, on the mistaken grounds that 'it doesn't matter what happens early in life'. Thus while the evidence does suggest that no mother of a very young child should feel bound to remain at home (provided satisfactory alternative caretaking arrangements can be made) equally, no mother should feel that her responsibilities diminish after her child becomes older. Nor does the evidence condone bad institutions, or 'problem families' or refugee camps, simply because their unfortunate effects can, in many cases, be reversed. Nor would we wish to see nursery schools either opened or closed as a result of this debate. That such schools fail to show long-term effects is no argument against their existence, both for the present benefit to the child and also to his mother. There is absolutely no implication that infancy and early childhood are unimportant, only that their long-term role is *by itself* very limited.

The way in which children are perceived and handled is intimately affected by the prevailing *zeitgeist*. In spite of the currently more humane attitude to children (mentioned above) they are not always accorded prime importance when their interests and those of their parents are in conflict. More usually, of course, such needs are in harmony.

What then are the main implications? First and foremost, the whole of development is important, not merely the early years. There is as yet no indication that a given stage is clearly more formative than others; in the long-term all may be important. We are now entering the era when empirical findings, based upon the newer and more powerful methodologies of the behavioural sciences, have the possibility of dictating appropriate policies. Thus our relative dependence upon fashions in child rearing may give way to a more careful empirical analysis of the needs of individual children, to the manner in which these needs can best be satisfied, to the methods by which the disadvantaged may best be helped, and indeed to diminishing the pathology of society. The widespread use of over-simple notions about children, of inadequate social action dependent on such notions, and the unwitting employment of self-fulfilling prophecies, need to give way to imaginative, yet independently and austerely evaluated experiments which depend only on the assumption that what one does for a child at any age, provided it is maintained, plays a part in shaping his development within the limits imposed by genetic and constitutional factors.

References

CHAPTER 1

AINSWORTH, M.D., ANDRY, R.G., HARLOW, R.G., LEBOVICI, S., MEAD, M., PRUGH, D.G. and WOOTTON, B. (1962) *Deprivation of Maternal Care: Reassessment of its Effects* (Geneva: World Health Organization)

BAERS, M. (1954) 'Women workers and home responsibilities', *International Labour Review* 69, 338-55

BLOOM, B.S. (1964) *Stability and Change in Human Characteristics* (London: John Wiley)

BOWLBY, J. (1951) *Maternal Care and Mental Health* (Geneva: World Health Organization)

BOWLBY, J., AINSWORTH, M.D., BOSTON, M. and ROSENBLUTH, D. (1956) 'The effects of mother–child separation: a follow-up study', *British Journal of Medical Psychology* 29, 211-47

BURTT, H.E. (1932) 'The retention of early memories', in W. Dennis (ed.) *Readings in Child Psychology*, 2nd ed. (Englewood Cliffs, N.J., 1963: Prentice-Hall)

CAMPBELL, D., SANDERSON, R.E. and LAVERTY, S.G. (1964) 'Characteristics of a conditioned response in human subjects during extinction trials following a single traumatic conditioning trial', *Journal of Abnormal and Social Psychology* 68, 627-39

CLARKE, A.D.B. (1968) 'Learning and human development – the 42nd Maudsley Lecture', *British Journal of Psychiatry* 114, 161-77

CLARKE, A.D.B. and CLARKE, A.M. (1954) 'Cognitive changes in the feebleminded', *British Journal of Psychology* 45, 173-9

CLARKE, A.D.B. and CLARKE, A.M. (1959) 'Recovery from the effects of deprivation', *Acta Psychologica* 16, 137-44

CLARKE, A.D.B. and CLARKE, A.M. (1960) 'Recent advances in the study of deprivation', *Journal of Child Psychology and Psychiatry* 1, 26-36

CLARKE, A.D.B. and CLARKE, A.M. (1972) 'Consistency and variability in the growth of human characteristics', in W.D. Wall and V.P. Varma (eds) *Advances in Educational Psychology I*, 32-52 (London: Univ. of London Press)

CLARKE, A.D.B., CLARKE, A.M. and REIMAN, S. (1958) 'Cognitive and social changes in the feebleminded – three further studies', *British Journal of Psychology* 49, 144–57

CLARKE, A.M. and CLARKE, A.D.B. (1976) 'Problems in comparing the effects of environmental change at different ages', in H. McGurk (ed.) *Ecological Factors in Human Development* (Amsterdam: North-Holland Publishing Company)

CONNOLLY, K. (1972) 'Learning and the concept of critical periods in infancy', *Developmental Medicine and Child Neurology* 14, 705–14

DENENBERG, V.H. (1972) (ed.) *Readings in the Development of Behaviour* (Stamford, Connecticut: Sinauer Associates)

DOBBING, J. and SMART, J.L. (1974) 'Vulnerability of developing brain and behaviour', in R.M. Gaze and M.J. Keating (eds) *Development and Regeneration in the Nervous System, British Medical Bulletin* 30 No 2, 164–8 (London: British Council)

DOUGLAS, J.W.B. (1975) 'Early hospital admissions and later disturbances of behaviour and learning', *Developmental Medicine and Child Neurology* 17, 456–80

FOGELMAN, K. and GOLDSTEIN, H. (1976) 'Social factors associated with changes in educational attainment between 7 and 11 years of age', *Educational Studies*, in press

FREUD, S. (1910) 'Infantile sexuality. Three contributions to the sexual theory', transl. A.A. Brill, *Nervous and Mental Disease Monographs*, No 7

FREUD, S. (1949) *An Outline of Psycho-analysis*, transl. J. Strachey (London: Hogarth Press)

FULLER, J.L. and WALLER, M.B. (1962) 'Is early experience different?', in E.L. Bliss (ed.) *Roots of Behaviour* (New York: Harper and Row), chapter 16

GOLDFARB, W. (1943) 'The effects of early institutional care on adolescent personality', *Journal of Experimental Education* 12, 106–29

HARLOW, H.F. and SUOMI, S.J. (1970) 'The nature of love – simplified', *American Psychologist* 25, 161–8

HEBB, D.O. (1949) *The Organization of Behavior* (New York and London: John Wiley)

JENSEN, A.R. (1969) 'How much can we boost IQ and scholastic achievement?', *Harvard Educational Review* 39, 1 123

KADUSHIN, A. (1970) *Adopting Older Children* (New York: Columbia Univ. Press)

KAGAN, J. and KLEIN, R.E. (1973) 'Cross-cultural perspectives on early development', *American Psychologist* 28, 947–61

KAGAN, J. and MOSS, H.A. (1962) *Birth to Maturity* (New York: John Wiley)

KLACKENBERG, G. (1956) 'Studies in maternal deprivation in infants' homes', *Acta Paediatrica* 45, 1–12

LENNEBERG, E.H. (1967) *Biological Foundations of Language* (New York and London: John Wiley)

LOCKE, J. (1632-1704) (1964) *Some Thoughts Concerning Education*, F.W. Garforth (ed.) (London: Heinemann)

MELLSOP, G.W. (1972) 'Psychiatric patients seen as children and adults: childhood predictors of adult illness', *Journal of Child Psychology and Psychiatry* 13, 91-101

MILL, J. (1816) 'Education', *Encyclopaedia Britannica*, 5th ed.; see also Burston, W.H. (1969) *James Mill on Education* (Cambridge: Cambridge Univ. Press)

MORGAN, P. (1975) *Child Care: Sense and Fable* (London: Temple Smith)

NOVAK, M.A. and HARLOW, H.F. (1975) 'Social recovery of monkeys isolated for the first year of life: I. Rehabilitation and therapy', *Developmental Psychology* 11, 453–65

O'CONNOR, N. (1956) 'The evidence for the permanently disturbing effects of mother–child separation', *Acta Psychologica* 12, 174–91

PINNEAU, S.R. (1955a) 'The infantile disorders of hospitalism and anaclitic depression', *Psychological Bulletin* 52, 429–52

PINNEAU, S.R. (1955b) 'Reply to Dr Spitz', *Psychological Bulletin* 52, 459–62

PLATO (428–348 B.C.) (1955) *The Republic*, transl. H.D.P. Lee (Harmondsworth: Penguin)

PRUGH, D.G., STAUB, E.M., SANDS, H.H., KIRSCHBAUM, R.M. and LENIHAN, E.A. (1953) 'A study of the emotional reactions of children and families to hospitalization and illness', *American Journal of Orthopsychiatry* 23, 70-106

QUINTILIAN (*c.* A.D 35–100) (1965) *On the Early Education of the Citizen-Orator*, transl. J.S. Watson, J.J. Murphy (ed.) (New York: Bobbs-Merrill)

RATHBUN, C., MCLAUGHLIN, H., BENNETT, O. and GARLAND, J.A. (1965) 'Later adjustment of children following radical separation from family and culture', *American Journal of Orthopsychiatry* 35, 604–9

ROBINS, L.N. (1966) *Deviant Children Grown Up* (Baltimore: Williams and Wilkins)

RUSSELL, B. (1959) *Wisdom of the West* (London: Macdonald)

RUTTER, M. (1972) *Maternal Deprivation Reassessed* (Harmondsworth: Penguin)

RUTTER, M., BIRCH, H.G., THOMAS, A. and CHESS, S. (1964) 'Temperamental characteristics in infancy and the later development of behaviour disorders', *British Journal of Psychiatry* 110, 651–61

RUTTER, M. and MADGE, N. (1976) *Cycles of Disadvantage* (London: Heinemann, for Social Science Research Council)

SAMEROFF, A.J. and CHANDLER, M.J. (1975) 'Reproductive risk and the continuum of caretaking casualty', in F.D. Horowitz, M. Hetherington, S. Scarr-Salapatek and G. Siegel (eds) *Review of Child Development Research*, vol. 4 (Chicago: Univ. of Chicago Press)

SCHAFFER, H.R. (1958) 'Objective observations of personality development in early infancy', *British Journal of Medical Psychology* 31, 174–83

SCHAFFER, H.R. (1976) *Mothering* (London: Open Books; New York: Harvard Univ. Press)

SCHLAEGEL, T.F. (1953) 'Visual experience and visual imagery', *Journal of Genetic Psychology* 83, 265–77

SCOTT, J.P. (1968) *Early Experience and the Organization of Behaviour* (Belmont, Calif.: Wadsworth)

SEGLOW, J., KELLMER PRINGLE, M. and WEDGE, P. (1972) *Growing Up Adopted* (Slough: National Foundation for Educational Research)

SKODAK, M. and SKEELS, H.M. (1949) 'A final follow-up study of one hundred adopted children', *Journal of Genetic Psychology* 75, 85–125

SLUCKIN, W. (1971) (ed.) *Early Learning and Early Experience* (Harmondsworth: Penguin)

SPITZ, R.A. (1945) 'Hospitalism: an inquiry into the genesis of psychiatric conditions in early childhood', *Psychoanalytic Study of the Child* 1, 53–74

SPITZ, R.A. (1946a) 'Hospitalism: a follow-up report', *Psychoanalytic Study of the Child* 2, 113–17

SPITZ, R.A. (1946b) 'Anaclitic depression', *Psychoanalytic Study of the Child* 2, 313–42

SPITZ, R.A. (1955) 'Reply to Dr Pinneau', *Psychological Bulletin* 52, 453–9

STORR, A. (1975) 'A human condition', review article, *Sunday Times*, 28 September

SUOMI, S.J. and HARLOW, H.F. (1972) 'Social rehabilitation of isolate-reared monkeys', *Developmental Psychology* 6, 487–96

TRASLER, G. (1960) *In Place of Parents: a Study of Foster Care* (London: Routledge and Kegan Paul)

WACHS, T.D. (1973) 'Reinstatement of early experiences and later learning: an animal analogue for human development', *Developmental Psychobiology* 6, 437–44

WATSON, J.B. (1928) *Psychological Care of Infant and Child* (New York: Norton)

WHITE, B.L. (1971) 'An analysis of excellent early educational practices: preliminary report', *Interchange: A Journal of Educational Studies* 2, 86–7 (Toronto: Ontario Institute for Studies in Education); quoted in L.J. Stone, H.T. Smith and L.B. Murphy (1974) (eds) *The Competent Infant* (London: Tavistock)

WOODS, P.J. (1959) 'The effects of free and restricted environmental experience on problem-solving behaviour in the rat', *Journal of Comparative and Physiological Psychology* 52, 399–402

WOODWARD, W.H. (1905) *Vittorino Da Feltre and other Humanist Educators* (Cambridge: Cambridge Univ. Press)

WORLD HEALTH ORGANIZATION (1951) *Expert Committee on Mental Health, Report on the Second Session,* Technical Report Series, No 31 (Geneva: World Health Organization)

YARROW, L.J. (1961) 'Maternal deprivation: toward an empirical and conceptual re-evaluation', *Psychological Bulletin* 58, 459–90

CHAPTER 2

BETTELHEIM, B. (1959) 'Feral children and autistic children', *American Journal of Sociology* 64, 455–67

CLARKE, A.D.B. (1972) 'Commentary on Koluchová's "Severe deprivation in twins: a case study" ', *Journal of Child Psychology and Psychiatry* 13, 103–6

DAVIS, K. (1940) 'Extreme social isolation of a child', *American Journal of Sociology* 45, 554–65

DAVIS, K. (1947) 'Final note on a case of extreme isolation', *American Journal of Sociology* 52, 432–7

DOBBING, J. and SMART, J.L. (1974) 'Vulnerability of developing brain and behaviour', in R.M. Gaze and M.J. Keating (eds) *Development and Regeneration in the Nervous System, British Medical Bulletin* 30 No 2, 164–8 (London: British Council)

GESELL, A. (1940) *Wolf Child and Human Child* (New York: Harper)

ITARD, J.M.G. (1932) *The Wild Boy of Aveyron,* transl. G. and M. Humphrey (New York: Appleton-Century-Crofts)

KOLUCHOVÁ, J. (1972) 'Severe deprivation in twins: a case study', *Journal of Child Psychology and Psychiatry* 13, 107–14

LENNEBERG, E.H. (1967) *Biological Foundations of Language* (New York and London: John Wiley)

LURIA, A.R. and YUDOVICH, F.Ia. (1971) *Speech and the Development of Mental Processes in the Child* (Harmondsworth: Penguin)

MASON, M.K (1942) 'Learning to speak after six and a half years of silence', *Journal of Speech Disorders* 7, 295–304

OGBURN, W.F. (1956) 'The wolf boy of Agra', *American Journal of Sociology* 64, 449-54

OGBURN, W.F. and BOSE, N.K. (1959) 'On the trail of the wolf-children', *Genetic Psychology Monographs* 60, 117-93

STONE, L.J. (1954) 'A critique of studies on infant isolation', *Child Development* 25, 9-20

TREDGOLD, R.F. and SODDY, K. (1956) *A Text-book of Mental Deficiency* (London: Baillière, Tindall and Cox)

CHAPTER 3

DAVIS, K. (1940) 'Extreme social isolation of a child', *American Journal of Sociology* 45, 554-65

MASON, M.K. (1942) 'Learning to speak after six and a half years of silence', *Journal of Speech Disorders* 7, 295-304

MAXFIELD, F.N. 'What happens when the social environment of a child approaches zero', unpublished manuscript

SINGH, J.A.L. and ZINGG, R.M. (1941) *Wolf-Children and Feral Man* (New York: Harper)

CHAPTER 4

LANGMEIER, J. and MATĚJČEK, Z. (1968) *Psychická deprivace v dětství* (Prague: S.Z.D.N.)

CHAPTER 5

CLARKE, A.D.B. (1972) 'Commentary on Koluchová's "Severe deprivation in twins: a case study" ', *Journal of Child Psychology and Psychiatry* 13, 103-6

KOLUCHOVÁ, J. (1972) 'Severe deprivation in twins: a case study', *Journal of Child Psychology and Psychiatry* 13, 107-14

LANGMEIER, J. and MATĚJČEK, Z. (1968) *Psychická deprivace v dětství* (Prague: S.Z.D.N.)

CHAPTER 6

BOWLBY, J. (1951) *Maternal Care and Mental Health* (Geneva: World Health Organization)

BOWLBY, J., AINSWORTH, M.D., BOSTON, M. and ROSENBLUTH, D. (1956) 'The effects of mother-child separation: a follow-up study', *British Journal of Medical Psychology* 29, 211-47

CLARKE, A.D.B. and CLARKE, A.M. (1953) 'How constant is the IQ?', *Lancet* 2, 877–80

CLARKE, A.D.B. and CLARKE, A.M. (1954) 'Cognitive changes in the feebleminded', *British Journal of Psychology* 45, 173–9

CLARKE, A.D.B. and CLARKE, A.M. (1959) 'Recovery from the effects of deprivation', *Acta Psychologica* 16, 137–44

CLARKE, A.D.B. and CLARKE, A.M. (1975) *Recent Advances in the Study of Subnormality: a Miniature Textbook* (London: National Association for Mental Health)

CLARKE, A.D.B., CLARKE, A.M. and REIMAN, S. (1958) 'Cognitive and social changes in the feebleminded – three further studies', *British Journal of Psychology* 49, 144–57

DAVIS, K. (1947) 'Final note on a case of extreme isolation', *American Journal of Sociology* 52, 432–7

DENNIS, W. (1973) *Children of the Crèche* (New York: Appleton-Century-Crofts)

DENNIS, W. and NAJARIAN, P. (1957) 'Infant development under environmental handicap', *Psychological Monographs* 71, 1–13

DOUGLAS, J.W.B. (1964) *The Home and the School* (London: MacGibbon and Kee)

DOUGLAS, J.W.B. (1975) 'Early hospital admissions and later disturbances of behaviour and learning', *Developmental Medicine and Child Neurology* 17, 456–80

DOUGLAS, J.W.B. and BLOMFIELD, J.M. (1958) *Children Under Five* (London: George Allen and Unwin)

DOUGLAS, J.W.B., ROSS, J.M. and SIMPSON, H.R. (1968) *All Our Future* (London: Peter Davies)

FREUD, A. and DANN, S. (1951) 'An experiment in group upbringing', *Psychoanalytic Study of the Child* 6, 127–68

GARDNER, D.B., HAWKES, G.R. and BURCHINAL, L.G. (1961) 'Development after non-continuous mothering', *Child Development* 32, 225–34

GOLDFARB, W. (1943) 'The effects of early institutional care on adolescent personality', *Journal of Experimental Education* 12, 106–29

KADUSHIN, A. (1970) *Adopting Older Children* (New York: Columbia Univ. Press)

KAGAN, J. and MOSS, H.A. (1962) *Birth to Maturity* (New York: John Wiley)

KOLUCHOVÁ, J. (1972) 'Severe deprivation in twins: a case study', *Journal of Child Psychology and Psychiatry* 13, 107–14

LEWIS, H. (1954) *Deprived Children* (London: Oxford Univ. Press)

MCNEMAR, Q. (1940) 'A critical examination of the University of Iowa studies of environmental influence upon the IQ', *Psychological Bulletin* 37, 63–92

PRUGH, D.G., STAUB, E.M., SANDS, H.H., KIRSCHBAUM, R.M. and LENIHAN, E.A. (1953) 'A study of the emotional reactions of children and families to hospitalization and illness', *American Journal of Orthopsychiatry* 23, 70–106

RATHBUN, C., DI VIRGILIO, L. and WALDFOGEL, S. (1958) 'The restitutive process in children following radical separation from family and culture', *American Journal of Orthopsychiatry* 28, 408–15

RATHBUN, C., MCLAUGHLIN, H., BENNETT, O. and GARLAND, J.A. (1965) 'Later adjustment of children following radical separation from family and culture', *American Journal of Orthopsychiatry* 35, 604–9

RUTTER, M. (1971) 'Parent–child separation: psychological effects on the children', *Journal of Child Psychology and Psychiatry* 12, 233–60

SCHAFFER, H.R. (1958) 'Objective observations of personality development in early infancy', *British Journal of Medical Psychology* 31, 174–83

SKEELS, H.M. (1966) 'Adult status of children with contrasting early life experiences: a follow-up study', *Monographs of the Society for Research in Child Development* 31 No 3, Serial No 105

TIZARD, B. and REES, J. (1974) 'A comparison of the effects of adoption, restoration to the natural mother, and continued institutionalization on the cognitive development of four-year-old children', *Child Development* 45, 92–9

TRASLER, G. (1960) *In Place of Parents: a Study of Foster Care* (London: Routledge and Kegan Paul)

WOLKIND, S., KRUK, S. and CHAVES, L. (1976) 'Childhood separation experiences and psycho-social status in primiparous women – preliminary findings', *British Journal of Psychiatry* 128, 391–6

CHAPTER 7

APPEL, L.F., COOPER, R.G., MCCARRELL, N., KNIGHT, J.S., YUSSEN, S.R. and FLAVELL, J.H. (1971) 'The developmental acquisition of the distinction between perceiving and memory', unpublished manuscript

BAXTER, B.L. (1966) 'Effect of visual deprivation during postnatal maturation on the electroencephalogram of the cat', *Experimental Neurology* 14, 224–37

CHOW, K.L. and STEWART, D.L. (1972) 'Reversal of structural and functional effects of long-term visual deprivation in cats', *Experimental Neurology* 34, 409–33

DENNIS, W. (1973) *Children of the Crèche* (New York: Appelton-Century-Crofts)

DENNIS, W. and NAJARIAN, P. (1957) 'Infant development under environmental handicap', *Psychological Monographs* 71, 1–13

GOMBER, J. and MITCHELL, G. (1974) 'Preliminary report on adult male isolation-reared rhesus monkeys caged with infants', *Developmental Psychology* 10, 298

GUILFORD, J.P. (1967) *The Nature of Human Intelligence* (New York: McGraw-Hill)

HAGGARD, E.A. (1973) 'Some effects of geographic and social isolation in natural settings', in J.E. Rasmussen (ed.) *Man in Isolation and Confinement* (Chicago: Aldine), 99–143

HARLOW, H.F. and HARLOW, M.K. (1966) 'Learning to love', *American Scientist* 54 No 3, 244–72

HARLOW, H.F., SCHILTZ, K.A. and HARLOW, M.K. (1969) 'The effects of social isolation on the learning performance of rhesus monkeys', in C.R. Carpenter (ed.) *Proceedings of the Second International Congress of Primatology*, vol. 1 (New York: Karger)

HESS, E.H. (1958) 'Imprinting in animals', *Scientific American* 198, 81–90

HESS, E.H. (1964) 'Imprinting in birds', *Science* 146, 1129–39

HESS, E.H. (1972) 'Imprinting in a natural laboratory', *Scientific American* 227, 24–31

HOLLOS, M. and COWAN, P.A. (1973) 'Social isolation and cognitive development: logical operations and role taking abilities in three Norwegian social settings', *Child Development* 44, 630–41

HOLTON, G. (1973) *Thematic Origins of Scientific Thought* (Cambridge, Mass.: Harvard Univ. Press)

KAGAN, J. (1971) *Change and Continuity in Infancy* (New York: John Wiley)

KAGAN, J. and KLEIN, R.E. (1973) 'Cross-cultural perspectives on early development', *American Psychologist* 28, 947–61

KAGAN, J., KLEIN, R.E., HAITH, M.M. and MORRISON, F.J. (1973) 'Memory and meaning in two cultures', *Child Development* 44, 221–3

KAGAN, J. and MOSS, H.A. (1962) *Birth to Maturity* (New York: John Wiley)

KARP, S.A. and KONSTADT, N.L. (1963) *Manual for the Children's Embedded Figures Test* (Brooklyn, New York: Cognitive Tests)

KOLUCHOVÁ, J. (1972) 'Severe deprivation in twins: a case study', *Journal of Child Psychology and Psychiatry* 13, 107–14

LORENZ, K.Z. (1965) *Evolution and the Modification of Behavior* (Chicago: Univ. of Chicago Press)

MASON, W.A. and KENNEY, M.D. (1974) 'Redirection of filial attachments in rhesus monkeys: dogs as mother surrogates', *Science* 183, 1209–11

MILLER, E.A., GOLDMAN, P.S. and ROSVOLD, H.E. (1973) 'Delayed recovery of function following orbital prefrontal lesions in infant monkeys', *Science* 182, 304–6

PIAGET, J. (1952) *The Origins of Intelligence in Children* (New York: International Universities Press)

RHEINGOLD, H.L. and BAYLEY, N. (1959) 'The later effects of an experimental modification of mothering', *Child Development* 30, 363-72

SCOTT, M.S. (1973) 'The absence of interference effects in pre-school children's picture recognition', *Journal of Genetic Psychology* 122, 121-6

SUOMI, S.J. and HARLOW, H.F. (1972) 'Social rehabilitation of isolate-reared monkeys', *Developmental Psychology* 6, 487-96

TIZARD, B. and REES, J. (1974) 'A comparison of the effects of adoption, restoration to the natural mother, and continued institutionalization on the cognitive development of four-year-old children', *Child Development* 45, 92-9

WILSON, P.D. and RIESEN, A.H. (1966) 'Visual developments in rhesus monkeys neonatally deprived of patterned light', *Journal of Comparative and Physiological Psychology* 61, 87-95

CHAPTER 8

AINSWORTH, M.D. (1962a) 'The effects of maternal deprivation: a review of findings and controversy in the context of research strategy', in *Deprivation of Maternal Care: a reassessment of its effects, Public Health Papers* (New York: World Health Organization) 14, 97-165

AINSWORTH, M.D. (1962b) 'Reversible and irreversible effects of maternal deprivation on intellectual development', in *Maternal Deprivation* (New York: Child Welfare League of America), 42-62

AL-ISSA, I. and DENNIS, W. (1970) *Cross-Cultural Studies of Behavior* (New York: Holt, Rinehart and Winston)

ASHER, E.J. (1935) 'The inadequacy of current intelligence tests for testing Kentucky mountain children', *Journal of Genetic Psychology* 46, 480-6

BOWLBY, J. (1952) *Maternal Care and Mental Health*, 2nd ed. (Geneva: World Health Organization, monog. series 2)

BURKS, B.S. (1928) 'The relative influence of nature and nurture upon mental development; a comparative study of foster-parent–foster-child resemblance and true-parent–true-child resemblance', *27th Yearbook of the National Society for the Study of Education*, vol. 1, 219-316

CASLER, L. (1961) *Maternal Deprivation; a critical review of the literature*, Monographs of the Society for Research in Child Development No 26

DENNIS, W. (1966) 'Goodenough scores, art experience and modernization', *Journal of Social Psychology* 68, 211-28

DENNIS, W. (1972) *Historical Readings in Developmental Psychology* (New York: Appleton-Century-Crofts)

EDWARDS, A.S. and JONES, L. (1938) 'An experimental and field study of North Georgia mountaineers', *Journal of Social Psychology* 9, 317–33

FREEMAN, F.N., HOLZINGER, K.J. and MITCHELL, B.C. (1928) 'The influence of environment on the intelligence, school achievement and conduct of foster children', *27th Yearbook of the National Society for the Study of Education*, vol. 1, 101–217

GOLDFARB, W. (1955) 'Emotional and intellectual consequences of psychological deprivation in infancy; a revaluation', in P.H. Hoch and J. Zubin (eds) *Psychopathology of Childhood* (New York: Grune and Stratton), 105–19

GORDON, H. (1923) *Mental and Scholastic Tests among Retarded Children*, Education Pamphlet 44 (London: Board of Education)

JENSEN, A.R. (1969) 'How much can we boost IQ and scholastic achievement?', *Harvard Educational Review* 39, 1–123

LEAHY, A.M. (1935) 'Nature-nurture and intelligence', *Genetic Psychology Monographs* 17, 235–308

POLLOCK, G.F. (1960) *Skyland* (Berryville, Va: Chesapeake Book Co.)

SHERMAN, M. and HENRY, T.R. (1933) *Hollow Folk* (New York: Thomas Y. Crowell)

SHERMAN, M. and KEY, C.B. (1932) 'The intelligence scores of isolated mountain children', *Child Development* 3, 279–90

SKEELS, H.M. (1940) 'Some Iowa studies of the mental growth of children in relation to differentials of the environment; a summary', in *Intelligence: Its Nature and Nurture, 39th Yearbook of the National Society for the Study of Education*, vol. 2, 281–308

SKEELS, H.M. (1942) 'A study of the effects of differential stimulation on mentally retarded children: a follow-up report', *American Journal of Mental Deficiency* 46, 340–50

SKEELS, H.M. and FILLMORE, E.A. (1937) 'The mental development of children from underprivileged homes', *Journal of Genetic Psychology* 50, 427–39

SKODAK, M. (1939) 'Children in foster homes', *Univ. of Iowa Studies on Child Welfare* 16 No 1

SKODAK, M. and SKEELS, H.M. (1945) 'A follow-up study of children in adoptive homes', *Journal of Genetic Psychology* 66, 21–58

SKODAK, M. and SKEELS, H.M. (1949) 'A final follow-up study of one hundred adopted children', *Journal of Genetic Psychology* 75, 85–125

SPITZ, R.A. (1945) 'Hospitalism: an inquiry into the genesis of psychiatric conditions in early childhood', *Psychoanalytic Study of the Child* 2, 53–74

SPITZ, R.A. (1946) 'Hospitalism: a follow-up report', *Psychoanalytic Study of the Child* 1, 113–17

WHEELER, L.R. (1932) 'The intelligence of East Tennessee mountain children', *Journal of Education and Psychology* 23, 351–71

WHEELER, L.R. (1942) 'A comparative study of the intelligence of East Tennessee mountain children', *Journal of Education and Psychology* 30, 321–34

CHAPTER 9

BAYLEY, N. (1966) 'Manual of directions for infant scales of development: mental, motor and behavior profiles', in *Bayley Scales of Infant Development* (New York: Psychological Corp.)

BOWLBY, J. (1951) *Maternal Care and Mental Health* (Geneva: World Health Organization)

CALDWELL, B.M. (1970) 'The effects of psycho-social deprivation on human development in infancy', *Merrill-Palmer Quarterly* 16, 260–77

CALDWELL, B.M., HEIDER, J. and KAPLAN, B. (1966) 'The inventory of home stimulation', paper presented at the meeting of the American Psychological Association, New York

CLARKE, A.D.B. (1968) 'Problems in assessing the later effects of early experience', in E. Miller (ed.) *Foundations of Child Psychiatry* (London: Pergamon)

GOLDFARB, W. (1945) 'Effects of psychological deprivation in infancy and subsequent stimulation', *American Journal of Psychiatry* 102, 18–33

RHEINGOLD, H.L. and BAYLEY, N. (1959) 'The later effects of an experimental modification of mothering', *Child Development* 30, 363–72

RUTTER, M. (1972) *Maternal Deprivation Reassessed* (Harmondsworth: Penguin)

SKEELS, H.M. (1966) 'Adult status of children with contrasting early life experiences: a follow-up study', *Monographs of the Society for Research in Child Development* 31 No 3, Serial No 105

SPITZ, R.A. (1949) 'The role of ecological factors in emotional development in infancy', *Child Development* 20, 145–55

STEIN, Z.A. and SUSSER, M. (1970) 'Mutability of intelligence and epidemiology of mild mental retardation', *Review of Educational Research* 40, 29–67

TIZARD, B., COOPERMAN, O., JOSEPH, A. and TIZARD, J. (1972) 'Environmental effects on language development: a study of young children in long-stay residential nurseries', *Child Development* 43, 337–58

TIZARD, B. and JOSEPH, A. (1970a) 'The cognitive development of young children in residential care', *Journal of Child Psychology and Psychiatry* 11, 177–86

TIZARD, B. and JOSEPH, A. (1970b) 'Today's foundlings', *New Society* 16 No 418, 584–5

TIZARD, J. and TIZARD, B. (1971) 'The social development of two-year-old children in residential nurseries', in H.R. Schaffer (ed.) *The Origin of Human Social Relations* (London: Academic)

CHAPTER 10

ABRAHAMS, M.J. and WHITLOCK, F.A. (1969) 'Childhood experience and depression', *British Journal of Psychiatry* 115, 833–88

AINSWORTH, M.D. (1962) 'The effects of maternal deprivation: a review of findings and controversy in the context of research strategy', in *Deprivation of Maternal Care: a reassessment of its effects, Public Health Papers* (Geneva: World Health Organization) 14, 97–165

AINSWORTH, M.D. (1967) *Infancy in Uganda: Infant Care and the Growth of Love* (Baltimore: Johns Hopkins Univ. Press)

ANDRY, R.G. (1960) *Delinquency and Parental Pathology* (London: Methuen)

ANTHONY, E.J. and KOUPERNIK, C. (1970) (eds) *The Child in His Family* (New York: Wiley-Interscience)

BAERS, M. (1954) 'Women workers and home responsibilities', *International Labour Review* 69, 338–55

BANDURA, A. (1969) 'Social-learning theory of identificatory processes', in D.A. Goslin (ed.) *Handbook of Socialization Theory and Research* (New York: Rand McNally)

BARRY, W.A. (1970) 'Marriage research and conflict; an integrative review', *Psychological Bulletin* 73, 41–54

BECKER, W.C. (1964) 'Consequences of different kinds of parental discipline', in M.L. Hoffman and L.W. Hoffman (eds) *Review of Child Development Research*, vol. 1 (New York: Russell Sage Foundation)

BELL, R.Q. (1964) 'The effect on the family of a limitation in coping ability in a child: a research approach and a finding', *Merrill-Palmer Quarterly* 10, 129–42

BELL, R.Q. (1968) 'A reinterpretation of the direction of effects in studies of socialization', *Psychological Review* 75, 81–95

BERGER, M. and PASSINGHAM, R.E. (1973) 'Early experience and other environmental factors: an overview', in H.J. Eysenck (ed.) *Handbook of Abnormal Psychology*, 2nd ed. (London: Pitman's Medical Press)

BIRTCHENALL, J. (1969) 'The possible consequences of early parent death', *British Journal of Medical Psychology* 42, 1–12

BIRTCHENALL, J. (1970) 'Depression in relation to early and recent parent death', *British Journal of Psychiatry* 116, 299–306

BOHMAN, M. (1970) *Adopted Children and their Families. A follow-up study of adopted children, their background, environment and adjustment* (Stockholm: Proprius)

BOWLBY, J. (1946) *Forty-four Juvenile Thieves: Their Characters and Home-life* (London: Baillière, Tindall and Cox)

BOWLBY, J. (1958a) 'Separation of mother and child', *Lancet* 1, 480

BOWLBY, J. (1958b) 'Separation of mother and child', *Lancet* 1, 1070

BOWLBY, J. (1958c) 'The nature of the child's tie to his mother', *International Journal of Psychoanalysis* 39, 350–73

BOWLBY, J. (1962) 'Childhood bereavement and psychiatric illness', in D. Richter, J.M. Tanner, L. Taylor and O.L. Zangwill (eds) *Aspects of Psychiatric Research* (London: Oxford Univ. Press)

BOWLBY, J. (1968) 'Effects on behaviour of disruption of an affectional bond', in J.M. Thoday and A.S. Parker (eds) *Genetic and Environmental Influences on Behaviour* (Edinburgh: Oliver and Boyd)

BOWLBY, J. (1969) *Attachment and Loss*, vol. 1 *Attachment* (London: Hogarth Press)

BOWLBY, J., AINSWORTH, M.D., BOSTON, M. and ROSENBLUTH, D. (1956) 'The effects of mother–child separation: a follow-up study', *British Journal of Medical Psychology* 29, 211–47

BOWLBY, J. and PARKES, C.M. (1970) 'Separation and loss within the family', in E.J. Anthony and C. Koupernik (eds) *The Child in His Family* (New York: Wiley-Interscience)

BRILL, N.Q. and LISTON, E.H. (1966) 'Parental loss in adults with emotional disorders', *Archives of General Psychiatry* 14, 307–14

BRONFENBRENNER, U. (1961) 'Some family antecedents of responsibility and leadership in adolescents', in L. Petrullo and B.M. Bass (eds) *Leadership and Interpersonal Behaviour* (New York: Holt)

BROWN, F. (1961) 'Depression and childhood bereavement', *Journal of Mental Science* 107, 754–77

BROWN, F. (1966) 'Childhood bereavement and subsequent psychiatric disorder', *British Journal of Psychiatry* 112, 1035–41

BROWN, G.W. and RUTTER, M. (1966) 'The measurement of family activities and relationships – a methodological study', *Human Relations* 19, 241–63

CALDWELL, B.M. (1964) 'The effects of infant care', in M.L. Hoffman and L.W. Hoffman (eds) *Review of Child Development Research*, vol. 1 (New York: Russell Sage Foundation)

CALDWELL, B.M., WRIGHT, C.M., HONIG, A.S. and TANNENBAUM, J. (1970) 'Infant day care and attachment', *American Journal of Orthopsychiatry* 40, 397–412

CAPLAN, M.G. and DOUGLAS, V.I. (1969) 'Incidence of parental loss in children with depressed mood', *Journal of Child Psychology and Psychiatry* 10, 225–32

CHRISTENSEN, H.T. (1964) *Handbook of Marriage and the Family* (Chicago: Rand McNally)

CHRISTENSEN, H.T. (1969) 'Normative theory derived from cross-cultural family research', *Journal of Marriage and the Family* 31, 209–22

CONGER, J.J. and MILLER, L. (1966) *Personality, Social Class and Delinquency* (New York: Wiley)

CRAIG, M.M. and GLICK, S.J. (1965) *A Manual of Procedures for Applications of the Glueck Prediction Table* (London: Univ. of London Press)

CUMMINGS, S.T., BAYLEY, H.C. and RIE, H.E. (1966) 'Effects of the child's deficiency on the mother: a study of mothers of mentally retarded, chronically ill and neurotic children', *American Journal of Orthopsychiatry* 36, 595–608

DAVENPORT, H.T. and WERRY, J.S. (1970) 'The effect of general anesthesia, surgery and hospitalization upon the behaviour of children', *American Journal of Orthopsychiatry* 40, 806–24

DENNEHY, C. (1966) 'Childhood bereavement and psychiatric illness', *British Journal of Psychiatry* 112, 1049–69

DOUGLAS, J.W.B. (1970) 'Broken families and child behaviour', *Journal of the Royal College of Physicians of London* 4, 203–10

DOUGLAS, J.W.B. (1975) 'Early hospital admissions and later disturbances of behaviour and learning', *Developmental Medicine and Child Neurology* 17, 456–80

DOUGLAS, J.W.B., ROSS, J.M., HAMMOND, W.A. and MULLIGAN, D.G. (1966) 'Delinquency and social class', *British Journal of Criminology* 6, 294–302

DOUGLAS, J.W.B., ROSS, J.M. and SIMPSON, H.R. (1968) *All Our Future* (London: Peter Davies)

FAUST, O.A., JACKSON, K., CERMAK, E.G., BURTT, M.M. and WINKLEY, R. (1952) *Reducing Emotional Trauma in Hospitalized Children*, Albany Residential Project, Albany, New York; cited by Yarrow (1964)

FLETCHER, R. (1966) *The Family and Marriage in Britain* (Harmondsworth: Penguin)

GIBSON, H.B. (1969) 'Early delinquency in relation to broken homes', *Journal of Child Psychology and Psychiatry* 10, 195–204

GLUECK, S. and GLUECK, E.T. (1950) *Unravelling Juvenile Delinquency* (Cambridge, Mass.: Harvard Univ. Press)

GLUECK, S. and GLUECK, E.T. (1962) *Family Environment and Delinquency* (London: Kegan Paul)

GRAHAM, P. and RUTTER, M. (1968) 'The reliability and validity of the psychiatric assessment of the child – II. Interview with the parent', *British Journal of Psychiatry* 114, 581–92

GRAHAM, P., RUTTER, M. and GEORGE, S. (1973) 'Temperamental characteristics as predictors of behavior disorders in children', *American Journal of Orthopsychiatry* 43, 328–39

GREGORY, I. (1965) 'Anterospective data following childhood loss of parent', *Archives of General Psychiatry* 13, 110–20

GREGORY, I. (1966) 'Retrospective data concerning childhood loss of a parent', *Archives of General Psychiatry* 15, 362–7

HANDEL, G. (1967) (ed.) *The Psychosocial Interior of the Family: a sourcebook for the study of whole families* (London: Allen and Unwin)

HEINICKE, C.M. and WESTHEIMER, I.J. (1965) *Brief Separations* (London: Longmans)

HILL, O. and PRICE, J. (1967) 'Childhood bereavement and adult depression', *British Journal of Psychiatry* 113, 743–51

HINDE, R.A. and SPENCER-BOOTH, Y. (1970) 'Individual differences in the responses of rhesus monkeys to a period of separation from their mothers', *Journal of Child Psychology and Psychiatry* 11, 159–76

HIRSCHI, T. and SELVIN, H.C. (1967) *Delinquency Research: an appraisal of analytic methods* (New York: Free Press)

ILLINGWORTH, R.S. and HOLT, K.S. (1955) 'Children in hospital: some observations on their reactions with special reference to daily visiting', *Lancet* 2, 1257–62

IRVINE, E.E. (1966) 'Children in kibbutzim: thirteen years after', *Journal of Child Psychology and Psychiatry* 7, 167–78

JONSSON, G. (1967) 'Delinquent boys, their parents and grandparents', *Acta Psychiatrica Scandinavica* 43, suppl. 195

KREITMAN, N., COLLINS, J., NELSON, B. and TROOP, J. (1970) 'Neurosis and marital interaction – I. Personality and symptoms', *British Journal of Psychiatry* 117, 33–46

LANGNER, T.S., GREENE, E.L., HERSON, J.H., JAMESON, J.D. and GOFF, J.A. (1969a) 'Mental disorder in a random sample of Manhattan children', unpublished paper, American Orthopsychiatry Association

LANGNER, T.S., GREENE, E.L., HERSON, J.H., JAMESON, J.D. and GOFF, J.A. (1969b) 'Psychiatric impairment in welfare and non-welfare city children', unpublished paper, American Psychological Association

LEVY, D.M. (1958) *Behavioural Analysis: Analysis of clinical observations of behaviour as applied to mother–newborn relationships* (New York: Thomas)

LEWIS, A.J. (1956) *Social Psychiatry – Lectures on the Scientific Basis of Medicine VI* (London: British Postgraduate Medical Federation)

LIN, T. and STANDLEY, C.C. (1962) *The Scope of Epidemiology in Psychiatry* (Geneva: World Health Organization)

McCORD, W. and McCORD, J. (1959) *Origins of Crime: a new evaluation of the Cambridge-Somerville Youth Study* (New York: Columbia Univ. Press)

MARRIS, P. (1958) *Widows and their Families* (London: Routledge)

MEAD, M. (1954) 'Some theoretical considerations of the problem of mother–child separation', *American Journal of Orthopsychiatry* 24, 471–83

MEDAWAR, P.B. (1967) *The Art of the Soluble* (London: Methuen)

MEDAWAR, P.B. (1969) *Induction and Intuition in Scientific Thought* (London: Methuen)

MILLER, L. (1969) 'Child rearing in the kibbutz', in J.G. Howells (ed.) *Modern Perspectives in International Child Psychiatry* (Edinburgh: Oliver and Boyd)

MOORE, T.W. (1963) 'Effects on the children', in S. Yudkin and A. Holme (eds) *Working Mothers and their Children* (London: Michael Joseph)

MORRIS, J.N. (1957) *Uses of Epidemiology* (Edinburgh: Livingstone)

MUNRO, A. (1966) 'Parental deprivation in depressive patients', *British Journal of Psychiatry* 112, 443–57

MUNRO, A. and GRIFFITHS, A.B. (1969) 'Some psychiatric non-sequelae of childhood bereavement', *British Journal of Psychiatry* 115, 305–11

NAESS, S. (1959) 'Mother–child separation and delinquency', *British Journal of Delinquency* 10, 22–35

NAESS, S. (1962) 'Mother–child separation and delinquency: further evidence', *British Journal of Criminology* 2, 361–74

NYLANDER, I. (1960) 'Children of alcoholic fathers', *Acta Paediatrica* 49, suppl. 121

O'CONNOR, N. (1956) 'The evidence for the permanently disturbing effects of mother–child separation', *Acta Psychologica* 12, 174–91

PETERSON, D.R., BECKER, W.C., HELLMER, L.A., SHOEMAKER, D.J. and QUAY, H.C. (1959) 'Parental attitudes and child adjustment', *Child Development* 30, 119–30

PITTS, F.N., MEYER, J., BROOKS, M. and WINOKUR, G. (1965) 'Adult psychiatric illness assessed for childhood parental loss and psychiatric illness in family members: a study of 748 patients and 250 controls', *American Journal of Psychiatry* 121, suppl. 1–10

POWER, M.J., ALDERSON, M.R., PHILIPSON, C.M., SHOENBERG, E. and MORRIS, J.N. (1967) 'Delinquent schools?', *New Society* 10, 542–3

PRUGH, D.G., STAUB, E.M., SANDS, H.H., KIRSCHBAUM, R.M. and LENIHAN, E.A. (1953) 'A study of the emotional reactions of children and families to hospitalization and illness', *American Journal of Orthopsychiatry* 23, 70–106

QUINTON, D. and RUTTER, M. (1976) 'Early hospital admissions and later disturbances of behaviour: an attempted replication of Douglas's findings' (submitted for publication)

ROBERTSON, J. and BOWLBY, J. (1952) 'Responses of young children to separation from their mother – II. Observations of the sequences of response of children aged 18–24 months during the course of separation', *Courrier* 2, 131–41

ROBINS, L.N. (1966) *Deviant Children Grown Up* (Baltimore: Williams and Wilkins)

ROBINS, L.N. (1969) 'Social correlates of psychiatric disorders: can we tell causes from consequences?', *Journal of Health and Social Behavior* 10, 95–104

ROBINS, L.N. and HILL, S.Y. (1969) 'Assessing the contributions of family structure, class and peer groups to juvenile delinquency', *Journal of Criminal Law, Criminology and Political Science* 57, 325–34

ROE, A. and BURKS, B.S. (1945) *Adult Adjustment of Foster Children of Alcoholic and Psychotic Parentage and the Influence of Foster Homes* (New Haven: Yale Univ. Press)

ROSANOFF, A.J., HANDY, L.M. and PLESSET, I.R. (1941) *The Etiology of Child Behavior Difficulties, Juvenile Delinquency and Adult Criminality, with Special Reference to their Occurrence in Twins*, Psychiatric Monographs No 1 (Sacramento: Department of Institutions)

ROWNTREE, G. (1955) 'Early childhood in broken families', *Population Studies* 8, 247–63

RUTTER, M. (1966) *Children of Sick Parents: an environmental and psychiatric study*, Maudsley Monographs No 16 (London: Oxford Univ. Press)

RUTTER, M. (1967) 'A children's behaviour questionnaire for completion by teachers: preliminary findings', *Journal of Child Psychology and Psychiatry* 8, 1–11

RUTTER, M. (1970a) 'Psychosocial disorders in childhood and their outcome in adult life', *Journal of the Royal College of Physicians of London* 4, 211–18

RUTTER, M. (1970b) 'Sex differences in children's responses to family stress', in E.J. Anthony and C. Koupernik (eds) *The Child in His Family* (New York: Wiley-Interscience)

RUTTER, M., BIRCH, H.G., THOMAS, A. and CHESS, S. (1964) 'Temperamental characteristics in infancy and the later development of behaviour disorders', *British Journal of Psychiatry* 110, 651–61

RUTTER, M. and BROWN, G.W. (1966) 'The reliability and validity of measures of family life and relationships in families containing a psychiatric patient', *Social Psychiatry* 1, 38–53

RUTTER, M., COX, A., TUPLING, C., BERGER, M. and YULE, W. (1975) 'Attainment and adjustment in two geographical areas – I. The prevalence of psychiatric disorder', *British Journal of Psychiatry* 126, 493–509

RUTTER, M. and GRAHAM, P. (1968) 'The reliability and validity of the psychiatric assessment of the child', *British Journal of Psychiatry* 114, 563–80

RUTTER, M., GRAHAM, P. and YULE, W. (1970) *A Neuropsychiatric Study in Childhood, Clinics in Developmental Medicine*, vols 35–36 (London: Spastics International Medical Publications)

RUTTER, M. and MADGE, N. (1976) *Cycles of Disadvantage* (London: Heinemann Educational, in press)

RUTTER, M., TIZARD, J. and WHITMORE, K. (1970) (eds) *Education, Health and Behaviour* (London: Longmans)

SACKETT, G.P. (1969) 'Abnormal behaviour in laboratory-reared rhesus monkeys', in M.W. Fox (ed.) *Abnormal Behaviour in Animals* (New York: Saunders)

SCHAFFER, H.R. and CALLENDER, W.M. (1959) 'Psychological effects of hospitalization in infancy', *Paediatrics* 24, 528–39

SCHAFFER, H.R. and EMERSON, P.E. (1964) 'The development of social attachments in infancy', *Monographs of the Society for Research in Child Development* 29 No 3, 1–77

SCHAFFER, H.R. and SCHAFFER, E.B. (1968) *Child Care and the Family* (London: Bell)

SCHLESINGER, B. (1969) *The One-Parent Family: Perspectives and annotated bibliography* (Toronto: Univ. Press)

SHEPHERD, M. and COOPER, B. (1964) 'Epidemiology and mental disorder: a review', *Journal of Neurology, Neurosurgery and Psychiatry* 27, 277–90

SHIELDS, J. (1954) 'Personality differences and neurotic traits in normal twin school children', *Eugenics Review* 45, 213–46

SHIELDS, J. (1968) 'Psychiatric genetics', in M. Shepherd and D.L. Davies (eds) *Studies in Psychiatry* (London: Oxford Univ. Press)

SPENCER-BOOTH, Y. and HINDE, R.A. (1971) 'Effects of six-day separation from mother on 18–32 week old rhesus monkeys', *Animal Behavior* 19, 174–91

SPROTT, W.J.H., JEPHCOTT, A.P. and CARTER, M.P. (1955) *The Social Background of Delinquency* (Nottingham: Univ. of Nottingham)

STACEY, M., DEARDEN, R., PILL, R. and ROBINSON, D. (1970) *Hospitals, Children and their Families: The report of a pilot study* (London: Routledge and Kegan Paul)

STENDLER, C.B. (1950) 'Sixty years of child training practices', *Journal of Pediatrics* 36, 122–34

TAIT, C.D. and HODGES, E.F. (1962) *Delinquents, their Families and the Community* (Springfield, Illinois: C.C. Thomas)

TANNER, J.M. (1962) *Growth at Adolescence* (Springfield, Illinois: C.C. Thomas)

TERRIS, M. (1964) (ed.) *Goldberger on Pellagra* (Baton Rouge: Louisiana State Univ. Press)

THOMAS, A., CHESS, S. and BIRCH, H.G. (1968) *Temperament and Behaviour Disorders in Children* (London: Univ. of London Press)

THOMAS, A., CHESS, S., BIRCH, H.G., HERTZIG, M. and KORN, S. (1963) *Behavioural Individuality in Early Childhood* (New York: New York Univ. Press)

VERNON, D.T.A., FOLEY, J.M., SIPOWICZ, R.R. and SCHULMAN, J.L. (1965) *The Psychological Responses of Children to Hospitalization and Illness* (Springfield, Illinois: C.C. Thomas)

WARDLE, C.J. (1961) 'Two generations of broken homes in the genesis of conduct and behaviour disorders in childhood', *British Medical Journal* 2, 349–54

WEST, D.J. (1967) *The Young Offender* (Harmondsworth: Penguin)

WEST, D.J. (1969) *Present Conduct and Future Delinquency* (London: Heinemann)

WOLFENSTEIN, M. (1953) 'Trends in infant care', *American Journal of Orthopsychiatry* 23, 120–30

WOLFF, S. and ACTON, W.P. (1968) 'Characteristics of parents of disturbed children', *British Journal of Psychiatry* 114, 593–601

WOOTTON, B. (1959) *Social Science and Social Pathology* (London: Allen and Unwin)

WORLD HEALTH ORGANIZATION (1951) *Expert Committee on Mental Health, Report on the Second Session 1951*, Technical Report Series, No 31, (Geneva: World Health Organization)

YARROW, L.J. (1961) 'Maternal deprivation: toward an empirical and conceptual re-evaluation', *Psychological Bulletin* 58, 459–90

YARROW, L.J. (1963) 'Research in dimensions of early maternal care', *Merrill-Palmer Quarterly* 9, 101–14

YARROW, L.J. (1964) 'Separation from parents during early childhood', in M.C. Hoffman and L.W. Hoffman (eds) *Review of Child Development Research*, vol. 1 (New York: Russell Sage Foundation)

YARROW, L.J. (1968) 'The crucial nature of early experience', in D.C. Glass (ed.) *Environmental Influences* (New York: Rockefeller Univ. Press and Russell Sage Foundation)

YUDKIN, S. and HOLME, A. (1963) *Working Mothers and their Children* (London: Michael Joseph)

CHAPTER 11

ALEXANDER, F. and FRENCH, T. (1946) *Psychoanalytic Therapy* (New York: W.W. Norton)

BOWLBY, J. (1951) *Maternal Care and Mental Health* (Geneva: World Health Organization)

CHILD WELFARE LEAGUE OF AMERICA (1960) *Adoption of Oriental Children by American White Families – An Interdisciplinary Symposium* (New York: C.W.L.A.)

ESCALONA, S.K. (1968) *The Roots of Individuality* (Chicago: Aldine)

FRIES, M. and WOOLF, P. (1953) 'Some hypotheses on the role of the congenital activity type in development', *Psychoanalytic Study of the Child* (New York: International Universities Press) 8, 48–62

HESTON, L.L., DENNY, D.D. and PAULEY, I.B. (1966) 'The adult adjustment of persons institutionalized as children', *British Journal of Psychiatry* 112, 1103–10

HOBBS, N. (1964) 'Sources of gain in psychotherapy', in W.G. Bennis, E.H. Schein, D.E. Berlew and F. Steel (eds) *Interpersonal Dynamics* (Homewood, Illinois: The Dorsby Press)

JOSSLYN, I. (1948) *Psychosocial Development of Children* (New York: Family Service Association of America)

KOHLBERG, L., LACROSS, J. and RICKS, D. (1970) 'The predictability of adult mental health from childhood behavior', in B. Wolman (ed.) *Handbook of Child Psychopathology* (New York: McGraw-Hill)

LAWDER, E. A., LOWER, K.D. and others (1966) *Post-placement Functioning in Adoptive Families, A Follow-up Study of Adoptions at the Children's Aid Society of Pennsylvania*, final report to the Children's Bureau, R-114, August 1966 (mimeo)

LEVIN, P. (1965) 'There are babies and babies', *New York Times Magazine*, 19 September

LIVSON, N. and PESKIN, H. (1967) 'The prediction of adult psychological health in a longitudinal study', *Journal of Abnormal and Social Psychology* 72, 509–18

MAAS, H. (1963) 'The young adult adjustment of twenty wartime residential nursery children', *Child Welfare* 42, 57–72

MEIER, E. (1962) *Former Foster Children as Adult Citizens*, unpublished Ph.D., Columbia University School of Social Work

MEIER, E. (1965) 'Current circumstances of former foster children', *Child Welfare* 44, 196–206

MORRIS, H.H., ESCOLL, P.J. and WEXLER, R. (1956) 'Aggressive behavior disorders of childhood: a follow-up study', *American Journal of Psychiatry* 112, 991–7

MORRIS, H.H., SOROKER, E. and BURRUS, G. (1954) 'Follow-up study of shy withdrawn children – I. Evaluation of later adjustment', *American Journal of Orthopsychiatry* 24, 743–54

RATHBUN, C. and others (1964) 'Later adjustments of children following radical separation from family and culture', paper presented at the Annual Meeting of the American Orthopsychiatric Association, Chicago

RESEARCH INSTITUTE FOR THE STUDY OF MAN (1964) *Final Report to Children's Bureau on Study of Adoption of Greek Children by American Foster Parents*, R-22, November, mimeo (New York)

RIPPLE, L. (1968) 'A follow-up study of adopted children', *Social Service Review* 42, 479–97

ROBINS, L.N. (1966) *Deviant Children Grown Up* (Baltimore: Williams and Wilkins)

ROE, A. (1945) 'The adult adjustment of children of alcoholic parents raised in foster homes', *Quarterly Journal of Studies on Alcohol* 5

ROE, A. and BURKS, B. (1945) *Adult Adjustment of Foster Children of Alcoholic and Psychotic Parentage and the Influence of Foster Homes, Memoirs of the Section on Alcohol Studies* (New Haven: Yale Univ. Press)

ROSENTHAL, R. (1966) *Experimenter Effects in Behavioral Research* (New York: Appelton-Century-Crofts)

SROLE, L. and others (1962) *Mental Health in the Metropolis – The Midtown Manhattan Study* (New York: McGraw-Hill)

THEIS, S. VAN (1924) *How Foster Children Turn Out* (New York: State Charity Aid Association)

THOMAS, A., BIRCH, H.G., CHESS, S., HERTZIG, M. and KORN, S. (1965) *Behavioral Individuality in Early Childhood* (New York: New York Univ. Press)

THOMAS, E.J. and GOODMAN, E. (1965) *Socio-biological Theory and Interpersonal Helping in Social Work* (Ann Arbor, Michigan: Campus Publishers)

TINKER, K. (1952)'Do children in foster care outgrow behavior problems?', *Minnesota Welfare* 8, Nos 4, 5, 6

WELTER, M. (1965) *Adopted Older Foreign and American Children* (New York: International Social Service)

WITKIN, H.A. and others (1962) *Psychological Differentiation* (New York: John Wiley)

WITMER, H., HERZOG, E., WEINSTEIN, E. and SULLIVAN, M. (1963) *Independent Adoptions* (New York: Russell Sage Foundation)

YARROW, L. J. (1962) 'Maternal deprivation: toward an empirical and conceptual reevaluation', in *Maternal Deprivation* (New York), 3–41

CHAPTER 12

BEREITER, C. and ENGELMANN, S. (1966) *Teaching Disadvantaged Children in the Preschool* (Englewood Cliffs, N.J.: Prentice-Hall)

BLANK, M. and SOLOMON, F.A. (1968) 'A tutorial language program to develop abstract thinking in socially disadvantaged pre-school children', *Child Development* 39, 379–89

BLANK, M. and SOLOMON, F.A. (1969) 'How shall the disadvantaged child be taught?', *Child Development* 40, 47–61

BLOOM, B.S. (1964) *Stability and Change in Human Characteristics* (London and New York: John Wiley)

BRONFENBRENNER, U. (1974) *A Report on Longitudinal Evaluations of Pre-school Programs*, vol. 2 *Is Early Intervention Effective?* (Washington, D.C.: D.H.E.W. Publication no [OHD] 74-25)

CLARKE, A.D.B. (1968) 'Learning and human development – the 42nd Maudsley Lecture', *British Journal of Psychiatry* 114, 1061–77

CLARKE, A.M. (1974) 'Compensatory education for the mildly subnormal', in J. Garside (ed.) *Report on Seminar: Recent Studies into Mental Retardation and their Practical Application* (Sydney: Australian Council for Rehabilitation of Disabled), 22–7

CLARKE, A.M. and CLARKE, A.D.B. (1974) *Mental Deficiency: the Changing Outlook*, 3rd ed. (London: Methuen)

DENNIS, W. (1973) *Children of the Crèche* (New York: Appelton-Century-Crofts)

GRAY, S. W. and KLAUS, R.A. (1965) 'An experimental pre-school program for culturally deprived children', *Child Development* 36, 887–98

GRAY, S. W. and KLAUS, R.A. (1970) 'The Early Training Project: a seventh-year report', *Child Development* 41, 909–24

HEBER, R. and GARBER, H. (1971) 'An experiment in prevention of cultural-familial mental retardation', in D.A. Primrose (ed.) *Proceedings of the 2nd Congress of the International Association for the Scientific Study of Mental Deficiency* (Warsaw: Polish Medical Publishers; Amsterdam: Swets and Zeitlinger), 31–5

HEBER, R. and GARBER, H. (1975) 'Progress Report II: an experiment in the prevention of cultural-familial retardation', in D.A. Primrose (ed.) *Proceedings of the 3rd Congress of the International Association for the Scientific Study of Mental Deficiency* (Warsaw: Polish Medical Publishers), vol. 1, 34–43

HESS, R.D. and SHIPMAN, V.C. (1965) 'Early experience and the socialization of cognitive modes in children', *Child Development* 36, 869–86

HUNT, J.McV. (1961) *Intelligence and Experience* (New York: Ronald Press)

JENSEN, A.R. (1969) 'How much can we boost IQ and scholastic achievement?', *Harvard Educational Review* 39, 1–123

KIRK, S.A. (1958) *Early Education of the Mentally Retarded* (Urbana, Illinois: Univ. of Illinois Press)

MCNEMAR, Q. (1940) 'A critical examination of the University of Iowa studies of environmental influence upon the IQ', *Psychological Bulletin* 37, 63–92

SKEELS, H.M. (1966) 'Adult status of children with contrasting early life experiences: a follow-up study', *Monographs of the Society for Research in Child Development* 31 No 3, Serial No 105

SKEELS, H.M. and DYE, H.B. (1939) 'A study of the effects of differential stimulation on mentally retarded children', *Proceedings of the American Association on Mental Deficiency* 44, 114–36

SKODAK, M. (1968) 'Adult status of individuals who experienced early intervention', in B.W. Richards (ed.) *Proceedings of the 1st Congress of the International Association for the Scientific Study of Mental Deficiency* (Reigate: Michael Jackson), 11–18

TIZARD, B. (1974) *Pre-School Education in Great Britain: a Research Review* (London: Social Science Research Council)

UNITED STATES COMMISSION ON CIVIL RIGHTS (1967) *Racial Isolation in the Public Schools*, vol. 1 (Washington, D.C.: U.S. Government Printing Office)

CHAPTER 13

GRAY, S.W. and KLAUS, R.A. (1965) 'An experimental pre-school program for culturally deprived children', *Child Development* 36, 887–98

GRAY, S.W., KLAUS, R.A., MILLER, J.O. and FORRESTER, B.J. (1966) *Before First Grade* (New York: Teachers College Press, Columbia Univ.)

KLAUS, R.A. and GRAY, S.W. (1968) 'The Early Training Project for disadvantaged children: a report after five years', *Monographs of the Society for Research on Child Development* 33 No 4, Serial No 120

LINDQUIST, E.F. (1953) *The Design and Analysis of Experiments in Psychology and Education* (Boston: Houghton Mifflin)

MILLER, J.O. (1970) 'Cultural deprivation and its modification; effects of intervention', in C.H. Haywood (ed.) *Social-cultural Aspects of Mental Retardation* (Boston: Appleton-Century-Crofts)

WESTINGHOUSE LEARNING CORPORATION (1969) *The Impact of Head Start: An Evaluation of the Head Start Experience on Children's Cognitive and Affective Development* (Ohio: Westinghouse Learning Corporation, Ohio Univ.)

CHAPTER 14*

AMIDON, A. and BRIM, O.G. (1972) 'What do children have to gain from parent education?', paper prepared for the Advisory Committee on Child Development, National Research Council, National Academy of Science

*We include here all the references quoted in the volume, not merely those mentioned in this excerpt. Research workers will find this list very useful.

BEE, H.L., VAN EGEREN, L.F., STREISSGUTH, A.P., NYMAN, B.A. and LECKIE, M.S. (1969) 'Social class differences in maternal teaching strategies and speech patterns', *Developmental Psychology* 1, 726–34

BELL, R.Q. (1968) 'A reinterpretation of the direction of effects in studies of socialization', *Psychological Review* 75, 81–95

BELLER, E.K. (1972) 'Impact of early education on disadvantaged children', in S. Ryan (ed.) *A Report on Longitudinal Evaluations of Preschool Programs* (Washington, D.C.: Office of Child Development)

BELLER, E.K. (1973) Personal communication

BEREITER, C. and ENGELMANN, S. (1966) *Teaching Disadvantaged Children in the Preschool* (Englewood Cliffs, N.J.: Prentice Hall)

BISSELL, J.S. (1970) *The Cognitive Effects of Preschool Programs for Disadvantaged Children* (Washington, D.C.: National Institute of Child Health and Human Development)

BISSELL, J.S. (1971) *Implementation of Planned Variation in Head Start: First Year Report* (Washington, D.C.: National Institute of Child Health and Human Development)

BLOOM, B.S. (1964) *Stability and Change in Human Characteristics* (New York: John Wiley)

BLOOM, B.S. (1965) *Compensatory Education for Cultural Deprivation* (New York: Holt, Rinehart and Winston)

BOGATZ, G.A. and BALL, S. (1971) *The Second Year of Sesame Street: A continuing evaluation,* vols 1 and 2 (Princeton, N.J.; Educational Testing Service)

BRAUN, S.J. and CALDWELL, B. (1973) 'Emotional adjustment of children in day care who enrolled prior to or after the age of three', *Early Child Development and Care* 2, 13–21

BRONFENBRENNER, U. (1961) 'The changing American child: a speculative analysis', *Merrill-Palmer Quarterly* 7, 73–84

BRONFENBRENNER, U. (1968a) 'Early deprivation: a cross-species analysis', in S. Levine and G. Newton (eds) *Early Experience in Behavior* (Springfield, Illinois: C.C. Thomas), 627–764

BRONFENBRENNER, U. (1968b) 'When is infant stimulation effective?', in D.C. Glass (ed.) *Environmental Influences* (New York: Rockefeller Univ. Press), 251–7

BRONFENBRENNER, U. (1970) *Two Worlds of Childhood: U.S. and U.S.S.R.* (New York: Russell Sage Foundation)

BRONFENBRENNER, U. (1972a) 'Developmental reasearch and public policy', in J.M. Romanshyn (ed.), *Social Science and Social Welfare* (New York: Council on Social Work Education)

BRONFENBRENNER, U. (1972b) 'The roots of alienation', in U. Bronfenbrenner (ed.) *Influences on Human Development* (Hinsdale, Illinois: Dryden Press), 658–77

BRONFENBRENNER, U. and BRUNER, J. (1972) 'The President and the children', *New York Times*, 31 January

COLEMAN, J.S. (1966) *Equality of Educational Opportunity* (Washington, D.C.: U.S. Office of Education)

DEUTSCH, M. (1960) *Minority Group and Class Status as Related to Social and Personality Factors in Scholastic Achievement*, Society for Applied Anthropology Monograph No 2 (Ithaca, New York: New York State School of Industrial and Labor Relations, Cornell Univ.)

DEUTSCH, M. and others (1971) *Regional Research and Resource Center in Early Childhood: Final Report* (Washington, D.C.: U.S. Office of Economic Opportunity)

DEUTSCH, M., TALEPOROS, E. and VICTOR, J. (1972) 'A brief synopsis of an initial enrichment program in early childhood', in S. Ryan (ed.) *A Report on Longitudinal Evaluations of Preschool Programs* (Washington, D.C.: Office of Child Development)

DI LORENZO, L.T. (1969) *Pre-kindergarten Programs for Educationally Disadvantaged Children: Final Report* (Washington, D.C.: U.S. Office of Education)

GARDNER, J. and GARDNER, H. (1970) 'A note on selective imitation by a six-week-old infant', *Child Development* 41, 1209–13

GILMER, B., MILLER, J.O. and GRAY, S.W. (1970) *Intervention with Mothers and Young Children: Study of intra-family effects* (Nashville, Tennessee: Demonstration and Research Center for Early Education [DARCEE])

GORDON, I.J. (1971) *A Home Learning Center Approach to Early Stimulation* (Gainesville, Florida: Institute for Development of Human Resources [Grant No MH 16037–02])

GRAY, S.W. and KLAUS, R.A. (1965) 'An experimental preschool program for culturally deprived children', *Child Development* 36, 887–98

GRAY, S.W. and KLAUS, R.A. (1970) 'The Early Training Project: a seventh-year report', *Child Development* 41, 909–24

HAYES, D. and GRETHER, J. (1969) 'The school year and vacation: when do students learn?', paper presented at the Eastern Sociological Convention, New York

HEBB, D.O. (1949) *The Organization of Behavior* (New York and London: John Wiley)

HEBER, R., GARBER, H., HARRINGTON, S. and HOFFMAN, C. (1972) *Rehabilitation of Families at Risk for Mental Retardation* (Madison, Wisconsin: Rehabilitation Research and Training Center in Mental Retardation, Univ. of Wisconsin)

HERTZIG, M.E., BIRCH, H.G., THOMAS, A. and MENDEZ, O.A. (1968) 'Class and ethnic differences in responsiveness of preschool children to cognitive demands', *Monographs of the Society for Research in Child Development* 33 No 1, Serial No 117

HERZOG, E., NEWCOMB, C.H. and CISIN, I.H. (1972a) 'Double deprivation: the less they have the less they learn', in S. Ryan (ed.) *A Report on Longitudinal Evaluations of Preschool Programs* (Washington, D.C.: Office of Child Development)

HERZOG, E., NEWCOMB, C.H. and CISIN, I.H. (1972b) 'But some are poorer than others: SES differences in a preschool program', *American Journal of Orthopsychiatry* 42, 4–22

HESS, R.D., SHIPMAN, V.C., BROPHY, J.E. and BEAR, R.M. (1968) *The Cognitive Environments of Urban Preschool Children* (Chicago: Univ. of Chicago Graduate School of Education)

HESS, R.D., SHIPMAN V.C., BROPHY, J.E., and BEAR, R.M. (1969) *The Cognitive Environments of Urban Preschool Children: Follow-up phase* (Chicago: Univ. of Chicago Graduate School of Education)

HODGES, W.L., McCANDLESS, B.R. and SPICKER, H.H. (1967) *The Development and Evaluation of a Diagnostically Based Curriculum for Preschool Psychosocially Deprived Children* (Washington, D.C.: US Office of Education)

HUNT, J.McV. (1961) *Intelligence and Experience* (New York: Ronald Press)

INFANT EDUCATION RESEARCH PROJECT, U.S. Office of Education Booklet No OE-37033 (Washington, D.C.: U.S. Office of Education)

KAGAN, J. (1971) *Change and Continuity in Infancy* (New York: John Wiley)

KAGAN, J. (1968) 'On cultural deprivation', in D.C. Glass (ed.) *Environmental Influence* (New York: Rockefeller University Press), 211–50

KARNES, M.B. (1969) *Research and Development Program on Preschool Disadvantaged Children: Final report* (Washington, D.C.: U.S. Office of Education)

KARNES, M.B. and BADGER, E.D. (1969a) 'Training mothers to instruct their infants at home', in Karnes (1969), 249–63

KARNES, M.B., HODGINS, A.S. and TESKA, J.A. (1969b) 'The effects of short-term instruction at home by mothers of children not enrolled in a preschool', in Karnes (1969), 197–203

KARNES, M.B., HODGINS, A.S. and TESKA, J.A. (1969c) 'The impact of at-home instruction by mothers on performance in the ameliorative preschool', in Karnes (1969), 205–12

KARNES, M.B., STUDLEY, W.M., WRIGHT, W.R. and HODGINS, A.S. (1968) 'An approach to working with mothers of disadvantaged preschool children', *Merrill-Palmer Quarterly* 14, 174–84

KARNES, M.B., TESKA, J.A., HODGINS, A.S. and BADGER, E.D. (1970) 'Educational intervention at home by mothers of disadvantaged infants', *Child Development* 41, 925–35

KARNES, M.B., ZEHRBACH, R.R. and TESKA, J.A. (1972) 'An ameliorative approach in the development of curriculum', in R.K. Parker (ed.) *The Preschool in Action* (Boston: Allyn and Bacon), 353–81

KIRK, S.A. (1958) *Early Education of the Mentally Retarded* (Urbana, Illinois: Univ. of Illinois Press)

KIRK, S.A. (1969) 'The effects of early education with disadvantaged infants', in Karnes (1969)

KLAUS, R.A. and GRAY, S.W. (1968) 'The Early Training Project for disadvantaged children: a report after five years', *Monographs of the Society for Research in Child Development* 33 No 4, Serial No 120

KRAFT, I., FUSHILLO, J. and HERZOG, E. (1968) *Prelude to School: An evaluation of an inner-city school program* Children's Bureau Research Report No 3 (Washington, D.C.: Children's Bureau)

LEVENSTEIN, P. (1970) 'Cognitive growth in preschoolers through verbal interaction with mothers', *American Journal of Orthopsychiatry* 40, 426–32

LEVENSTEIN, P. (1972a) Personal communication

LEVENSTEIN, P. (1972b) 'But does it work in homes away from home?', *Theory into Practice* 11, 157–62

LEVENSTEIN, P. and LEVENSTEIN, S. (1971) 'Fostering learning potential in preschoolers', *Social Casework* 52, 74–8

LEVENSTEIN, P. and SUNLEY, R. (1968) 'Stimulation of verbal interaction between disadvantaged mothers and children', *American Journal of Orthopsychiatry* 38, 116–21

MOSS, H.A. (1967) 'Sex, age, and state as determinants of mother–infant interaction', *Merrill-Palmer Quarterly* 13, 19–36

RADIN, N. (1969) 'The impact of a kindergarten home-counseling program', *Exceptional Children* 36, 251–6

RADIN, N. (1972) 'Three degrees of maternal involvement in a preschool program: impact on mothers and children', *Child Development* 43, 1355–64

RADIN, N. and WEIKART, D. (1967) 'A home teaching program for disadvantaged preschool children', *Journal of Special Education* 1, 183–90

REHABILITATION OF FAMILIES AT RISK FOR MENTAL RETARDATION (1971) *A Progress Report* (Madison, Wisconsin: Rehabilitation Research and Training Center in Mental Retardation, Univ. of Wisconsin)

RHEINGOLD, H.L. (1969) 'The social and socializing infant', in D.A. Goslin (ed.) *Handbook of Socialization Theory and Research* (Chicago: Rand McNally), 779–90

SCHAEFER, E.S. (1968) *Progress Report: Intellectual Stimulation of Culturally Deprived Parents* (National Institute of Mental Health)

SCHAEFER, E.S. (1970) 'Need for early and continuing education', in V.H. Denenberg (ed.) *Education of the Infant and Young Child* (New York: Academic Press), 61–82

SCHAEFER, E.S. (1972a) Personal communication

SCHAEFER, E.S. (1972b) 'Parents as educators: evidence from cross-sectional, longitudinal and intervention research', *Young Children* 27, 227–39

SCHAEFER, E.S. and AARONSON, M. (1972) 'Infant education research project: implementation and implications of the home-tutoring program', in R.K. Parker (ed.) *The Preschool in Action* (Boston: Allyn and Bacon), 410–36

SCHOGGEN, M. and SCHOGGEN, P. (1971) *Environmental Forces in Home Lives of Three-year-old Children in three Population Sub-groups,* DARCEE Papers and Reports, vol. 5 No 2 (Nashville, Tennessee: George Peabody College for Teachers)

SKEELS, H.M. (1966) 'Adult status of children from contrasting early life experiences: a follow-up study', *Monographs of the Society for Research in Child Development* 31 No 3, Serial No 105

SKEELS, H.M. and DYE, H.B. (1939) 'A study of the effects of differential stimulation on mentally retarded children', *Proceedings of the American Association on Mental Deficiency* 44, 114–36

SKEELS, H.M., UPDEGRAFF, R., WELLMAN, B.L. and WILLIAMS, H.M. (1938) 'A study of environmental stimulation: an orphanage preschool project', *University of Iowa Studies in Child Welfare* 15 No 4

SKODAK, M. and SKEELS, H.M. (1949) 'A final follow-up study of one hundred adopted children', *Journal of Genetic Psychology* 75, 85–125

SMITH, M.B. (1968) 'School and home: focus on achievement', in A.H. Passow (ed.) *Developing Programs for the Educationally Disadvantaged* (New York: Teachers College Press), 89–107

SOAR, R.S. (1966) 'An integrative approach to classroom learning', (NIMH Project Number 5-R11MH01096 to the Univ. of South Carolina and 7-R11MH02045 to Temple Univ.)

SOAR, R.S. (1972) *Follow-Through Classroom Process Measurement and Pupil Growth (1970–71)* (Gainesville, Florida: College of Education, Univ. of Florida)

SOAR, R.S. and SOAR, R.M. (1969) 'Pupil subject matter growth during summer vacation', *Educational Leadership Research Supplement* 2, 577–87

SPRIGLE, H. (1972) 'Learning to learn program', in S. Ryan (ed.) *A Report on Longitudinal Evaluations of Preschool Programs* (Washington, D.C.: Office of Child Development)

STANFORD RESEARCH INSTITUTE (1971a) *Implementation of Planned Variation in Head Start: Preliminary evaluation of planned variation in Head Start according to Follow-Through approaches (1969-70)* (Washington, D.C.: Office of Child Development, U.S. Department of Health, Education and Welfare)

STANFORD RESEARCH INSTITUTE (1971b) *Longitudinal Evaluation of Selected Features of the National Follow-Through Program* (Washington, D.C.: Office of Education, U.S. Department of Health, Education and Welfare)

TULKIN, S.R. and COHLER, B.J. (1971) 'Child rearing attitudes on mother-child interaction among middle and working class families', paper presented at the 1971 Meeting of the Society for Research in Child Development

TULKIN, S.R. and KAGAN, J. (1970) 'Mother–child interaction: social class differences in the first year of life', *Proceedings of the 78th Annual Convention of the American Psychological Association*, 261–2

VAN DE RIET, V. (1972) *A Sequential Approach to Early Childhood and Elementary Education* (Gainesville, Florida: Department of Clinical Psychology, Univ. of Florida)

WEIKART, D.P. (1967) *Preschool Intervention: A preliminary report of the Perry Preschool Project* (Ann Arbor, Michigan: Campus Publishers)

WEIKART, D.P. (1969) 'A comparative study of three preschool curricula', paper presented at the bi-annual meeting of the Society for Research in Child Development, Santa Monica, California

WEIKART, D.P. and others (1970) *Longitudinal Results of the Ypsilanti Perry Preschool Project* (Ypsilanti, Michigan: High Scope Educational Research Foundation)

WEIKART, D.P., KAMII, C.K. and RADIN, N. (1964) *Perry Preschool Progress Report* (Ypsilanti, Michigan: Ypsilanti Public Schools)

CHAPTER 15*

BOWLBY, J. (1951) *Maternal Care and Mental Health* (Geneva: World Health Organization)

CLARKE, A.M. and CLARKE, A.D.B. (1976) 'Problems in comparing the effects of environmental change at different ages', in H. McGurk (ed.) *Ecological Factors in Human Development* (Amsterdam: North-Holland Publishing Company)

KAGAN, J. and KLEIN, R.E. (1973) 'Cross-cultural perspectives on early development', *American Psychologist* 28, 947–61

MORGAN, P. (1975) *Child Care: Sense and Fable* (London: Temple Smith)

*Where authors' work is discussed in this chapter with cross-references to earlier parts of the book, the references are not repeated here.

RUTTER, M. (1972) *Maternal Deprivation Reassessed* (Harmondsworth: Penguin)

SAMEROFF, A.J. and CHANDLER, M.J. (1975) 'Reproductive risk and the continuum of caretaking casualty', in F.D. Horowitz, M. Hetherington, S. Scarr-Salapatek and G. Siegel (eds) *Review of Child Development Research*, vol. 4 (Univ. of Chicago Press)

SCHAFFER, H.R. (1976) *Mothering* (London: Open Books; New York: Harvard Univ. Press)

VERNON, P.E. (1964) *Personality Assessment: a Critical Survey* (London: Methuen)

WADDINGTON, C.H. (1966) *Principles of Development and Differentiation* (New York: Macmillan)

Author index

Subject index